A Message from The Drucker Foundation

Peter F. Drucker, Honorary Chairman of the Drucker Foundation, and our Board of Governors join me in applauding your commitment to leadership development. By enrolling in the Dale Carnegie® Training course, *Leadership Training for Managers*, you are demonstrating your desire to fulfill your leadership potential.

We live in a time of unprecedented social, demographic, and economic change. It is the era of the knowledge worker. To keep pace, we must be flexible and ready to change our strategy and actions, but the fundamentals of leadership remain constant.

Leaders today face an entirely new set of challenges. As you will read in these pages, leadership today is far more than managing people or projects, developing plans, and achieving goals. Leaders are responsible for building organizations and partnerships that bring value to their customers, employees, investors, and communities.

Peter Drucker has told us that "there may be 'born leaders,' but there are surely far too few to depend on them." I agree, and through my own leadership experience and observation of leaders from all three sectors around the world, I have discovered that:

- Leadership is a matter of how to be, not how to do it.
- Leadership is the ability to manage for the organization's mission and to mobilize people around the mission.
- Effective leaders lead from the front—they do not push from the rear.
- Leaders disperse leadership throughout every level of the organization.
- And as Peter Drucker tells us, leaders "make the strengths of people effective, and their weaknesses irrelevant."

The chapters of *Leader to Leader* explore these ideas and provide many other diverse perspectives and valuable insights that we hope will enhance your *Leadership Training for Managers* journey.

In an uncertain future, leadership development is the one imperative that will make the critical difference. By participating in training opportunities like this, you are not only enriching yourself—you are helping to ensure the viability of your organization and our society.

Sincerely,

Frances Hesselbein

Dale Carnegie® is a registered trademark and service mark of Dale Carnegie & Associates, Inc. All Rights Reserved.

OTHER PUBLICATIONS FROM THE DRUCKER FOUNDATION

Organizational Leadership Resource

The Drucker Foundation Self-Assessment Tool

The Drucker Foundation Future Series

The Leader of the Future, *Frances Hesselbein, Marshall Goldsmith, Richard Beckhard, Editors*

The Organization of the Future, *Frances Hesselbein, Marshall Goldsmith, Richard Beckhard, Editors*

The Community of the Future, *Frances Hesselbein, Marshall Goldsmith, Richard Beckhard, Richard F. Schubert, Editors*

The Drucker Foundation Wisdom to Action Series

Leading Beyond the Walls, *Frances Hesselbein, Marshall Goldsmith, Iain Somerville, Editors*

Leading for Innovation, *Frances Hesselbein, Marshall Goldsmith, Iain Somerville, Editors*

More Books from the Drucker Foundation

Hesselbein on Leadership, *Frances Hesselbein*

On Mission and Leadership, *Frances Hesselbein, Rob Johnston, Editors*

On Leading Change, *Frances Hesselbein, Rob Johnston, Editors*

On High-Performance Organizations, *Frances Hesselbein, Rob Johnston, Editors*

On Creativity, Innovation, and Renewal, *Frances Hesselbein, Rob Johnston, Editors*

Video Training Resources

Excellence in Nonprofit Leadership Video, *featuring Peter F. Drucker, Max De Pree, Frances Hesselbein, and Michele Hunt. Moderated by Richard F. Schubert.*

Lessons in Leadership Video, *with Peter F. Drucker*

Leading in a Time of Change workbook and video, *a conversation with Peter F. Drucker and Peter M. Senge*

Peter Drucker: An Intellectual Journey, *Ken Witty*

Journal

Leader to Leader Journal

Online Resources

www.leaderbooks.org

LEADER TO LEADER

**DRUCKER FOUNDATION
LEADERBOOKS**

ABOUT THE DRUCKER FOUNDATION

The Peter F. Drucker Foundation for Nonprofit Management, founded in 1990, takes its name and inspiration from the acknowledged father of modern management. By providing educational opportunities and resources, the foundation furthers its mission "to lead social sector organizations toward excellence in performance." It pursues this mission through the presentation of conferences, video teleconferences, the annual Peter F. Drucker Award for Nonprofit Innovation, and the annual Frances Hesselbein Fellows Program, as well as through the development of management resources, partnerships, and publications.

Since its founding, the Drucker Foundation's special role has been to serve as a broker of intellectual capital, bringing together the finest leaders, consultants, authors, and social philosophers in the world with the leaders of social sector voluntary organizations.

The Drucker Foundation believes that a healthy society requires three vital sectors: a public sector of effective governments, a private sector of effective businesses, and a social sector of effective community organizations. The mission of the social sector and its organizations is to change lives. It accomplishes this mission by addressing the needs of the spirit, mind, and body of individuals, the community, and society. This sector and its organizations also create a meaningful sphere of effective and responsible citizenship.

The Drucker Foundation aims to make its contribution to the health of society by strengthening the social sector through the provision of intellectual resources to leaders in business, government, and the social sector. In the first eight years after its inception, the Drucker Foundation, among other things:

- Presented the Drucker Innovation Award, which each year generates several hundred applications from local community enterprises; many applicants work in fields where results are difficult to achieve.

- Held twenty conferences in the United States and in countries across the world.

- Developed four books; a *Self-Assessment Tool* (revised 1998) for nonprofit organizations, and three books in the Drucker Foundation Future Series: *The Leader of the Future* (1996), *The Organization of the Future* (1997), and *The Community of the Future* (1998).

- Developed *Leader to Leader,* a quarterly journal for leaders from all three sectors.

- Gave rise to similar organizations in Argentina, Australia, and Canada.

For more information on the Drucker Foundation, contact:

The Peter F. Drucker Foundation for Nonprofit Management
320 Park Avenue, Third Floor
New York, NY 10022-6839
Telephone: (212) 224-1174
Fax: (212) 224-2508
E-mail: info@pfdf.org
Web address: www.pfdf.org

LEADER TO LEADER

Enduring Insights on Leadership
from the
Drucker Foundation's
Award-Winning Journal

FRANCES HESSELBEIN
PAUL M. COHEN

EDITORS

JOSSEY-BASS
A Wiley Imprint
www.josseybass.com

Copyright © 1999 The Peter F. Drucker Foundation for Nonprofit Management, 320 Park Avenue, 3rd floor, New York, New York 10022. www.drucker.org

Published by Jossey-Bass
A Wiley Imprint
989 Market Street, San Francisco, CA 94103-1741   www.josseybass.com

No part of this publication may be reproduced, stored in a retrieval system, or transmitted in any form or by any means, electronic, mechanical, photocopying, recording, scanning, or otherwise, except as permitted under Section 107 or 108 of the 1976 United States Copyright Act, without either the prior written permission of the Publisher, or authorization through payment of the appropriate per-copy fee to the Copyright Clearance Center, Inc., 222 Rosewood Drive, Danvers, MA 01923, (978) 750-8400, fax (978) 750-4470, or on the web at www.copyright.com. Requests to the Publisher for permission should be addressed to the Permissions Department, John Wiley & Sons, Inc., 111 River Street, Hoboken, NJ 07030, (201) 748-6011, fax (201) 748-6008, e-mail: permcoordinator@wiley.com.

The chapters in this collection originally appeared as articles in various issues of the journal *Leader to Leader*.

Credits are on page 398.

Jossey-Bass books and products are available through most bookstores. To contact Jossey-Bass directly call our Customer Care Department within the U.S. at (800) 956-7739, outside the U.S. at (317) 572-3986 or fax (317) 572-4002.

Jossey-Bass also publishes its books in a variety of electronic formats. Some content that appears in print may not be available in electronic books.

Dale Carnegie edition ISBN 0-7879-5349-0

Library of Congress Cataloging-in-Publication Data

Leader to Leader : enduring insights on leadership from the Drucker Foundation's award-winning journal / Frances Hesselbein, Paul M. Cohen, editors.
    p. cm.
  A collection of essays from the journal, Leader to leader.
  Includes index.
  ISBN 0-7879-4726-1 (acid-free paper)
  1. Leadership. 2. Management. 3. Organizational change. 4. Peter F. Drucker Foundation for Nonprofit Management. 1. Hesselbein, Frances. II. Cohen, Paul M., date. III. Leader to leader.
  HM141 .L3742 1999
  303.3'4—dc21
                                                    98-51224

Printed in the United States of America
FIRST EDITION
HB Printing   10 9 8 7

CONTENTS

Introduction   xi
    Frances Hesselbein

Part I   On Leaders and Leadership

1 **My Mentors' Leadership Lessons**   3
    Peter F. Drucker

2 **Managing in a World That Is Round**   9
    Frances Hesselbein

3 **The Leader's Legacy**   15
    Max De Pree

4 **Ten Lessons from Presidents**   25
    Doris Kearns Goodwin

5 **Finding Your Leadership Voice**   37
    James M. Kouzes

6 **The Best Lesson in Leadership**   43
    Herb Kelleher

Part II   Leading Innovation and Transformation

7 **The Discipline of Innovation**   53
    Peter F. Drucker

8 **The Practice of Innovation**   57
    Peter M. Senge

9 **Making Change Happen** 69
John P. Kotter

10 **Strategic Innovation in the Quest for New Wealth** 81
Gary Hamel, Jim Scholes

11 **Making Change Stick** 95
Douglas K. Smith

Part III Leadership in the New Information Economy

12 **The Shape of Things to Come** 109
Peter F. Drucker

13 **The Search for Meaning** 121
Charles Handy

14 **Women and the New Economy** 133
Sally Helgesen

15 **Aligning Corporate Culture to Maximize High Technology** 143
Esther Dyson

16 **Good-bye, Command and Control** 151
Margaret Wheatley

17 **The Soul of the Network Economy** 163
Kevin Kelly

Part IV Competitive Strategy in a Global Economy

18 **How Locals Can Win Global Contests** 175
Rosabeth Moss Kanter

19 **Leadership Secrets of a Venture Capitalist** 183
Ann Winblad

20	**Strategy in a World Without Borders** Kenichi Ohmae	**189**
21	**The Success Syndrome** David A. Nadler, Mark Nadler	**201**

Part V Leading for High Performance

22	**The Habits of Effective Organizations** Stephen R. Covey	**215**
23	**GE's Collective Genius** Steven Kerr	**227**
24	**Aligning Action and Values** Jim Collins	**237**
25	**Building Companies Worthy of Devotion** Charlotte Beers	**247**
26	**The Mark of a Winner** Noel Tichy	**255**
27	**Creating an Energized Workplace** Bob Nelson	**265**
28	**The Real Keys to High Performance** Jeffrey Pfeffer	**275**
29	**Developing the Star Performer** Linda A. Hill	**287**
30	**Leading for the Long Term** Leonard Berry	**301**

Part VI Building Great Teams

31	**The Secrets of Great Groups** Warren Bennis	**315**

Contents

32 Making Teams Work at the Top   323
Jon R. Katzenbach

33 Why Teams Don't Work   335
J. Richard Hackman

34 Coaching for Better Teamwork   349
Marshall Goldsmith

Part VII Leadership Across the Sectors

35 Leadership in the Cities   357
John W. Gardner

36 Full Disclosure: A Strategy for Performance   365
Regina Herzlinger

37 The Invisible Side of Leadership   375
James E. Austin

Index   389

INTRODUCTION

Times of great change are always times of anxiety—but also of great opportunity and hope. That reality has led to an extraordinary hunger for new insights and understandings in all institutions of our society. To help fulfill that need, the Drucker Foundation has invited highly respected leaders from business, government, and social sector enterprises to share their ideas with others who want to make a difference.

If we learn anything from Peter Drucker and the other thought leaders who have contributed to *Leader to Leader*, the Drucker Foundation's management quarterly, it is that we need to learn and unlearn more things more quickly than we ever have before. Despite—perhaps because of—the information overload we all experience, the need is great for a forum that brings together the best thinking of the moment. And we believe that the time is right for collaborative action across the public, private, and social sectors. A healthy society depends on all three sectors performing effectively and with high productivity.

Amid the unprecedented social, demographic, and economic change that Peter Drucker describes in his interview in Chapter Twelve, one thing remains constant for leaders: our obligation is to enhance our constituents' performance and to deliver results. Many of the voices in this volume remind us that the leader's new challenge in a society of knowledge workers is to define a motivating mission and vision for the organization. "Knowledge people are volunteers," says Peter Drucker in the interview. "And we know what attracts and holds volunteers. The first thing is a clear mission. People need to know what their organization stands for and is trying to accomplish."

In a time of ambiguity and anxiety, it seems that everything is in a state of flux. Yet two threads run through successful organizations, and these pages. First, leadership is the ability to manage for the organization's mission and to mobilize people around that mission. Second, although strategy and tactics change all the time, the fundamentals of leadership do not. My observations of great leaders; my own work as chief executive of the Girl Scouts of the USA, a three-million-member organization; and my current efforts with the Drucker Foundation have led me to conclude the following:

- *Leadership is a matter of how to be, not how to do.* We spend most of our lives mastering how to do things, but in the end it is the quality and character of the individual that defines the performance of great leaders.
- *Leaders succeed through the efforts of their people.* The basic task of the leader is to build a highly motivated, highly productive workforce. This means moving across the boundaries both within and outside the organization, investing in people and resources, and exemplifying—demanding—personal commitment to a common task.
- *Leaders build bridges.* The boundaries between sectors, organizations, employees, customers, and others are blurring. The challenge for leaders is to build a cohesive community both within and outside the organization, to invest in relationships, and to communicate a vision that speaks to a richly diverse workforce and marketplace.

Leaders today have to be healers and unifiers. They are responsible for what lies outside the walls as well as what lies within. True leaders throughout the organization understand that a deteriorating, fragmented community is not going to provide the kind of engaged, energetic, high-performance workforce that competition—and our own missions and goals—demand.

They understand, too, that in a world where no individual can possibly have all the answers, it is the inclusive organization that excels. Leaders of such organizations know that they must disperse leadership across the organization, banish the hierarchy, and create more circular, flexible, and fluid management systems based on collaborative relationships and mutual respect.

People want to be part of something that makes a difference, that transcends the ordinary—they want a star to steer by. The need for a clear, compelling mission, a reason for being, a purpose, cuts across every organization, whether a government agency, a nonprofit organization, or a corporation. Yet to achieve any mission, the organization has to be managed and led. It is essential that leaders of an organization be able to articulate the organization's values, to mobilize people around those values, and to embody those values personally as they manage for the mission.

People both in this country and around the world also have an enormous hunger for ideas; that's why three years ago the Drucker Foundation launched *Leader to Leader*, a journal of ideas by leaders for leaders. This hunger among millions of working executives demonstrates their concern for the future and a commitment to make a difference. The incisive thinkers and remarkable leaders who have contributed to the journal and to this book open doors, spark ideas, raise signal flags, and help satisfy that universal hunger. These extraordinary contributors have taught us, among other things, that great thought leaders do not live in ivory towers; they are engaged with and deeply care about others. They measure their own success by the real-world impact of their work. That people throughout our society and our organizations want to contribute to a better world has been a major premise of *Leader to Leader*.

We learned, too, that astonishing things happen when you give smart, creative people a free hand. Never have we approached our authors with an assigned topic or reviewed their work before an advisory board; when you're working with the best in the world, you don't need to do that. Rather, we simply asked, What's on your mind? What issues will most affect leaders, organizations, or communities in the coming years?

From that unfettered process several coherent themes emerged with astonishing clarity. They are evident in the seven sections of this book. Part One collects the enduring principles of effective leadership from those who have devoted themselves to its study or who have themselves led large and world-respected organizations. Part Two provides insights on what is perhaps leaders' most daunting task—guiding organizational change in a fast-moving world. Part Three looks at the breathtaking changes that in a few short years have transformed the way people work and generate financial and social wealth. Part Four showcases the strategic leadership of business, government, and nonprofit organizations worldwide. Part Five reminds us that the ultimate responsibility of organizations and their leaders is to achieve results, and it suggests ways to do just that. Part Six helps leaders to sharpen what is potentially the most powerful but often the most underutilized tool in modern organizations—their people. Finally, Part Seven spotlights innovative leadership in the public and social sector organizations we count on to build strong families, healthy children, and cohesive communities.

In tenuous times, thoughtful people know that there are no quick or easy answers. But they also know that the quality of their ideas and the authenticity of their actions can shape the future. Our goal is to enhance the quality of leadership by provoking thought, supporting action, and inspiring hope—knowing, as Peter Drucker reminds us, that for leaders the focus must be on results. Our promise is that the contributors to this book provide knowledge that can make a difference in the way you think and act. In a world of information overload, it's a simple but exacting order. Like any real leader, you will accept no less.

Easton, Pennsylvania Frances Hesselbein
December 1998

Part I

ON LEADERS AND LEADERSHIP

1 PETER F. DRUCKER

MY MENTORS' LEADERSHIP LESSONS

Peter F. Drucker has been a teacher, writer, and adviser to senior executives for more than fifty years. Author of thirty books, he is honorary chairman of the Drucker Foundation and Clarke Professor of Social Sciences at the Claremont Graduate University in Claremont, California.

The three people from whom I learned the most in my work were all very different. The first two were exceptionally demanding; the third was exceptionally brilliant. All three taught me a lot.

My first boss founded the economics department in a European private bank. He went to France when Hitler came to power, rose to be a full general under De Gaulle, and commanded French resistance troops in Africa. My second boss was among the last in the great nineteenth-century tradition of liberal journalism in Europe— a stern disciplinarian. I learned more from him than from anybody else. My third boss was a London banker who built a private bank from scratch. It became the first newcomer to the London Clearinghouse Association—the club of private banks—in fifty years, and today is part of a financial conglomerate.

Five lessons I learned from those remarkable men still apply today:

- *Treat people differently, based on their strengths.* My first boss, the banker, simply did not know that there were such things as beginners, so he had me work out a merger of the European artificial silk industry—the makers of rayon, the first synthetic fabric. It was a merger of the German, Dutch, Italian, and French companies. And at age nineteen I worked it out, period. I was a securities analyst trainee and knew nothing about anything. When I went in to ask a question he looked at me and said, "Have you looked it up? Don't come and ask me a question until after you have looked it up." So I looked things up, and I learned something.

There were four or five of us, and he treated each of us differently—the way we needed to be treated, which for me was very rough. He demanded enormous things from me. He looked at people, what they should be doing, and then demanded it at a high professional level, far beyond our capacity, and did not stop until we did work that had that quality.

- *Set high standards, but give people the freedom and responsibility to do their jobs.* My next job was for Frankfurt's leading afternoon newspaper. It was the second-largest afternoon paper on the continent—with a circulation of 600,000 and an editorial staff of fourteen people. We didn't know enough to know that we were overworked; we just loved what we were doing.

I went to work as financial and foreign writer on my twentieth birthday. The oldest staff member was perhaps twenty-six—largely because this was ten years after the end of World War I and the people who should have held those jobs were lying in officers' graves all over Europe. There were no educated thirty-year-olds—virtually none.

You began work at 6:00 in the morning. I took the first streetcar, which stopped outside the office at 6:02. My first morning I climbed the three stairs to the editorial offices and there was the editor, six-foot-five, whom I had never met—the publisher had hired me—with a watch in his hand, looking at me. He said, "Young man, if you don't come in five minutes to six tomorrow morning you don't have to come in at all." I explained that the first streetcar didn't leave until 5:35. He picked up the telephone at 6:00 in the morning and got the mayor of Frankfurt out of bed. The next day the first streetcar left at 5:07, and I was on it.

I had a 6:50 deadline each morning—less than an hour in which to write the second and third editorials each day, six days a week. One needed to be nine hundred words, the other six hundred words. The editor had to approve them, but the topics were entirely up to me—and did I learn! The discipline this imposed forced me to be resourceful but allowed me to be creative. Yes, the editor was stern, forbidding, demanding, relentless. But his demands were based not on the mindless exercise of authority but on accountability and the delivery of results.

- *Performance review must be honest, exacting, and an integral part of the job.* The same editor provided a very powerful performance-assessment model. The fourth Saturday of every month, instead of going home at noon, when the paper had gone to press, we adjourned to a private room in a tavern and stayed until 2:00 in the morning. We paid for the sausages they served; the beer was furnished by the paper.

So we began the review around the table. The first to speak was usually the one woman on the staff, because her name began with a B. We each made a presentation about the last month's work, what we thought we had done outstandingly well and why, what we thought needed improvement, where we had botched things, and what we could learn from those mistakes.

It was not just a performance review, it was a performance, period. Each of us—all fourteen—took twenty or thirty minutes. That's seven hours. The editor didn't say a word; we all asked questions, and he took only a few notes. When we were finished, we had another round of sausage and beer. Then the editor asked for comments—ten minutes or fifteen minutes from each of us. Finally, he summed up for three hours without once looking at the notes. We just loved it—and learned everything there was to know about where we stood and how to do better.

- *People learn the most when teaching others.* My third employer was the youngest of three senior partners of a bank. I worked for him mostly as the firm's economist and London securities analyst.

Once a week or so he would sit down with me and talk about the way he saw the world. He used me as an audience, and in the process he demonstrated how to think. He talked the same subject over and over again until it clicked. I learned an enormous amount listening to him and seeing a first-rate mind work. The clarity, the aesthetic rigor he demanded of himself was a joy to behold.

He insisted that because I was the firm's economist I had better learn some economics, which as a brash young man I thought was quite unreasonable. But he used his influence to get me into a prestigious economics seminar at Cambridge. When I left the firm I told him, "I'm not going to be a banker; money bores me silly." He said, "I've known that all along." He simply needed someone who could listen, who could allow him to work out his ideas. In the end, I think he learned more than I did from our little talks.

- *Effective leaders earn respect—but they don't need to be liked.* Each of my three mentors won my respect, but I doubt that any of them considered himself my friend. It would never have occurred to the editor, for instance, to feel affection for a staff member; it was irrelevant. At the end he made me one of three senior editors, but I never even had lunch with him. I never sat down with him except on business. Yet I knew that if I did my job, I could trust him totally—and that if I didn't, I would be out, period.

When I went back to Europe in 1953 for the first time since the war, I went to Frankfurt and called on him. He was very gracious, and I told him how much he had taught me in those monthly review sessions, how much I had learned. And he looked at me and said, "That never occurred to me. The only thing I was interested in was next month's papers." The only bond we had was the task at hand.

Each of these three leaders taught me valuable lessons. But they were, to use an often-abused phrase, "just doing their job." They focused on performance and responsibility for results. Intuitively they understood that the manager's job is to make human strength effective and human weakness irrelevant. Perhaps that was the biggest lesson of all.

2 FRANCES HESSELBEIN

MANAGING IN A WORLD THAT IS ROUND

Frances Hesselbein is editor in chief of Leader to Leader, *chairman of the Drucker Foundation, and former chief executive of Girl Scouts of the USA.*

Five hundred years ago, Renaissance Man discovered that the world was round. Three hundred and fifty years later, Organization Man developed the practice of management. But as this practice evolved, he forgot that his world was round, and he built a management world of squares and boxes and pyramids. His world had a special language that matched its structure: the language of command and control, of order and predict, of climb the ladder, of top and bottom, of up and down.

In every large organization for the next one hundred years, rank equaled authority. And for the most part the old hierarchy that boxed people and functions in squares and rectangles, in rigid structures, worked well. It even developed the famous pyramid with the CEO sitting on the pointed top looking down as his workforce looked up.

And then a period of massive historic change began, a period of global competition and blurred boundaries, of old answers that did not fit the new realities. In organizations in all three sectors there grew a new cynicism about our basic institutions. With government agencies, corporations, and voluntary or social sector organizations trying to ride the winds of change, a different philosophy began to move across the landscape of organizations, and with it came a new language, a new approach, and a new diversity of leadership.

In the 1970s and 1980s, some leaders in the private and the voluntary sectors saw that the hierarchies of the past did not fit the present in which they were living or the future they envisioned—so they took people and functions out of the boxes and, in doing so, liberated the human spirit and transformed the organization.

Today we begin to see the new leaders, the leaders of the future, working in fluid and flexible management structures; and we hear a new language from these leaders—they understand the power of language:

"Mission-focused, values-based, demographics-driven"

"Learning to lead people and not to contain them"

"Management is a tool—not an end"

"Followership is trust"

We hear corporate leaders using more felicitous and inclusive language—for example, Jack Welch of General Electric: "Ten years from now, we want magazines to write about GE as a place where people have the freedom to be creative, a place that brings out the best in everybody, an open, fair place where people have a sense that what they do matters, and where that sense of accomplishment is rewarded in both the pocketbook and the soul. That will be our report card." A powerful corporate leader speaking of soul? The times are changing!

From my own experience in 1976, when I left the mountains of western Pennsylvania to begin my work as CEO of Girl Scouts of

Managing in a World That Is Round 11

the USA, the largest organization for girls and women in the world, I knew that the old structures were not right for the next decade, let alone for the next century. So volunteers and staff together unleashed our people through a flat, circular, fluid management system (see Figure 2.1). In the new organizational structure, people and functions moved across three concentric circles, with the CEO in the middle looking across, not at the top looking down. Five minutes after it was presented, a colleague dubbed it "the bubble chart" and an observer called it "the wheel of fortune." Our people moved across the circles of the organization—never up and down—and the result was high performance and high morale.

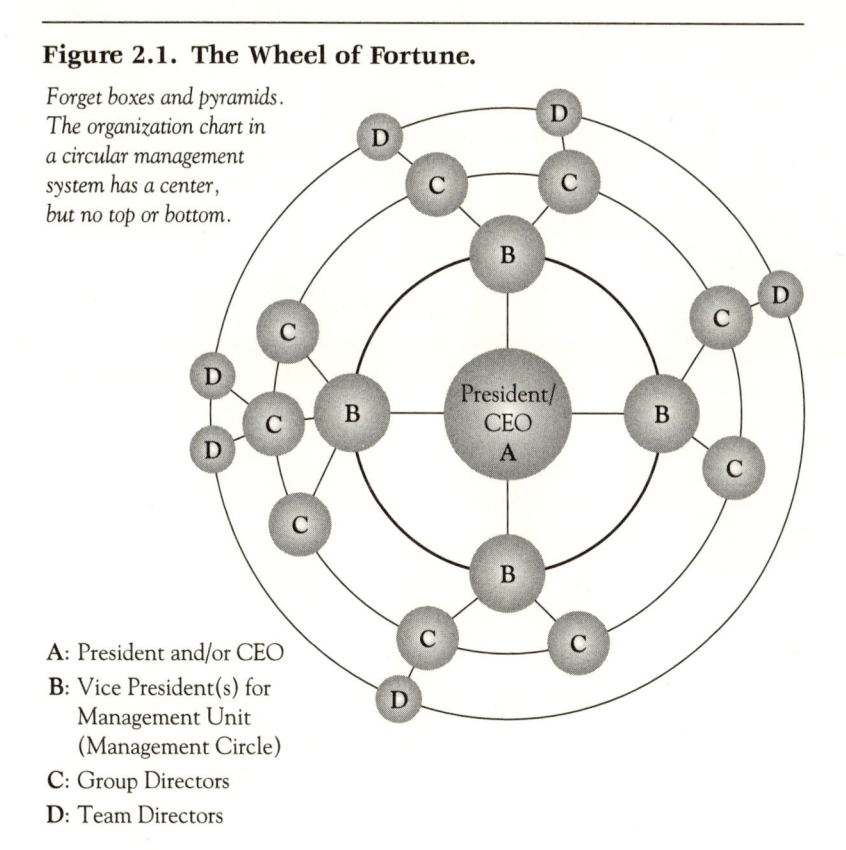

Figure 2.1. The Wheel of Fortune.

Forget boxes and pyramids. The organization chart in a circular management system has a center, but no top or bottom.

A: President and/or CEO
B: Vice President(s) for Management Unit (Management Circle)
C: Group Directors
D: Team Directors

I am often asked by management students and middle managers in the organizations with which I work, "How can we free up the organization and make the changes you talk about if we are not at the top?" I reply, "You can begin where you are, whatever your job. You can bring new insight, new leadership to your team, your group."

That advice applies equally—or especially—to senior executives. As Peter Senge has noted, when it comes to sustaining meaningful change, senior executives have considerably less power than most people think. But one place where they can effect change is in their own work groups and everyday activities.

With the return to organizations of a more fluid, circular view of the world, the days of turf battles, the star system, and the Lone Ranger are over. The day of the partnership is upon us. Leaders who learn to work with other corporations, with government agencies, and with social sector organizations will achieve new energy, new impact, and new significance in their organization's work. But to manage effective partnerships, leaders will have to master three imperatives—managing for the mission, managing for innovation, and managing for diversity.

Managing for the mission. Understanding one's mission is the essence of effective strategy, for the small nonprofit enterprise as well as for the Fortune 500 company. Consider the power of three questions that Peter Drucker offers those who are formulating an organizational mission:

What is our business/mission?

Who is our customer?

What does the customer value?

We devoted many pages of the first issue of *Leader to Leader* to the power of a motivating, aligned mission, so I'll add just a simple observation. An effective mission statement, as Drucker notes, must fit on a T-shirt, and it must give people a clear, compelling, and motivating reason for the organization's existence. For example, "To serve the most vulnerable," the mission of the International Red Cross, satisfies both criteria and succeeds brilliantly; "To maximize shareholder value," the de facto mission of many corporations, satisfies only the first criterion, and fails miserably.

Managing for innovation. Peter Drucker defines innovation as "change that creates a new dimension of performance." If we build innovation into how we structure the organization, how we lead the workforce, how we use teams, and how we design the ways we work together, then innovation becomes a natural part of the culture, the work, the mind-set, the "new dimension of performance." At the same time, we must practice "planned abandonment" and give up programs that may work today but will have little relevance in the future.

Managing for diversity. Perhaps the biggest question in today's world is, How do we help people deal with their deepest differences? Every leader must anticipate the impact of an aging, richly diverse population on the families, work organizations, services, and resources of every community. Headlines and television tell us that governance amid diversity is the world's greatest challenge.

Those headlines also remind us of the grinding reality that no single entity—whether public, private, or nonprofit—can restore our cities to health or create a healthy future for all of our citizens. But in the partnerships that are emerging across all three sectors, we see remarkable openness and results. We need thousands more such partnerships. All of us are learning from one another. Thousands of dedicated public sector employees overcome daunting odds every day to improve their corner of the world. A huge social sector—with more than a million voluntary organizations in the United States and more than twenty million worldwide—shows what dedicated people can do, even on woefully inadequate budgets. And the incredible resources, energy, and expertise of the private sector remind us that behind every problem there really is an opportunity. It is the leader's job to identify the critical issues in which his or her organization can make a difference, then to build effective partnerships based on mission, innovation, and diversity to address those issues.

We need to remember that we can do little alone and yet much together. To be effective, leaders must look beyond the walls of the corporation, the university, the hospital, the agency—and work to build a cohesive community that embraces all of its people—knowing that there is no hope for a productive enterprise within the walls if the community outside the walls cannot provide the healthy, energetic workforce that is essential in a competitive world.

3 MAX DE PREE

THE LEADER'S LEGACY

Max De Pree is chairman emeritus of office furniture manufacturer Herman Miller, a leader in both product design and organizational innovation. De Pree pioneered the use of profit sharing, gain sharing, work teams, and other participatory management practices. In 1997 De Pree was honored by the Business Enterprise Trust with its lifetime achievement award. He is a member of Fortune *magazine's Business Hall of Fame and is the best-selling author of* Leadership Is an Art, Leadership Jazz, *and* Leading Without Power.

Long-time chairman and CEO of Herman Miller—one of the most innovative and most admired companies in America—Max De Pree has won the praise of business and community leaders. His writings and leadership practices have inspired millions of people to think differently about work and life. In February 1997 De Pree was honored by President Clinton and the Business Enterprise Trust with a Lifetime Achievement Award. Just a few weeks later the De Pree Leadership Institute was established at Fuller Theological Seminary. Afterwards, he spoke with Editor in Chief Frances Hesselbein about the many roles and responsibilities of leaders.

FRANCES HESSELBEIN: *Max, you have spoken eloquently about the obligations of leadership and the need for leaders to leave a legacy for their colleagues, customers, and communities. Too few people are helping us see the significance of this philosophy. What do you mean by leaving a legacy, and why is it important?*

MAX DE PREE: One should think first of all about the difference between strategic planning and the concept of a legacy. A strategic plan—understanding the value you provide to customers, your competitive strengths—is necessary but insufficient to the full task of leadership. Leaving a legacy—articulating and bringing to life the kind of organization or community that you want to be a part of—is very different. And it is every bit as important.

At Herman Miller, for instance, leaving a legacy meant, first of all, that there was a common good that we were all connected to and had a right to. And second, that we did not have categories of people based on either performance or natural gifts. Rather, we had a community of people who got to be as good as they could be because we were able to sort out their gifts and assign tasks according to those gifts. The dream was that we would then create results that were quite rich. It wasn't an effort to create results that could be measured only in terms of the conventional wisdom of accountants. Those measurements are important but they're never enough if you're thinking about a community. One has to think about what kind of place we work in, what kind of relationships we have within the workplace, what effect work has on the families we go home to, and what effect the family has on the work we do.

On the one hand, as a leader you always seek a certain level of simplicity; on the other hand, you want to be aware that the workplace is a very complex setting and that there is a range of achievements you'd like to shoot for. We as leaders don't do a good enough job of explaining to people that the quality of the community cannot be seen in terms of the best-off part of the community; it's measured in terms of how the most vulnerable people are doing.

FH: *Yes. That has great significance for so many of us who are concerned about what is going to happen to those who are least able to compete. So what you have to say about building community is extremely helpful. You alluded to the new contexts for work and for leaders. What do you see as these contexts for the leaders of the future?*

MD: The knowledge and information era, as we call it, is clearly changing work tremendously. For instance, the physical dispersal of work, our relationships to the organization and one another, and the demands that we place on certain jobs are all changing. A part of the new context that we're in today is a result of the downsizing that has gone on. We have gone from a corporate society in which we used to say, "Yes, there is a place for you here," to now saying, "No, there may not be a place for you, at least not in the long term."

Corporate leadership, for a variety of reasons, is withdrawing what used to be a meaningful commitment. One of the results of that is that we have stopped trusting one another; we don't find meaning in work the way we used to. These are real losses, which we are not yet facing up to. We're also losing our corporate poise. Even twenty years ago you could sense a certain poise in which people in corporations trusted one another, cared about one another. They had self-confidence, and you could always count on people to be able to work on their own when necessary. But when you lose your corporate poise, people no longer feel able to do that. That's a part of a new context.

We're seeing a movement among leaders in American corporate life toward more individualism, and to me at least that signifies less concern for the common good. You see this when leaders place their own interests above those of all other stakeholders—for instance, with extravagant compensation packages even for executives who have performed poorly. Leaders also have to be concerned about the fragmentation of society in general. Instead of seeing a coming together of community and family and educational systems, with the corporation playing a role, we're seeing those groups driving one another apart. We're seeing young people coming up who are actually quite dangerous. I'm not at all sure that the corporations are as well equipped to handle that kind of problem. That is yet another new context we must face.

FH: *This new corporate context is so different from the call in your earlier writing for a covenant between management and the workforce. We seem to be going in the other direction, with every man, woman, and child for himself or herself. But when you talk about the need to build community, you talk about the need to first get your own house in order. We use that phrase at the Drucker Foundation as well, but in what sense do you mean it?*

MD: Getting one's house in order, in a family or a really good school or a great corporation, has to begin with one's beliefs about people. In my case, it stems from the belief that each of us is made in the image of God, but there are many who have a high view of people that doesn't stem from a religious source. The important thing is that we need to understand that each person is authentic—is an individual with a legitimate place in the world—regardless of whether we hire that person. As long as a person is in your work community, is a legitimate part of that community, she's indispensable to the group. Then you have to work in such a way that your relationships reflect that belief.

If you want to build trust and if you want to have covenantal relationships, you always have to start with respect. Another way leaders can get their own house in order is to describe to themselves what I call an ethical space within which they're going to operate. If that's rooted in good values, then they can build trust and build covenantal relationships that are enormously productive, both in terms of the bottom line and in terms of the kind of communities we want to live and work in.

FH: *Even the language motivates and inspires people when you talk about covenantal relationships. You're saying that before we can look at* *strategy and structure in terms of getting the institutional house in order, we have to look within and put our personal houses in order.*

MD: Yes. Another way to say that is we have to know who we are. It's very difficult. Most of us have also been followers; we didn't come out of the nursery as leaders. And we have learned along the way a great deal about people who wanted to lead us but had no idea who they were. It's tough to follow somebody who doesn't have that sense of himself.

FH: *Max, in talking about knowing who we are, you have done some provocative thinking on the importance of personal restraint. Tell me why you think personal restraint in today's world has significance?*

MD: I think about personal restraint in terms of the moral tone that has to be applied to the way we use our environment. We share the world with a lot of people who have the same rights that we do. We have to understand that there is a relatively small but significant segment of the world who have been given a larger share of all its riches. Philosophically we need to learn how to ask, "Was all this favored stuff given to me for *me*?"

Another side to that question is, "OK, I've got everything I need in life and there's a large world out there." Not everybody has that. So then the question one asks is not "How much do I give away?" but "What may I keep?" I'm here for seventy, seventy-five, eighty years if things go well. I have a certain purview as a leader. The question of what I may keep is to me quite an important one, especially for leaders to ask. When leaders indulge themselves with lavish perks and the trappings of power, they're not showing appropriate restraint, and they're damaging their standing as leaders.

FH: *We hear a lot about shared leadership responsibility and the new role of leaders. But from your experience, what are the few things that a leader may not delegate?*

MD: That's an important question. First of all, from the perspective of the people within most organizations, the only one who is able to hold the organization accountable is the leader. So the leader may not delegate that role. There are some other elements of good corporate life that have to be seen as core elements of leadership. When I was very young, I was an operating room scrub nurse in World War II in France and Germany. Although the relatively untrained scrub nurses could do a lot under severe stress, there were certain things the surgeons could never delegate. It's the same in business. Really good restaurants, for instance, seem to have an owner looking over everything; the great restaurant owner doesn't delegate that oversight. That means providing the kind of visibility and personal engagement that cannot be delegated. I say that one of the functions of a leader is to stop: just as you can't have a conversation with somebody riding by in a car, if you're going to interact with a leader, she has to understand she needs to stop—and listen.

Nor can a leader delegate the final decision on what it is we're going to measure. In a good organization we measure outputs, but in a better organization we also measure inputs. The buck has to stop with somebody on what we're going to measure, because that's going to have an enormous influence on the health of the community down the road. But there is one more thing. The leader has to set the tone for the quality of relationships. If he doesn't care about the quality of relationships, everybody catches on quickly. But if he cares deeply, everybody catches on to *that* quickly. It's almost impossible to think about an organization in which people down the line can set that particular tone.

FH: *If you are my leader and I am your follower, what do you owe me?*

MD: As a leader, to start with, I owe you a respect and an understanding that you're legitimate in that relationship, that I cannot do very much without you. I also owe you a perceivable level of fairness. I'm going to make promises over time. You as a follower have to see those promises kept. The leader owes the follower productive conversations about the gifts that the follower brings to the organization and about the kinds of contributions the follower wishes to make—so that tasks can be designed that give that person hope. In organizations that work, hope is a very functional force, and understanding the function of hope in an organization is essential.

We're talking about two things. One is choice, and choice is always directly connected to hope. The other thing in a productive organization is the design of the task. It's very hard for workers to succeed if they never see how their task is designed. If they can't succeed they can't have hope. And if they can't have hope, it's going to be, at best, a very ordinary organization.

A leader owes followers one more thing: to point them in the direction in which our personal and our group potential lies. As a leader, you've got to understand and explain the environment in which your organization and people are operating. You provide an agenda of things to be working on that are going to have an effect on your future. You should be able to say to people, the company is moving in such and such a direction and will require new skills and knowledge, so we're developing educational programs to help those of you who want to fit in to do this.

FH: *One of the things that raises anxiety in an organization is risk taking: what is risk, who should be taking it, and how much? What does risk taking mean to you, and can we lead without taking risks?*

MD: We cannot either lead or learn without taking risks. As you gain more and more responsibility in organized life, you become more and more of an amateur, because you're less and less specialized. Because of the complexity of work, you have to count more on others. But that also means you're more exposed to risk. When you get to be the CEO, nobody gives you a perfect setting in which to make a decision. They only give you gray areas. All the black and white decisions are made elsewhere. So as the black and white choices merge into gray choices, the level of risk rises. You're also more at risk because you don't have as much time as you used to. But that's part of the job—and the risk—of leadership.

FH: *You have talked about another kind of risk taking in your books, one that makes some people uneasy: moving toward greater openness. The notion of being open and vulnerable to the talents of others is very uplifting as we look at the uncertainty of the future. How did you develop this view?*

MD: Dr. Carl Frost, who is an industrial psychologist and was a consultant at Herman Miller for many years, taught us a lot about participative management. He helped me understand the need to be abandoned to the strengths that others bring. It's similar to what happens when you raise children. When your child turns, say, sixteen, you suddenly discover that you've lost your influence. You've done everything you could do, and now you're at the mercy of the child. It's a little frightening, but when the children turn out well, it's terribly rewarding. You learn that being abandoned to the strengths this child has developed is a really wonderful way to live together as parent and child.

Another mentor in my life was David Hubbard, who for many years was president of Fuller Theological Seminary. He used to talk about two things in particular that taught me a lot. He said leaders don't inflict pain, they bear pain. And he said, the primary purpose of power is not to use it but to share it. A special kind of power develops when it's shared, as compared to when it's used.

FH: *That makes enormous sense. So much of what you talk about has to do with relationships, and I think all of us have learned so much by a simple thing that you did at Herman Miller—you did not have a vice president for human resources; you had a vice president for people. And you've said that if you had been there longer it would have been vice president for people and families.*

MD: You're a great one, Frances, for pointing out to all of us the importance of language and how it influences our behavior in an organization. What we were simply searching for was a way to assign significant responsibility to somebody who is not an overseer of people but an advocate of people. That comes back to the whole idea that what we're working on here is potential, not simply achieving today's goals. For most people in good organizations, achieving their goals is not so difficult. For years we have underestimated people.

We never had a senior officer for human resources before Michele Hunt became vice president for people. We consciously avoided putting that into our structure until we understood that it had to be a senior position of advocacy. It's interesting, Frances, that once you understand the language you're searching for, then you can really describe what you want to achieve.

FH: *Max, as a CEO, how did you help people throughout the enterprise understand your mission? How did you communicate that sense of purpose—why you did what you did, not just the what of the business?*

MD: At Herman Miller, that came out of the convictions that we shared. My dad was founder of the company, and then my brother was the CEO for seventeen years. The company grew nicely and in about 1970 became a public company, which changed things a lot. Through all of that, there was a red thread running through what we were trying to do. It was a thread of moral purpose. In addition to establishing and nurturing good relationships, we tried to do the right thing in the way we researched and developed products. This meant, for instance, that if we were going to perform a leadership role in the design of new products, we had to have connections with the very best people. One of the great gifts of my father and brother is that they were so good at identifying people like Charles Eames and George Nelson and Bob Propst and Bill Stumpf. These are really talented people who gave product leadership to the company over a long period. But we always tried to determine our potential as a group, and we always had a clear sense of mission. We always talked about a more complex set of results that we wanted, including results in our community.

There were other manifestations of this red thread. When it came time for us to establish a major manufacturing operation in Georgia, we sent Michele Hunt, an African American woman, to get that started. We went through a period with the all-white male city council, when they would send Michele out of the meeting and say go call the home office and get a decision. And she'd go out, wait a few minutes, and walk back in and give them the decisions. After a while they caught on, and we ended up with a wonderful relationship with the city of Roswell.

FH: *Max, I have one more question. If you could have just one wish for today's and tomorrow's leaders, what would you wish for them?*

MD: I'd wish that at a younger stage of life these leaders would know in their hearts that what they're figuratively ready to die for is going to change. If they could live in light of that knowledge, they would think differently about their jobs and the world. When we're fifty-two and we've just been made the CEO or chief financial officer in a good-sized company, we honestly believe we'd be ready to die for earnings per share or return on investment. But in about ten years that's going to change. We'd be better leaders if we understood that what we were ready to die for is going to change.

FH: *Max, it's fascinating. We began this conversation talking about change, and we are ending it talking about change. I'd like to express enormous gratitude for this dialogue and for all you bring to all of us who try to make a difference.*

4 DORIS KEARNS GOODWIN

TEN LESSONS FROM PRESIDENTS

Doris Kearns Goodwin is author of the best-sellers The Fitzgeralds and the Kennedys, Lyndon Johnson and the American Dream, *and* No Ordinary Time, *which won the 1995 Pulitzer Prize for history. Her most recent book is the baseball memoir* Wait till Next Year. *She served as an assistant to President Johnson during his last year in office and taught for ten years at Harvard University.*

There are as many styles of leadership as there are leaders. That is evident simply by looking at the forty-two men who have reached the highest office in the land. It is especially clear from three presidents whose legacies loom large thirty years and more after they left office: Lyndon Johnson, John F. Kennedy, and the greatest president of this century, Franklin Roosevelt.

Lyndon Johnson

Johnson's great strength as a leader was his superb understanding of the process of government, specifically the legislative process. That was the key to the landmark legislative program of his early years in office—the Civil Rights Act of 1964, the Voting Rights Act of 1965, Medicare, and aid to education. He had spent his life in the House and the Senate, and he respected the give-and-take of congressional politics. He took seriously and understood the needs of each representative and senator, and worked hard to build relationships with them. When Johnson was a senator, for instance, he knew that Sundays were a lonely time for the leader of the Senate, Richard Russell, a bachelor. So Johnson visited Russell every Sunday morning to read the *New York Times* and keep him company. Not surprisingly, Russell later helped Johnson become majority leader of the Senate.

As president, Johnson mastered one of the great skills of leadership—knowing when to go forward with each of his goals. He had an instinctive sense of timing about when to introduce a bill, and a sense of which ones would create momentum rather than divisiveness for the next bill. For instance, Johnson introduced the Voting Rights Act on the heels of the bloody march on Selma, Alabama, when police assaulted peaceful demonstrators and Congress faced overwhelming public pressure to act. On the wall of the Oval Office Johnson kept a map that showed him which bills were in which committee at every moment. He would come to his office at 5:00 A.M. and start calling the congressmen and senators who he knew were going to have to vote on a provision of the bill that day. If they didn't answer the phone, he'd talk to their wife, husband, son, daughter, or grandchild, saying, "Now you get the Senator to go with me on this bill," and he would make each senator (and his family) feel that the senator was the key to success.

Johnson was also able to share credit with members of both parties. He understood that he had to make Congress feel that his landmark legislation was their triumph as well. He assured Minority Leader Everett Dirksen, for instance, that Dirksen's support for the Civil Rights Bill would make him a hero to millions. This approach succeeded brilliantly. By the middle of 1965, America was on course, as Johnson might have said, for the largest social reform since the New Deal. And because Roosevelt was his idol, that was Johnson's goal.

Sadly, in the midst of these great triumphs, he made a fatal decision with respect to the war in Vietnam. Initially he was reluctant to get involved in the war; his whole heart was in domestic policy. But by July 1965 it was clear that he either had to escalate our commitment or gradually withdraw. He decided, of course, to escalate, to commit hundreds of thousands of troops and millions of dollars. But it was the way he made that decision that proved his undoing. Some people within his administration had argued that he should mobilize the American public behind the war effort by going to Congress for a declaration of war, making a series of speeches explaining his position, imposing a war tax to create a sense of shared participation, and calling up the reserves.

But Johnson rejected all these ideas. Instead he decided to finance the war with the current level of appropriations (while putting in secret Defense Department appropriations) and keeping from Congress and the public the very pessimistic estimates about how much time and human effort it would take to win the war. His first goal was always to keep his Great Society moving forward, and he didn't trust the American people or the Congress to support him if the full scope of the war were understood.

Of course, a leader cannot break trust. It's a disastrous decision in any institution, but particularly when lives are at risk. In his speeches Johnson kept promising that there was light at the end of the tunnel—a promise that proved fatal when he was unable to keep his word. The public was not prepared for the long and difficult war that emerged, and Johnson's credibility was destroyed. Divisions in the society deepened, the peace movement grew, and North Vietnam's successful Tet offensive provoked a challenge in the 1968 primaries from Eugene McCarthy and Robert Kennedy, leading eventually to Johnson's withdrawal from the presidential race. His retirement was almost unbearable to him, because he knew how he had failed at the moment that his triumph had almost been achieved. In the end, his greatest enemy was not his political or military adversaries, but his own arrogance.

John Kennedy

Lyndon Johnson and his predecessor, John Kennedy, present a remarkable contrast in style. Kennedy's strengths and weaknesses as a leader were the mirror image of Johnson's. Whereas Johnson was brilliant in small groups, making deals with individual congressmen, making Congress feel part of a team effort to create the Great Society, Kennedy was never really comfortable with the world of legislative politics. He didn't enjoy the backroom schmoozing and didn't believe in the process of political give-and-take. His ambitions were always a step beyond the House and Senate, and his colleagues there felt that he wasn't really one of them. He also did not possess the instinctive sense of timing that allowed Johnson to capitalize on dramatic moments and build on each success. By contrast, Kennedy introduced a series of bills when he first came into office that by the time of his death were stymied (though Johnson eventually passed many of them).

Yet whereas Lyndon Johnson was unable to mobilize the public at large, unable to generate trust in the people, unable to sustain the dignity of the presidency and the credibility of his word, John Kennedy understood the power of language, the importance of symbolism, humor, and image to give the public a sense of connection to the presidency. He made millions of people feel that they were part of the New Frontier. That's the mystery and the art of leadership—the ability to mobilize people to feel included and to care about the tasks ahead. Kennedy made politics exciting and fulfilling. He conveyed the most important sense that a leader can convey: that the problems of society, however large they might seem, can be solved by public action. In so doing, he gave energy to a growing number of movements of the 1960s, even some that were not particularly friendly to him: the civil rights movement, the women's movement, the consumer movement, and the environmental movement. Indeed, his strongest legacy was that he made young people feel that politics was an honorable profession and a rich adventure. Kennedy's concept of public service brought thousands of young people into the Peace Corps and VISTA, creating a desire on the part of the younger generation to play a role in improving human society.

There have been cycles in American history when people have wanted to be part of the large issues of the day. They have marched, they have argued, they have discussed the problems with friends and family. At other times, such as in the past decade or so, private life has taken precedence. Kennedy helped to create social momentum; that is an exceptional ability even for gifted leaders, and may be his greatest legacy.

Perhaps one of his best temperamental qualities, however, in contrast to Lyndon Johnson, was his ability to learn from mistakes. For example, after he made the disastrous mistake at the Bay of Pigs, authorizing an ill-advised, ill-prepared intervention in Cuba, he reshaped his foreign policy decision-making structure. Never again would he depend on a narrow group of advisers who may have had their own agendas. He learned to question others' assumptions and values, to examine critically the information and intelligence brought to him. He was not just skeptical; he was genuinely curious. He was able to reach down into the bureaucracy by calling State Department desk officers who had never been called by a president before, to get unfiltered information. This approach contributed to his success in handling the Cuban Missile Crisis, which proved to be a twentieth-century political turning point.

Kennedy also accepted responsibility for the failure at the Bay of Pigs—and surprisingly to him, his public opinion ratings went up as a result. In fact, he said at that point, "I don't understand it. The worse I do, the more they love me." Of course, the public was responding not to his mistakes but to his willingness to shoulder responsibility.

Franklin Roosevelt

But as compelling as Johnson's and Kennedy's leadership legacies were, no president I've studied offers a better case study in leadership than Franklin Roosevelt. Probably his greatest gift as a leader was his absolute confidence in himself and, more important, in the American people. It was a confidence shaped in part by his parents, by the possession of his talents, and by the transforming experience of triumphing over his polio. It was a confidence so deep that it provided an inner well of security through the worst days of World War II. Once, in the middle of the war, he told a friend, "When I go to sleep at night and I think of all the decisions that I've made that day, I say to myself, 'Well, old top, you've probably done as best you can.' And I roll over and go straight to sleep." Contrast that with Lyndon Johnson waking in the night, worrying about whether the bombing targets he had chosen had been right.

Roosevelt's confidence allowed him to be flexible, to try everything and meet defeat with serenity, knowing he'd do better next time. He tolerated ambiguity in ways that often baffled and sometimes angered those around him. He was so skilled at anticipating what others wanted from him that, it was said, he would seem to agree with people at meetings by nodding his head amiably at anything that was said, leaving confusion as to what he really believed. Perhaps if he had been more blunt he would have lost fewer friends, one disillusioned aide said. His ambiguity didn't stop him from taking action, however. He never lost the essential qualities of leadership, which are to observe, discuss, assess, understand—and then take responsibility and move forward.

Moreover, Roosevelt's supreme confidence proved contagious, for he was somehow able to transmit his strength outward—first to his cabinet officers, who wrote that during the darkest days of the war they felt buoyed by his strength, his optimism, and his belief in them. But ultimately Roosevelt extended his optimism to the American people at large, in the mysterious ways that great leaders engage others. He did this primarily through a remarkable series of radio addresses—the "fireside chats"—in which he shaped, educated, and molded public opinion rather than merely reflecting it, as leaders too often do today.

I'd always imagined that Roosevelt was on the radio every week as today's presidents are, but actually he delivered just two or three fireside chats a year. He waited for a dramatic moment to go before the people. These addresses were so powerful and inspiring that afterward he received thousands of telegrams urging him to go on the radio every day to sustain morale. But with knowing insight he wrote back to one of his listeners, saying that if his speeches ever become routine they would lose their effectiveness. That is yet another of the leadership challenges that he so well understood: when to go before the people, how to seize a dramatic moment to ask for certain things, and how to avoid overexposure.

If you've ever felt overwhelmed by the complexity of a problem, think of what Roosevelt faced in 1940. With war approaching, the United States had virtually no military capacity—we became the seventeenth largest military power only after Holland surrendered to Germany and lost its spot on the list. We had just 500,000 soldiers compared to 6 million in the German Army. Roosevelt understood that Germany's threat was to Western civilization; he had to mobilize an isolationist country and move from a peacetime economy to a wartime economy. His first step was to reach out to the business community with whom he had endured hostile relations in the 1930s. But he knew that government couldn't build the tanks, the weapons, the planes, the ships—only the business community could. He asked business leaders to run the war production agencies, and as "dollar a year men" they became heroes during the war.

He gave generous loans and tax incentives to help build the factories that would produce war materials, forging perhaps the most extraordinary government-business partnership ever and creating a miracle of industrial production. Between 1940 and 1942, America produced more weaponry than all of the Axis powers and other Allied powers combined. In terms of total output, some have calculated, it was like building a Panama Canal every week. Roosevelt also knew the importance of making each factory feel that it was an integral part of this production effort. He visited the plants and shipyards, conferred awards of excellence, and understood the power of symbolism. There was a pilot, for instance, who had been shot down in the South Pacific but whose plane somehow carried him to safety. With Roosevelt, the decorated pilot visited the Boeing plant where his plane had been built and told the workers they had saved his life. Naturally they redoubled their efforts.

In contrast to Lyndon Johnson, Roosevelt never promised that victory would be quick or easy. After giving people his sober estimates, however, he said he was certain that eventually a democracy would beat out a dictatorship because a democracy releases the free energies of a free people while the most efficient dictatorship never can. He brought his point to life by highlighting American history—Washington at Valley Forge running out of provisions but persevering, the pioneers' struggles to settle the West, the hardships of the Civil War, and the Industrial Revolution. Like most presidents before him—and unlike most since—Roosevelt understood that history can be a powerful leadership tool.

He also understood the need for personal renewal, and he drew sustenance from a remarkable group of people around him. Imagine what the modern media would make of the Roosevelt White House: a secretary in love with the president; a woman reporter in love with the First Lady; a beautiful Norwegian princess visiting on weekends; the prime minister of England in residence for months at a time, drinking from morning to night, and yet saving his country in the process. We have seen recently how destructive the airing of such subjects can be. But these relationships were essential to Roosevelt's leadership. His conversations with the people who lived with him in the White House allowed him to relax and replenish his energies to face the struggles of the day.

More than any leader I have studied, Roosevelt knew how to structure relaxation into his working days. For instance, he had a cocktail hour every night, with one rule: you could not talk about politics. The only person who violated the rule, it was said, was

Eleanor, who somehow couldn't help but bring up slum clearance or civil rights during these social hours. But most of the time he was able to relax, and he could often work several hours more at night after the cocktail hour, replenished by those conversations. In the midst of the worst days of the war, he would hold marathon poker games with his cabinet officers, where the only thing he thought about was how to win the next hand. And almost unimaginable today, in the midst of the war Roosevelt went on several fishing trips, one of which lasted ten days. He argued that the prevailing assumptions, the group-think, the obstacles to change, made creative thinking impossible in Washington. Indeed, some of his most important initiatives, such as the Lend-Lease program that sustained England in the early years of the war, were conceived during these getaways.

It is also useful to consider Roosevelt's complicated and difficult relationship with Eleanor. It was a historic partnership that points up the importance for all leaders to have a counterpoint to themselves, someone who mirrors their strengths and weaknesses, as in many ways Eleanor did for Franklin. She was always concerned with what should be done, he was concerned with what could be done. She was the idealist, he was the practical force. To be sure, the partnership between Franklin and Eleanor was not without flaws on both sides. But after his death she understood that much of her vision had been realized, that the war had become a vehicle for social reform at home. The United States had been transformed from a weak, isolationist, socially stratified country into a powerful, productive, prosperous society, more just than ever before in its history.

Presidents as Leaders

As leaders, all three of these presidents knew the importance of assembling a strong inner circle, of knowing the talents, skills, and weaknesses of people and matching them to the demands of the job. Johnson, for instance, had almost a psychiatrist's capacity to understand the people with whom he was dealing—especially when he served in the Senate—and he knew how to translate colleagues' needs into votes. Of course, presidents, more than most chief executives, often make compromises in recruiting their senior managers; Fortune 500 presidents don't need congressional approval for their teams. Yet all effective leaders still choose a strength over a weakness.

To be sure, every leader uses talent differently. Roosevelt deliberately appointed to his cabinet people of diverse points of view who weren't afraid to challenge one another, or him. Indeed, their public squabbles often deflected criticism away from him. Starting with Kennedy, however, the White House staff began to eclipse the cabinet as the president's central policymaking team. It's an important distinction because cabinet officers, although appointed by the

---

Ten Lessons for Leaders

Lyndon Johnson, John Kennedy, and Franklin Roosevelt were three very different people and presidents. But their stories offer at least ten useful lessons for leaders of today's organizations:

- *Timing is (almost) everything.* Knowing when to introduce an initiative, when to go before one's constituents—and when to hold off—is a crucial skill.

- *Anything is possible if you share the glory.* Giving others a chance to claim credit is an easy and effective way to get results.

- *Trust, once broken, is seldom restored.* It is the most fragile yet essential attribute of leadership. No leader can afford to take his word lightly.

- *Leadership is about building connections.* Effective leaders make people feel they have a stake in common problems.

- *Leaders learn from their mistakes.* To succeed, leaders must acknowledge and understand and improve on their shortcomings.

president, represent to some extent their own constituency; they manage agencies and that gives them a certain power vis à vis the president. White House staffers, on the other hand, are beholden only to the president and are less likely to challenge the boss.

The mistake that Johnson made was keeping most of Kennedy's cabinet. It included some very capable people, and Johnson thought that after Kennedy's shocking death the nation needed continuity. But that meant he never really felt that these were his people. As the war escalated and criticism mounted, he hunkered down; instead of dealing with the full cabinet and inviting debate, he dealt with a smaller and smaller group of advisers. By 1968, the cabinet

- *Confidence—not just in oneself—counts.* Most leaders are self-confident, sometimes to a fault; the real gift is the ability to extend faith in oneself to others. That means actually believing in their gifts.
- *Effective partnerships require devotion to one's partners.* Attention to the needs of the remote plant or institution pays off with energetic commitment.
- *Renewal comes from many sources.* Leaders must know themselves and find their own sources of strength.
- *Leaders must be talent brokers.* The ability to identify, recruit, and effectively manage the best and brightest people—including people unlike oneself—is itself a key talent.
- *Language is one's most powerful tool.* Without the ability to communicate, leaders can possess all the other attributes and still fail to have an impact.

was hardly meeting; Johnson's major decisions were made with only two or three people. That's a tendency for all leaders when things get tough, but it's precisely the wrong tendency. Johnson's isolation deprived him of new ideas and led to his undoing.

At their best, all effective leaders share a gift for defining a vision, for moving people toward the future. For some, that movement is propelled by a crisis. By the time Roosevelt came into office, for instance, the Depression had reached such a depth that people were ready for change. But in the absence of a crisis that helps to mobilize the public, leaders must find other opportunities. For instance, when Kennedy was elected in 1960, there was no overwhelming crisis. The Cold War had become a state of grinding normalcy; but by talking about poverty, about public service, Kennedy was able to lift expectations and make people feel part of a noble cause.

Great leaders have that capacity, but it's not simply charisma; it can be words. Lyndon Johnson didn't have charisma—but when he stood before a joint session of Congress in March 1965 and spoke about history and fate coming together at Lexington and Concord and then in Selma, he told people that the time had come to right a terrible wrong. That was a moment when a leader's words reached out and connected him to a powerful social movement. The Voting Rights Act passed within six weeks. It's up to the leader to know how to use words to channel people's best impulses into positive outcomes. That is another trait shared by Johnson, Kennedy, and Roosevelt. Their strengths lay in their extraordinary ability to reach out and move others; their weaknesses were simply those of any human being.

In the end, leaders and followers trying to make sense of—and a difference in—today's world face the same task as historians trying to understand the past. The real challenge of history is to resist the tendency, so prevalent today, to label, to stereotype, to expose, to denigrate—and instead bring common sense and empathy to our work so that the past can truly come alive, even if just for a few moments, in all its beauty, sorrow, and glory.

5 JAMES M. KOUZES

FINDING YOUR LEADERSHIP VOICE

James M. Kouzes is chairman of Tom Peters Group Learning Systems, based in Palo Alto, California. A renowned speaker and educator, he is coauthor with Barry Posner of The Leadership Challenge, Credibility, *and* Encouraging the Heart.

One of the most persistent myths in our culture associates leadership with rank. But leadership isn't a position; it's a process. It's an observable, understandable, learnable set of skills and practices available to everyone, anywhere in the organization.

I was making that case to a group of senior managers at a recent workshop when across the room a hand shot up. "I'd like to challenge that statement," said the participant. "I've been pondering this lately. Can anyone really learn to lead? If so, with all the leadership training that exists, why are there so few effective leaders?"

"Fair enough," I answered. "But let me respond by asking you something first: Can *management* be learned?"

"Yes," was the unanimous response from the group.

"Interesting, isn't it?" I continued. "I've been asked in almost every workshop if leadership can be learned, but I've never been asked if management can be learned. Never!"

That Special Leadership Something

Now why is that? What is it about management that allows us to assume that it can be learned, and what is it about leadership that constantly raises questions about our capacity to learn it? Tell me, what is that unique something about leadership?

Here are a few representative responses to these questions from workshop participants:

"Soul."

"Spirit."

"It's inside yourself."

"Managers do things right, leaders do the right things."

"Ethics."

"Value system."

Is there anything on this list that you cannot learn? Maybe some of these things can't be taught, but can you *learn* them? Soul? Spirit? Ethics? Values? Can you learn what's in your soul? Can you learn what gives you spirit? Can you learn what is right? Can you learn what you hope the future will be? Can you learn what you value most? Not for everyone, not for society, but for *you*?

The scary part is that we fear the answer is no. We're afraid that we have no spirit. That we have no soul. No deeply held beliefs. We've mastered all the techniques, but we've missed the guts.

In his witty book *Management of the Absurd,* psychologist and business executive Richard Farson writes, "In both parenthood and management, it's not so much what we *do* as what we *are* that counts.... There is no question that parents can and should do worthwhile things for their children, but it's what they are that will really matter.... The same dynamic occurs in management and leadership. People learn—and respond to—what we are." Farson has nailed it. All the techniques and all the tools that fill the pages of all the management and leadership books are not substitutes for who and what you are. In fact they boomerang if thrown by some "spinmeister" who has mastered form but not substance.

My colleague Barry Posner and I have been collaborating on leadership research for fifteen years, and we keep learning the same thing over and over. We keep rediscovering that *credibility is the foundation of leadership*. People don't follow your technique. They follow you—your message and your embodiment of that message.

In *Leadership Jazz,* Max De Pree, former chair and chief executive officer of the Michigan furniture maker Herman Miller, illustrates this point with a moving story about tending his prematurely born granddaughter, Zoe, during the first days of her fragile life. On his initial visit to the neonatal intensive care unit, De Pree encountered a compassionate nurse named Ruth, who gave him this advice: "I want you to come to the hospital every day to visit Zoe, and when you come, I would like you to rub her body and her legs and her arms with the tip of your finger. While you're caressing her, you should tell her over and over how much you love her, because she has to be able to connect your voice to your touch."

In that instant, De Pree realized that nurse Ruth was giving him not only the best advice for care of Zoe but also "the best possible description of the work of a leader. At the core of becoming a leader is the need always to connect one's voice to one's touch."

Leadership credibility is about connecting voice and touch, about doing what you say you will do. But De Pree insists that there's a prior task to connecting voice and touch. It's *"finding* one's voice in the first place."

Why Language Matters

Finding your voice is absolutely critical if you are to be an authentic leader. If you do not find your voice, you will find yourself with a vocabulary that belongs to someone else, mouthing words that were written by a speech writer who is nothing like you at all. If you doubt the importance of choosing your own vocabulary, consider these phrases from a speech by a banking manager Barry Posner and I observed during the course of our research:

- "Keep your capital, and keep it dry."
- "We'll act like SWAT teams."
- "We're going to beat their brains out."
- "We won't tolerate the building of fiefdoms."
- "There will be only a few survivors."

Contrast his words with these phrases from *The Body Shop,* by founder Anita Roddick:

- "We communicate with passion—and passion persuades."
- "I think all businesses' practices would improve immeasurably if they were guided by 'feminine' principles—qualities like love and care and intuition."
- "What we need is optimism, humanism, enthusiasm, intuition, curiosity, love, humor, magic, fun, and that secret ingredient—euphoria."
- "I believe that service—whether it is serving the community or your family or the people you love or whatever—is fundamental to what life is about."

What do these words communicate about the individuals speaking them—about their guiding beliefs and assumptions? Would any of these words be in your lexicon? Would you want them used in your organization? Only by finding your voice will you know.

Beyond Tools and Techniques

Every artist knows that finding one's voice is most definitely not a matter of technique alone. It's a matter of time and a matter of searching—soul searching.

I remember several years back attending a retrospective of painter Richard Diebenkorn's work with my wife and an artist friend. Toward the end of our gallery walk, our friend observed, "There are three periods in an artist's life. In the first, we paint exterior landscapes. In the second, we paint interior landscapes. In the third, they come together into an artist's unique style. In the third period, we paint our selves." I consider this the most important art appreciation lesson I've ever received. It applies equally to the appreciation of the art of leadership.

When first learning to lead, we paint what we see outside ourselves—the exterior landscape. We read biographies and autobiographies of famous leaders, attend speeches by decorated military officers, buy tapes by motivational speakers, and participate in classes led by skilled facilitators. We do all this to master the fundamentals, the tools, and the techniques. We're clumsy at first, failing more than succeeding, but soon we can give a speech with ease, conduct a meeting with grace, and praise an employee with style. It's an essential period; an aspiring leader can no more skip the fundamentals than can an aspiring painter.

Then it happens. Somewhere along the way we notice how mechanically rote that last speech sounded, what a boring routine that last meeting was, and how terribly sad and empty that last encounter felt. We awaken to the frightening thought that the words aren't ours, that the technique is out of a text, not straight from the heart.

This is a truly terrifying moment. We've invested so much time and energy in learning to do all the right things, and we suddenly see that they are no longer serving us well. They seem hollow. We stare into the darkness of our inner territory and begin to wonder what lies inside.

For aspiring leaders, this awakening initiates a period of intense exploration—a period of going beyond technique, beyond training, beyond copying what the masters do, beyond taking the advice of others. And if you surrender to it, after exhausting experimentation and often painful suffering, there emerges from all those abstract strokes on the canvas an expression of self that is truly your own.

So I'll have to amend what I said to the workshop participants a few weeks back. Yes, you can learn to lead, but don't confuse leadership with position and place. Don't confuse leadership with skills and systems or with tools and techniques. They are not what earn you the respect and commitment of your constituents. What earns you their respect in the end is whether you are you. And whether what you are embodies what they want to become. So just who are you, anyway?

6 HERB KELLEHER

THE BEST LESSON IN LEADERSHIP

Herb Kelleher, chairman, president, and CEO of Southwest Airlines, has been called perhaps the best CEO in America by Fortune *magazine. Under his leadership, Southwest has become the most consistently profitable, productive, and cost-efficient carrier in the industry. It has also earned the Triple Crown award for best on-time performance, baggage handling, and customer satisfaction for four years in a row.*

What's the secret to building a great organization? How do you sustain consistent growth, profits, and service in an industry that can literally change overnight? And how do you build a culture of commitment and performance when the notion of loyalty—on the part of customers, employees, and employers—seems like a quaint anachronism? I can answer in two words: *be yourself*.

That is both a simple and a profoundly difficult goal. It means spending less time benchmarking best practices and more time building an organization in which personality counts as much as quality and reliability. It also means cultivating an ability to embrace paradox.

Southwest Airlines has a reputation as the wild and crazy guy of commercial aviation. Yet in many ways we are the most conservative company in our industry. We have always maintained a strong balance sheet, watched our costs, and paid as much attention to our financial fitness in good times as in bad. That discipline lets us move quickly when opportunities come our way. From 1990 to 1994, for instance, when the airline industry lost $12.5 billion, we were able to buy more planes and enhance our capacity to compete in today's growing market.

But you can't just lead by the numbers. We've always believed that business can and should be fun. At far too many companies, when you come into the office you put on a mask. You look different, talk different, act different—which is why most business encounters are, at best, bland and impersonal. But we try not to hire people who are humorless, self-centered, or complacent, so when they come to work we want *them*, not their corporate clones. They are what makes us different from other airlines, and in most enterprises different is better.

Culture Defines Personality

A financial analyst once asked me if I was afraid of losing control of our organization. I told him I've never had control and I never wanted it. If you create an environment where the people truly participate, you don't *need* control. They know what needs to be done and they do it. And the more that people will devote themselves to your cause on a voluntary basis, a willing basis, the fewer hierarchies and control mechanisms you need.

We're not looking for blind obedience. We're looking for people who on their own initiative want to be doing what they're doing because they consider it to be a worthy objective. I have always believed that the best leader is the best server. And if you're a servant, by definition you're not controlling.

In an organization like ours, you're also likely to be a step behind the employees. The fact that I cannot possibly know everything that goes on in our operation—and don't pretend to—is a source of competitive advantage. The freedom, informality, and interplay that people enjoy allows them to act in the best interests of the company. For instance, when our competitors began demanding tens of millions of dollars a year for us to use their travel agents' reservations systems, I said, forget it; we'll develop an electronic, ticketless system so travel agents won't have to handwrite Southwest tickets—and we won't be held hostage to our competitors' distribution systems. It turned out that people from several departments had already gotten together, anticipated such a contingency, and begun working on a system, unbeknownst to me or the rest of our officers. That kind of initiative is possible only when people know that our company's success rests with them, not with me.

Personality Is Strategy

When you start out, as we did, having to operate as an intrastate airline, that pretty well dictates your market niche. You build a low-cost, high-frequency, point-to-point operation rather than the hub-and-spoke system that others have. And you make that apparent market weakness into an operational strength.

With deregulation, this market strategy was in question. Suddenly any carrier was free to compete with any other. We could have brought in 747s and flown nonstop from New York to Los Angeles, or Dallas to London. It was a defining moment. Howard Putnam, our president and CEO at the time, wisely asked people throughout the company to think about our future and the kind of organization we wanted to be. We decided not to go head to head with the international carriers but to build on the strategy that had worked so well for us in the past.

Over the years we have developed not only a different strategy but also a different strategic planning process. Basically, we just don't do it. In an industry where a two-week plan is likely to become obsolete, to spend days debating whether we're to serve Trenton, New Jersey, in 2005 is a meaningless exercise. Life is chaotic; in the airline business it's anarchic. So rather than trying to predict what we'll do, we try to define who we are and what we want, in terms of market niche, operational strategy, and financial health. We reflect, observe, debate—and we don't use our calculators.

Several years ago, for instance, our marketing group met with one item on the agenda: What is the next decade going to be like in the United States socially? We concluded that people were going to be much more value-conscious than they were during the 1980s. That ran in our favor—and helped validate our strategy. So our strategic planning is an effort to establish flexible goals and guideposts, not detailed action steps: What kind of debt-equity ratio do we want on our balance sheet? When do we want to deviate from that? Are we doing so for a good reason?

I have seen brilliant entrepreneurial strategies falter as an organization grows and matures. Obviously you manage a $25 billion company differently than you do a $25 million company. But you change your *practices*, not your principles. You learn how to communicate with large numbers of employees by using videotapes, newsletters, weekly updates, and frequent visits to the field. You share not only what's going on in the company but also what's going on in the industry and in the marketplace. You are careful that people don't preoccupy themselves with cosmetic things like offices and titles. You delegate more and more, and make yourself available as a troubleshooter. You go to meetings not to issue orders or instructions; you go to learn the problems people are having and to see if you can help. You remember that systems are not masters—they're servants in helping you carry out your mission. And that nothing comes ahead of your people.

If you take an ongoing, genuine interest in the well-being of your people, outside as well as inside the workplace, you eventually create trust. That leads to such things as our extraordinary pilots contract, with the pilots taking stock options for five years instead of pay increases. (To show good faith, I also took a five-year wage and bonus freeze.) But that kind of community building is not formulaic; if you try to program it, you destroy it.

Working for a Worthy Cause

Our real accomplishment is that we have inspired our people to buy into a concept, to share a feeling and an attitude, to identify with the company—and then to execute. Because our low-fare strategy is so central to who we are, our employees are enormously cost-conscious. We don't have the traditional budget struggles at the end of the year. That's not to say that we don't argue over budget allocations, but it's rare that a manager submits an inflated budget, thinking, "If I ask for 200 percent more, maybe I'll get 100 percent." That's just not us.

But you need to spend more time on the intangibles than on the tangibles to create that kind of buy-in. For example, I have told our people in the field—mostly young people—that my hope is that when they're talking to their grandchildren they say that Southwest Airlines was one of the finest experiences they ever had, that it helped them grow beyond anything they thought possible. We are not afraid to talk to our people with emotion. We're not afraid to tell them, "We love you," because we do.

One of the managers in our People Department once said, "The important thing is to take the bricklayer and make him understand that he's building a home, not just laying bricks." So we take the building-a-home approach: this is what you're doing not only for yourself but for society—giving people who'd otherwise not be able to travel the opportunity to do so; making it possible for grandparents to see their grandchildren for holidays, or for a working mom to take her son to see the World Series—for less than the cost of a ticket to the game. We constantly hold up examples of customer experiences and of employee efforts to make a difference.

Building Employee Partnership

You can't have a culture of commitment and performance without equitable employee compensation, and that includes executive compensation. Our officers—whom I consider the best in the business—

are paid 30 percent less, on average, than their counterparts at other airlines and at companies of similar size in other industries. On the other hand, most of our employees are at or above average pay levels in our industry. We try to make up that difference to our officers with stock options, but of course that depends on how well the company does.

We also have provided profit sharing to all employees for the past twenty-four years. We want them to have a significant ownership of Southwest Airlines. We want them to share our success. We want to offer top-notch benefit programs. But in return for this we want our people to be productive, and we achieve productivity through people's enthusiasm and dedication, to be sure—but also through work rules that encourage flexibility and cooperation up, down, and across our organization. I think it says a lot that we have had no layoffs and only one strike in our twenty-five-year history.

Our most important tools for building employee partnership are job security and a stimulating work environment. Our union leadership has recognized that we provide job security, and there hasn't been a lot of that in the airline industry. Certainly there have been times when we could have made substantially more profits in the short term if we had furloughed people, but we didn't. We were looking at our employees' and our company's long-term interests. And as it turns out, providing job security imposes additional discipline, because if your goal is to avoid layoffs, then you hire very sparingly. So our commitment to job security has actually helped us keep our labor force smaller and more productive than those of our competitors.

But it's not enough to try to assure people a job; equally important is allowing them to feel liberated when they come to work—to be creative, to think outside the lines. To foster problem solving and cooperation, for example, we have the Walk a Mile program, in which any employee can do somebody else's job for a day. The operations agents cannot fly the planes, but the pilots can—and do—work as operations agents. (They also, on their own, have held barbecues for all our mechanics, to thank them for keeping our planes flying.) Seventy-five percent of our twenty thousand people have participated in the job-swapping program. It's an administrative nightmare, but one of the best tools I know for building understanding and collaboration.

Training is another way you forge committed partnership. Naturally an airline must train every employee, but our most important training is not in how to manage or administer but in how to lead. Originally that training was part of our pilots' crew-resource management program; it focused on how the first officer and the pilot relate to each other, how they exchange information, and how they focus on the task at hand—in short, how they work as a team. Today we have reservation sales agents, flight attendants, mechanics, and administrative staff in those classes, as well as the cockpit crews.

Above all, you have to seize everyday opportunities to build bridges between people, especially in moments of crisis. Some years ago, for instance, one of our employee groups in effect voted itself out of its union. Many of the rank and file were feeling insecure about their future, so we gave them a personal contract signed by me. It provided for a grievance procedure, arbitration procedure, and so on. Several labor lawyers and professors called me and asked if that was legal. (I thought it was *their* job to tell *me*.) But they missed the point. Our agreement with the employees was a matter of good faith; it didn't need to be legally enforceable. We didn't set up an iota of the structure that the experts recommended, and a year later we had no grievances pending. They were all handled informally, by people with good will getting together and talking to each other.

Why Competition Helps Us

Fifteen years ago competitors were saying, "We're going to be the next Southwest Airlines." But they didn't really understand who we were. Most of them did not really imitate Southwest Airlines; they ended up creating new versions of themselves. But today we have a new wave of competition. Everybody's had an additional decade to learn—and many carriers, including the majors, are very precisely defining new niches and executing their strategy very well. The competition is tougher than ever. But in virtually every market in which we compete, the market has grown. In California, for instance, where Shuttle by United has invested millions of dollars to win a piece of our business, we have maintained our 50 percent share of the market—but we are now carrying many more passengers than we did three years ago. That's because, despite what the experts say, air travel is not a commodity business. We market ourselves based on our personality and spirit. That sounds like an easy claim, but in fact it is a supremely dangerous position to stake out, because if you're wrong, customers will let you know—with a vengeance. Customers are like a force of nature—you can't fool them, and you ignore them at your own peril.

In that regard, our approach has changed little in the past twenty-five years. My best lesson in leadership came during my early days as a trial lawyer. Wanting to learn from the best, I went to see two of the most renowned litigators in San Antonio try cases. One sat there and never objected to anything but was very gentle with witnesses and established a rapport with the jury. The other was an aggressive, thundering hell-raiser. And both seemed to win every case. That's when I realized that there are many different paths, not one right path. That's true of leadership as well. People with different personalities, different approaches, different values succeed not because one set of values or practices is superior but because their values and practices are *genuine*. And when you and your organization are true to yourselves—when you deliver both results and a singular experience—customers can spot it from thirty thousand feet.

Part II

LEADING INNOVATION AND TRANSFORMATION

7 PETER F. DRUCKER

THE DISCIPLINE OF INNOVATION

Peter F. Drucker has been a teacher, writer, and adviser to senior executives for more than fifty years. Author of thirty books, he is honorary chairman of the Drucker Foundation and Clarke Professor of Social Sciences at the Claremont Graduate University in Claremont, California.

The goal of most organizations—certainly of philanthropic organizations—is not just to deliver services but also to foster change and improve lives. After World War II we thought that this was the job of government, and for forty years we saw an enormous expansion of government programs for the community. Few of them have been very successful.

We are now about to enter a new era of community building with local organizations working on specific opportunities in the community. Increasingly, it is up to community organizations to innovate. In a time of rapid change, the opportunities for improving, for getting results, are also changing rapidly. Things that were impossible or unnecessary yesterday suddenly become possible, and things that made great sense yesterday no longer make sense. We have to learn in our organizations what is needed to perform and to innovate.

To master the discipline of innovation we must do three things:

- Focus on the mission
- Define the results we are after
- Assess what we're doing and how we are doing it

One of the tasks of leaders is to make sure that we constantly put our scarce resources (people and money) where they do the most good. We have to be results-focused and opportunity-focused. Good intentions are no longer enough.

This is best illustrated by a hypothetical example. For several years I have been working closely with a group in a major industrial city that started out to provide mentoring for youngsters who were floundering in high school. The program attracted many volunteers, especially young people who had postponed having their own children yet liked to work with children. After three or four years the organization had an oversupply of volunteers and no financial problems. Yet it had practically no results. It took us a few years to realize that if a youngster hasn't learned how to learn by the ninth or tenth grade, it's too late. So the organization has shifted its emphasis to grade school and kindergarten.

We confirmed something that educators have known all along—that the child who is far behind grade level in third or fourth grade is unlikely ever to catch up. This child is discouraged, turned off. But when the volunteers began to focus their efforts on children under the age of ten, their results went sky high. From almost no results with tenth graders, the group was seeing 60 percent success with second to fourth graders. But in time we saw that even among these younger children one group still showed poor results. We found that about one-sixth of elementary school children who fall behind are fully capable intellectually but have undiagnosed health problems—vision, hearing, or learning disabilities. We changed our focus once again and now concentrate on that small number of students whose problems often elude traditional testing but, once diagnosed, are easily remedied. We have refocused heavily on developing diagnostic tools, on training school nurses to give the tests, and on having a mobile clinic visit schools at the beginning and end of each year to test children.

We are now seriously considering abandoning the original aim of mentoring children who lack support at home; perhaps we will spin off that program to another organization. Yes, the learning-disabled children we now focus on need mentors, too, but by and large they achieve dramatic breakthroughs by suddenly being able to read, to hear, and to listen. Having regained full function, they require much less help. They just need a cheering section. We are about to extend this program beyond the local community, and within five years we'll have something that can be replicated in every school district in the country. This organization is in the process of designing the simple tools that would make a major difference to children and communities.

What we have really done is learn the discipline of innovation. That means having a clear mission. It means defining what we mean by results. It means being able and willing to abandon efforts that don't get results—either because we don't know how to produce results or because we are misdirecting our efforts, providing remedial services to tenth graders who have been defeated since first grade. In such cases, real results are most unlikely. But when you find a unique opportunity to make a real difference, you focus on it and constantly reassess results. This is a discipline. Innovation is not being brilliant, it's being conscientious. It's not looking at need alone, but looking at need and opportunity. Business, voluntary, and public sector organizations all address tremendous needs, but leaders must understand how their organizations can make the greatest difference and must focus their efforts toward that end.

Thus my friends and I will concentrate where we know how to produce significant results with our volunteers; with the school nurses, ophthalmologists, and audiologists who donate their services; and with the little money we have available. We know that we have already made a difference in one metropolitan area; we expect in ten years to have eliminated the problem in most of our metropolitan areas. We need the discipline of innovation because in a rapidly changing society our problems are changing. Society created the problems of the homeless, for instance, when we closed obsolete mental hospitals without providing halfway houses for people who are mentally ill. New problems demand innovative solutions.

We live in a world of rapid change. When I was born in 1909, all but 5 percent of humanity lived on the land and made their living in manual work. In developed countries, only 5 percent now live on the land and only between a fifth and a quarter make a living in manual work. We've urbanized developed countries in less than a century. These are tremendous changes, and most are occurring in the developing countries as well.

We need the organization that is out to make a difference, the organization that works on the local level with local volunteers and gives them opportunities to make a difference. These volunteers are successful professionals who seek significance—in both their professional and their community work. They expect to see results, especially results that show all of us that we can change things, that we can get a return on our hard work, on our good intentions, on our citizenship. This is what the discipline of innovation is all about.

8 PETER M. SENGE

THE PRACTICE OF INNOVATION

Peter M. Senge is a senior lecturer at the Massachusetts Institute of Technology and chairman of the Society for Organizational Learning, a global community of corporations, researchers, and consultants dedicated to the interdependent development of people and institutions. He is the author of the widely acclaimed book The Fifth Discipline *and coauthor of* The Fifth Discipline Fieldbook.

Peter Drucker has elegantly presented the three ingredients of the discipline of innovation (see Chapter Seven): focus on mission, define significant results, and do rigorous assessment. But if it sounds so simple, why is it so difficult for institutions to innovate?

There are two possible explanations, representing dramatically different worldviews. These opposing outlooks were first clarified nearly forty years ago by Douglas McGregor in his groundbreaking *Human Side of Enterprise:* Theory X (employees as unreliable and uncommitted, chasing a paycheck) versus Theory Y (employees as responsible adults wanting to contribute).

One possibility for difficulties with innovating is that most people really don't care about innovation. After all, Theory X is still the prevailing philosophy in most large institutions—certainly in the American corporate world. Few people in positions of authority would admit to that view, but our practices belie our espoused values. If we look honestly at how organizations manage people, most appear to operate with the belief that people cannot work without careful supervision. As Arie de Geus has shown in *The Living Company*, we treat the business enterprise as a machine for making money rather than as a living community. Consequently, we view people as "human resources" waiting to be employed (or disemployed) to meet the organization's needs. (The word *resource* literally means "standing in reserve, waiting to be used.")

From the Theory X perspective, institutions fail to innovate because most people lack the desire to innovate. Forget Drucker's theory of innovation. The answer to the problem is simple: find more capable people. But that's a never-ending story. "We don't have the right people" is an excuse that suits all times and all circumstances; it is a refuge for scoundrels. Moreover, it obscures leaders' fundamental task of helping people do more together than they could individually.

If, on the other hand, we take the Theory Y perspective, that most people come to work (or at least came to work at one time) truly desiring to make a difference, to gain, as Peter Drucker puts it, a "return on their citizenship," then the failure to innovate becomes a bigger puzzle. It cannot be laid off on not having the right people. It must have more to do with why Peter Drucker's three core practices are more difficult than meets the eye. It requires that we try to understand how good people, desiring to learn and innovate, can consistently fail to produce what they intend.

Know Your Purpose

We can start by inquiring into what we mean by mission anyway. It is very hard to focus on what you cannot define, and my experience is that there can be some very fuzzy thinking about mission, vision, and values.

Most organizations today have mission statements, purpose statements, official visions, and little cards printed with the organization's values. But precious few of us can say that our organization's mission statement has transformed the enterprise. And there has grown an understandable cynicism about lofty ideals that don't match the realities of organizational life.

The first obstacle to understanding mission is a problem of language. Many leaders use *mission* and *vision* interchangeably, or think that the words—and the differences between them—matter little. But words do matter. Language is messy by nature, which is why we must be careful how we use it. As leaders, after all, we have little else with which to work. We typically don't use hammers and saws, heavy equipment, or even computers to do our real work. The essence of leadership—what we do with 98 percent of our time—is communication. To master any management practice, we must start by bringing discipline to the domain in which we spend most of our time, the domain of words.

The dictionary—which unlike the computer *is* an essential leadership tool—contains multiple definitions of the word *mission*; the most appropriate here is "purpose, reason for being." *Vision*, by contrast, is "a picture or image of the future we seek to create," and values articulate how we intend to live as we pursue our mission. Paradoxically, if an organization's mission is truly motivating, it is never really achieved. Mission provides an orientation, not a checklist of accomplishments. It defines a direction, not a destination. It tells the members of an organization why they are working together, how they intend to contribute to the world. Without a sense of mission there is no foundation for establishing why some intended results are more important than others.

But there is a big difference between having a mission statement and being truly mission-based. To be truly mission-based means that key decisions can be referred back to the mission—our reason for being. It means that people can and should object to management edicts that they do not see as connected to the mission. It means that thinking about and continually clarifying the mission is everybody's job because, as de Geus points out, it expresses the aspirations and fundamental identity of a human community. By contrast, most mission statements are nice ideas that might have some meaning for a few but communicate little to the community as a whole. In most organizations, no one would dream of challenging a management decision on the grounds that it does not serve the mission. In other words, most organizations serve those in power rather than a mission.

This also gives some clue as to why being mission-based is so difficult. It gets to the core of power and authority. It is profoundly radical. It says, in essence, that those in positions of authority are not the source of authority. It says, rather, that the source of legitimate power in the organization is its guiding ideas. Remember "We hold these truths to be self-evident . . ."? The cornerstone of a truly democratic system of governance is not voting or any other particular mechanism. It is the belief that power ultimately flows from ideas, not from people. To be truly mission-based is to be democratic in this way, to make the mission more important than the boss, something that not too many corporations have yet demonstrated an ability to do.

Although this might appeal to our ideals, living this way is extraordinarily challenging. We are all closet authoritarians. For most of us it is the only system of management we have ever known, starting in school. To be mission-based, to be values-guided, is to hold up lofty standards against which every person's behavior can be judged. Moreover, mission is inherently fuzzy and abstract. It is so much easier to make decisions based on "the numbers," habit, and unexamined emotions. To be mission-based requires everyone to think continuously.

But it can be done, and when done it can work. The largest commercial enterprise in the world, in terms of market value, is not Microsoft, General Electric, or Matsushita. It is VISA International, whose annual volume exceeded $1.25 trillion in 1997. If its different member organizations' balance sheets of VISA products were combined and assessed according to common banking practices, it is estimated that its market value would exceed $333 billion. But VISA is not a typical corporation. It's a network of twenty-thousand owner-members, who are simultaneously one another's "customers, suppliers, and competitors," in the words of founding CEO Dee Hock. VISA's innovative governance system grew from an extraordinary effort to clarify purpose, which after several years emerged as "to create the world's premier system for the exchange of value." "Truly clarifying purpose and the principles which elaborate our deepest beliefs can be the hardest work you will ever do," says Hock. "But without it, there is no way to create an enterprise that can truly self-organize, where you can balance broadly distributed decision-making function and control at the most local level with coherence and cohesion at any scale up to the global."

Define Vision

The second requirement for innovation—define results—is easier in some ways. Managers are by nature pragmatic; ultimately they are concerned about results and must concentrate on how, not just why. The danger is that short-term goals can obscure larger purposes. Here again, language matters. After all, vision—an image of the future we seek to create—is synonymous with intended results. As such, vision is a practical tool, not an abstract concept. Visions can be long term or intermediate term. Multiple visions can coexist, capturing complementary facets of what people seek to create and encompassing different time frames. Leaders who lack vision fail to define what they hope to accomplish in terms that can ultimately be assessed. Although mission is foundational, it is extraordinarily difficult to assess how we are doing by looking only at the mission, because of its nature. To do this we need to stick out our necks and articulate "an image of the future we seek to create."

Results-oriented leaders must therefore have both a mission and a vision. Results mean little without purpose, for a very practical and powerful reason: a mission instills both the passion and the patience for the long journey. While vision inspires passion, many failed ventures are characterized by passion without patience.

Clarity about mission and vision is both an operational and a spiritual necessity. Mission provides a guiding star, a long-term purpose that allows you to balance the inevitable pressures between the short term and the long term. Vision translates mission into truly meaningful intended results—and guides the allocation of time, energy, and resources. In my experience, it is only through a compelling vision that a deep sense of purpose comes alive. People's passions flow naturally into creating something that truly excites them. Taken together, mission and vision fill a deep need: all human beings have a purpose, a reason for being. Most of us believe that there is something more important than what you can buy, acquire, or market. The passion at the heart of every great undertaking comes from the deep longing of human beings to make a difference, to have an impact. It comes from what you contribute rather than from what you get.

Now, these ideas might sound good, but if we take a deeper look we realize that they are radical statements in today's society. The return-on-investment orientation—the view that people go to work primarily for material gain—is the bedrock of our beliefs about people in contemporary industrial society. Thus the real discipline of innovation not only threatens established power relations, it runs counter to our cultural norms.

Consider, for example, the saying "People do what they're rewarded for." What management is about in many people's minds is creating the right set of incentives and rewards so people will do what the enterprise needs them to do. As W. Edwards Deming saw clearly, our system of management—in all organizations—is based almost totally on extrinsic motivation. It is pure Theory X thinking. It is why, in the last years of his life, Deming said that "our system of management has destroyed our people." This may not be our intent, but it is the consequence of our actions. If we didn't view the human being as an amoeba that does only what it's rewarded to do, then why would we spend so much time worrying about incentives?

Just ask people in the organization if they think the senior management really believes that people come to work every day, as Deming said, "seeking joy in work." That's intrinsic motivation, and it's assumed by today's management to be in scarce supply. Joy in work comes from being true to your purpose. It is the source of the passion, patience, and perseverance we need to thrive as individuals and as organizations. People cannot, however, define results that relate to their deeper passions unless leaders cultivate an environment in which those passions can be safely articulated.

Although there are some extraordinarily principled and value-driven organizations, the defining characteristic of far too many enterprises is cynicism. And cynicism comes from disappointment. As the saying goes, "Scratch the shell of any cynic and you'll find a frustrated idealist." Make speeches to your organization about upholding high ideals or contributing to a better world and most people will roll their eyes (if they're in corporations they'll almost certainly roll their eyes). That reaction is the product of thwarted expectations, and it is the reason that so many organizations fail to innovate. They are afraid to let the genie—passionate purpose—out of the bottle. With good cause. Passion is a powerful force, but when frustrated, it is also dangerous.

Assess Results

The third dimension of innovation is assessment. We must continually gauge how we can best use our scarce resources. As managers we all know what assessing is about; it's one of the fundamental activities of all management.

Assessment has two components: measurement and interpretation. The problem is that the second and more difficult component of assessment—interpretation—requires understanding, participation, and physical presence. Statistical measures of an activity may be disappointing, but if you're actually involved you may see that people are engaged and learning. They may be on the brink of a breakthrough. Incomplete or premature assessment destroys learning. As Bill O'Brien, retired CEO of Hanover Insurance, says, "managers are always pulling up the radishes to see how they're growing." Thus assessment is fundamentally about awareness and understanding, without which any set of measures can mislead. Someone sitting on the outside judging, rather than fully understanding, can make effective assessment impossible.

But with awareness comes yet another problem, as Drucker has pointed out: after assessing results, we must be willing to abandon what doesn't work. Abandonment often precedes innovation. It clears the decks for trying something new. Again, this sounds so simple. Yet how many of us have ever found that it is difficult for organizations to abandon what isn't working? To stop doing something that has been done for years? To remove from a position a person who really does not have credibility with his or her colleagues? "I worry about organizations that cannot fire one person but can fire a thousand," says O'Brien. There are good reasons why abandonment is a challenging organizational practice.

The first step in practicing abandonment is openness—creating an environment in which, at a critical moment, somebody with lots at stake can tell a boss, "This is not working." Building a culture in which people can express their views without fear of reprisal is a huge challenge for most organizations.

How often, for instance, have you noticed that when a group of people gets together informally the night before a staff meeting, their conversation bears almost no resemblance to the same group's discussion at the official meeting the next day? How many meetings have you attended where the real meeting takes place not in the conference room but in the hallway or the rest room afterward, when the very people who asked lots of intelligent questions in the meeting say, "What nonsense." Furthermore, when people do feel safe enough to speak openly in a meeting, insiders, those with the most on the line, tend to discount what is said. When, for instance, a junior salesperson, a young woman (or an old one), tells the boss that something is not working, you see how quickly an ostensibly open organization can reject unwelcome news.

I've never seen an institution that isn't deeply afflicted with these dynamics. Even the best-managed corporations in the world fall short of their full potential, mostly because people know that the official meeting is not where the issues are really discussed or decided.

The litmus test for measuring openness is simple: How fast does bad news travel upward? In most organizations good news travels upward faster than the speed of light. But failure is denied before the word can be spoken: "Whose failure? What failure? That wasn't a failure, we just didn't have enough funding." Make no mistake, the process of innovation is a process of failure. By nature, innovation is a continual learning process. You must experiment, assess, reflect on mission, identify results, experiment some more. Yet from an early age in school, and continuing in work, we have been trained to avoid failure, and thus real learning.

Chris Argyris, in his 1991 *Harvard Business Review* article "Teaching Smart People How to Learn," lays out a basic problem of learning in organizations. He notes that most people in organizations are quite smart, but that to succeed they've learned to find correct answers and cover up incorrect ones. This undermines the inquiry skills essential to real innovation and leadership because these skills revolve around how to "uncover" what isn't working in ways that do not invoke defensiveness.

Consider this true story: A top management team of exceptionally bright, committed people is discussing key issues facing a major American corporation. In three hours, not a single genuine question is asked. Of course, trivial questions get asked, such as "Didn't we go over this issue two years ago?" or "Don't our experienced salespeople disagree with that view?" or "When's lunch?" Each question implies that we are wasting our time with the subject, that we already have the answer.

Genuine inquiry starts when people ask questions to which they do not have an answer. That is rare in organizations. In most large corporations, people rise to the top because they're very good at a combination of two factors: merit and gamesmanship. In a good organization the mix may be fifty-fifty; in a great one, eighty-twenty. The problem is that even the best leaders—those who create a terrific impression and get results—actually know very little. In today's world, how could they know much? Obviously organizations want people at all levels who can produce results. But often the most important act of executive leadership is the ability to ask a question that hasn't been asked before—the ability to inquire, not just dictate or advocate. Unfortunately, most people in executive leadership positions are great at advocacy but poor at inquiry.

These are just a few of the issues revolving around effective assessment. This is an extraordinarily complex challenge, with complex intellectual issues (How do we know how long the radishes should take to grow?), complex emotional issues (Who is not attached to ideas they believe in, many of which are wrong?), complex interpersonal issues (I didn't want to tell him what I really think because it would hurt his feelings), and complex political issues (But it is the boss's pet program that is not working, and the company has invested millions in it). It is one thing for an organization with Peter Drucker advising it to "abandon practices that are not working." It is another for the rest of us who can learn only from peers.

For these reasons, assessment is a core research initiative within the new Society for Organizational Learning (SoL)—a group of leading companies, researchers, and consultants working together to advance the state of the art of how organizations learn. We are coming to believe that there is a big difference between "assessment for learning" and "assessment for evaluation." Because most of the assessment we have encountered in our lives was the latter, the very words tend to invoke defensiveness. But no learning can take place without continuous assessment. The key is that the assessment is done by the learners and the purpose is to learn, that is, to enhance capacity to produce intended outcomes, not to judge someone else.

From Habit to Discipline

Taken together, mission, vision, and assessment create an ecology, a set of fundamental relationships forming the bedrock of real leadership. These tools allow people, regardless of job title, to help shape their future. The failure of Industrial Age institutions to embrace the three components of innovation shows how far there is to go to meet the challenge of the next century. Moreover, Drucker is exactly right that innovation is a "discipline," a word having its root in the Latin *disciplina*, one of the oldest words for "to learn." Many have talent, but real learning requires discipline, the process through which we draw out our potential through commitment, practice, passion, patience, and perseverance.

It is a difficult process, but there is reason for hope. The discipline of innovation is practiced successfully in many domains of human affairs, notably the arts and science. Interestingly, when it is practiced effectively it is invariably done within communities, among diverse individuals who share a common purpose. Energized communities, for example, characterize most periods of innovation in the arts, such as the birth of impressionism, or modern dance, or jazz. Likewise, science at its best is an intensely collaborative undertaking; even when the collaborators are strong individuals competing with one another, their competition occurs within a larger mediating community. Likewise in business, real innovation is often much more collaborative than at first appears. For example, studies such as those by MIT's Eric von Hippel have shown that many of the best new-product innovations come from customers. The problem is that most companies are not organized to tap this source of innovative thinking.

My guess is that mastering the discipline of innovation will require organizations to work together, to learn from one another's efforts. We must learn to do what artists have done for millennia, what scientists do when science works. To do something new, people invariably experience periods of profound discomfort. Confronting the threat and uncertainty such change brings is best done together, not in isolation.

Several years ago, at one of the early meetings of SoL (then called the MIT Center for Organizational Learning), a manager approached me and said, "I see exactly what you're talking about, all these organizations learning from one another. This is Alcoholics Anonymous for Managers." I laughed, but I think he hit the nail on the head. We are all addicted to maintaining control, to avoiding failure, to doing things the way we always have. We can't help it. And we need one another to break the habit.

9 JOHN P. KOTTER

MAKING CHANGE HAPPEN

John P. Kotter is Konosuke Matsushita Professor of Leadership at Harvard Business School and a frequent speaker at top management meetings around the world. He is the author of six best-selling business books, including Leading Change *and* A Force for Change: How Leadership Differs from Management. *His most recent book is* Matsushita Leadership.

No organization today—large or small, local or global—is immune to change. To cope with new technological, competitive, and demographic forces, leaders in every sector have sought to alter fundamentally the way their organizations do business. These change efforts have paraded under many banners—total quality management, reengineering, restructuring, mergers and acquisitions, turnarounds.

Yet according to most assessments, few of these efforts accomplish their goals. Fewer than fifteen of the one hundred or more companies I have studied have successfully transformed themselves. The particulars of every case vary, but I have found that the change process involves eight critical steps (see box). Mismanaging any one of these steps can undermine an otherwise well-conceived vision, but four mistakes in particular are the source of most failures.

1. *Writing a memo instead of lighting a fire.* At least half of failed change efforts bungle the first vital step—establishing a sense of urgency. Too often leaders launch their initiatives by calling a meeting or circulating a consultant's report, then expect people to rally to the cause. It doesn't happen that way. To increase urgency, I sug-

---

Eight Steps to Transform Your Organization

1. *Establish a sense of urgency.*
   Examine market and competitive realities.
   Identify and discuss crises, potential crises, or major opportunities.

2. *Form a powerful guiding coalition.*
   Assemble a group with enough power to lead the change effort.
   Encourage the group to work as a team.

3. *Create a vision.*
   Create a vision to help direct the change effort.
   Develop strategies for achieving that vision.

4. *Communicate the vision.*
   Use every vehicle possible to communicate the new vision and strategies.
   Teach new behaviors by the example of the guiding coalition.

5. *Empower others to act on the vision.*
   Get rid of obstacles to change.
   Change systems or structures that seriously undermine the vision.
   Encourage risk taking and nontraditional ideas, activities, and actions.

gest you gather a group of key people for a day-long retreat. First, identify every possible factor that contributes to complacency. If you work at it, you will come up with twenty-five to fifty. Then brainstorm specific ways to counter each factor. Finally, develop an action plan to implement your ideas. If you attack all twenty-five or fifty items, your chances of creating a sense of urgency—and building necessary momentum—improve immeasurably. However, the effort involved in creating a sense of urgency is usually several times what

---

6. *Plan for and create short-term wins.*
   Plan for visible performance improvements.
   Implement those improvements.
   Recognize and reward employees involved in the improvements.

7. *Consolidate improvements and produce still more change.*
   Use increased credibility to change systems, structures, and policies that don't fit the vision.
   Hire, promote, and develop employees who can implement the vision.
   Reinvigorate the process with new projects, themes, and change agents.

8. *Institutionalize new approaches.*
   Articulate the connections between the new behaviors and organizational success.
   Develop the means to ensure leadership development and succession.

leaders expect. They slide through this first crucial step, and when the effort stalls six months later, they wonder why.

2. *Talking too much and saying too little*. Most leaders undercommunicate their change vision by a factor of ten. And the efforts they do make to convey their message are of the least convincing variety—speeches and memos. An effective change vision must include not only new strategies and structures but also new, aligned behaviors on the part of senior executives. Leading by example means just that—spending dramatically more time with customers, cutting wasteful spending in the executive suite, or pulling the plug on a pet project that doesn't measure up. People watch their bosses—particularly their immediate bosses—very closely. It doesn't take much in the way of inconsistent behavior by a manager to fuel the cynicism and frustration of his or her direct reports.

3. *Declaring victory before the war is over*. When a project is completed or an initial goal is met, it is tempting to congratulate everyone involved and proclaim the advent of a new era. Although it is important to celebrate results along the way, kidding yourself or others about the difficulty and duration of organizational transformation can be catastrophic. I met recently with a capable, intelligent management group that has begun to see encouraging results in a difficult initiative. They are only six months into what is probably a three-year process, but they are already talking about "wrapping this thing up in a few months." Such talk is nonsense. They are far from where they need to be, and in danger of losing the ground they have gained.

People look forward to completion of any task. The problem is, the results of a change vision are not directly proportional to the effort invested. That is, one-third of your way into a change process you are unlikely to see one-third of the possible results; you may see only one-tenth of the possible results. If you settle for too little too soon, you will probably lose it all. Celebrating incremental improvements is a great way to mark progress and sustain commitment—but don't forget how much work is still to come.

4. *Looking for villains in all the wrong places.* The perception that large organizations are filled with recalcitrant middle managers who resist all change is not only unfair but also untrue. In professional service organizations and in most organizations with an educated workforce, people at every level are engaged in change processes. Often it's the middle level that brings issues to the attention of senior executives. In fact, I have found that the biggest obstacles to change are not middle managers but, more often, those who work just a level or two below the CEO—vice presidents, directors, general managers, and others who haven't yet made it to the top and may have the most to lose in a change. That's why it is crucial to build a guiding coalition that represents all levels of the organization. People often hear the president or CEO cheerleading a change and promising exciting new opportunities. Most people in the middle want to believe that; too often their managers give them reasons not to.

Key Tasks for Change Leaders

These common mistakes suggest three key tasks for change leaders: managing multiple time lines, building coalitions, and creating a vision.

Managing Multiple Time Lines

To establish a sense of urgency and avoid declaring premature victory, leaders must manage a key strategic resource—time. Responding quickly while also accepting the long-term nature of the change process sounds like a paradox. But effective leaders make it clear that meaningful change takes years. At the same time, they create short-term wins and continuously remind people that the need for change is urgent precisely because it takes so long. When, for example, Konosuke Matsushita started the Matsushita Institute of Government and Management—his graduate school for people who want to go into public service—he explained that his vision was to help Japanese politics become less corrupt and more visionary. When a skeptical reporter asked how long that would take, he said, "In my judgment, about four hundred years—which is why it's so important that we start today."

The best leaders I have known balance short-term results with long-term vision. (When it comes to organizational change, I define *short term* as six to twelve months.) They engage directors, investors, employees, and other constituents in the excitement of delivering both long- and short-term results. They operate in multiple time frames.

Results and vision can be plotted on a matrix (see Figure 9.1). Poor results and weak vision spell sure trouble for any organization. Good short-term results with a weak vision satisfy many organizations—for a while. A compelling vision that produces few results is usually abandoned. Only good short-term results with an effective, aligned vision offer a high probability of sustained success.

Some leaders fear that they have too little time to manage long-term change, and they therefore focus only on quarterly or annual results. Yet many now reach senior leadership positions at age fifty or younger and have an opportunity to lead a number of transforma-

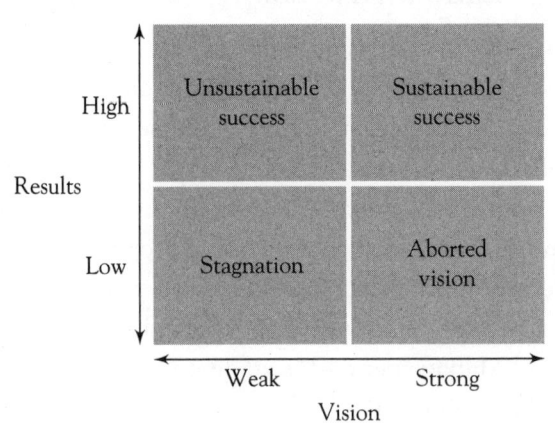

Figure 9.1. Vision, Results, and Sustainable Success.

	Weak	Strong
High	Unsustainable success	Sustainable success
Low	Stagnation	Aborted vision

Results (vertical axis) / Vision (horizontal axis)

tions necessary to long-term leadership. Jack Welch, for instance, has led at least three major change visions at General Electric. Of course, he had the benefit of starting early and keeping his job a long time—but he has kept the job precisely because he has made organizational change an ongoing, multiphase process.

Transforming an organization is the ultimate test of leadership, but understanding the change process is essential to many aspects of a leader's job. Two skills in particular—building coalitions and creating a vision—are especially relevant to our times.

Building Coalitions

In today's less hierarchical but more complex organizations, leaders must win the support of employees, partners, investors, and regulators for many types of initiatives. Because you are likely to meet resistance from unexpected quarters, building a strong guiding coalition is essential. There are three keys to creating such alliances.

1. *Engaging the right talent.* Coalition building is not simply reaching out to whoever happens to be in charge of a department, organization, or other constituency; it is also assembling the necessary skills, experience, and chemistry. A coalition of twenty people who are decent managers but ineffective leaders is unlikely to create meaningful change—or much else that is new. You don't necessarily start with the president or CEO as your partner; it may be the executive vice president who brings more to the party and yet still connects you to the line organization. The most effective partners usually have strong position power, broad experience, high credibility, and real leadership skills.

2. *Growing the coalition strategically.* Like a good board of directors, an effective guiding coalition needs a diversity of views and voices. Once a core group coalesces, the challenge is how to expand the scope and complexity of the coalition. It often means working with people outside your organization—even for an internal change effort. Leaders must not only reach beyond the confines of their enterprise but also know where and how to build support. That may

mean, for instance, giving others credit for success, but also accepting blame for failures oneself. It means showing a genuine care for individuals, but also a tough-mindedness about results—because getting results is the best way to recruit allies.

3. *Working as a team, not just a collection of individuals.* Leaders often say they have a team when in fact they have a committee or a small hierarchy (see Chapters Thirty-Two and Thirty-Three). The more you do to support team performance, the healthier the guiding coalition will be and the more able it will be to achieve its goals. Especially during the stress of change, leaders throughout the enterprise need to draw on reserves of energy, expertise, and most of all, trust. Personnel problems—all too easily ignored during placid times—often lurk beneath the surface of a team and come to the fore during times of change. The pressures of transformation make a strong team essential. Beyond the customary team-building retreats and events, real teams are built by doing real work together, sharing a vision and commitment to a goal.

Creating a Vision

Leading by example is essential to communicating a vision. But how do you actually build a vision? Because it relates to the future, people assume that vision building should resemble the long-term planning process: design, organize, implement. I have never seen it work that way. Defining a vision of the future does not happen according to a timetable or flowchart. It is more emotional than rational. It demands a tolerance for messiness, ambiguity, and setbacks, an acceptance of the half-step back that usually accompanies every step forward.

Day-to-day demands inevitably pull people in different directions. Conflict is inevitable. Having a shared vision does not eliminate tension between, say, sales and product-development groups, but it does help people make appropriate trade-offs. The alternative is to bog down in I-win, you-lose fights that can paralyze an organization. Thus leaders must convey a vision of the future that is clear in intention, appealing to stakeholders, and ambitious yet attainable. Effective visions are focused enough to guide decision making yet flexible enough to accommodate individual initiative and changing circumstances.

For example, a narrowly defined but effective change vision was developed by the operations group of a financial services company: "We want to reduce our costs by 30 percent and increase the speed with which we respond to customers by 40 percent. When this is

---

The Ways Change Happens

Organizations change of necessity and for a variety of reasons. But the single biggest impetus for change in an organization tends to be a new manager in a key job. These change leaders range from the middle to the top of an organization; it is often a new division-level manager or a new department head—someone with a fresh perspective—who sees that the status quo is unacceptable.

Although there is no single source of change, there is a clear pattern to failure. Most often, it is the result of a leader's attempt to shortcut a critical phase of the change process. Certainly there is room for flexibility in the eight steps that underlie successful change—but not a lot of room. When people say, for instance, "We're going to empower employees to act entrepreneurially—but we don't need to spend a lot of time changing our whole organization," they are almost bound to fail.

Producing change is about 80 percent leadership—establishing direction, aligning, motivating, and inspiring people—and about 20 percent management—planning, budgeting, organizing, and problem solving. Unfortunately, in most of the change efforts I have studied in the past twenty years, these percentages are reversed. Our business schools and work organizations continue to produce great managers; we need to do as well at developing great leaders.

completed, in approximately three years, we will have . . . better satisfied customers, increased revenue growth, more job security, and the enormous pride that comes from great accomplishment."

Traits of Effective Leaders

Leaders exist at all levels of an organization. At the edges of the enterprise, of course, leaders are accountable for less territory. Their vision may sound more basic; the number of people to motivate may be two. *But they perform the same leadership role as their more senior counterparts.* They excel at seeing things through fresh eyes and at challenging the status quo. They are energetic and seem able to run through, or around, obstacles.

I have found that people who provide great leadership are also deeply interested in a cause or discipline related to their professional arena. A leader in a pharmaceutical firm, for example, might have a passion for reducing suffering based on personal experience, perhaps with a parent or loved one, and be motivated by deep emotions and not just intellect. Such leaders also tap the deep convictions of others and connect those feelings to the purpose of the organization; they help people see what their everyday work means to that larger purpose.

The most notable trait of great leaders, certainly of great change leaders, however, is their quest for learning (see Chapter Twenty-Six). They show an exceptional willingness to push themselves out of their own comfort zones, even after they have achieved a great deal. They continue to take risks, even when there is no obvious reason for them to do so. And they are open to people and ideas, even at a time in life when they might reasonably think—because of their successes—that they know everything. Often they are driven by goals or ideals that are bigger than what any individual can accomplish, and that gap is an engine pushing them toward continuous learning.

Most leaders invest tremendous talent, energy, and caring in their change efforts, yet few see the results for which they had hoped. There is a good reason why so few organizations have transformed themselves. Today's leaders simply don't have much practice at large-scale change. Thirty years ago few organizations were thinking about radical reinvention, so there is little practical experience to be passed on to a new generation of managers. The good news is, the percentages are bound to improve. The kinds of changes routinely undertaken by today's organizations—producing ever better products more quickly at ever lower cost—were unimaginable thirty years ago. Over the next decade, thousands of leaders will guide equally remarkable changes. That is more than a safe prediction; it is a social and economic necessity. All institutions need effective leadership, but nowhere is the need greater than in the organization that is seeking to transform itself.

10 GARY HAMEL
JIM SCHOLES

STRATEGIC INNOVATION IN THE QUEST FOR NEW WEALTH

Gary Hamel is founder and chairman of Strategos, a consulting firm focused on strategy innovation. He is visiting professor of strategic and international management at London Business School and author or coauthor of several influential articles and books, including the best-seller Competing for the Future. *Jim Scholes is founder and European director of Strategos. His strategy work spans a variety of public and private sector organizations in the United States, Europe, and Asia. He has coauthored a book and articles on the practical application of soft systems thinking to complex organizational problems.*

We live in a discontinuous world. Digitalization, deregulation, and globalization are profoundly reshaping the industrial landscape. The convergence of these forces has produced an explosion of new organizational models, institutional relationships, and value-creating possibilities. What we see today is a dramatic proliferation of new economic life forms, virtual organizations, extended enterprises, global consortia, Internet-based commerce, ad infinitum.

Joseph Schumpeter's gale of "creative destruction" has become a hurricane. Inevitably, the economic sea change now under way will drive an extraordinary amount of wealth creation over the next few decades—just as the move from the agrarian economy to the industrial economy generated enormous new wealth around the turn of the century. Wealth will also get destroyed as new business models drive out the old. That much is obvious.

But there is a deeper question in this. *Who* will capture the new wealth? On the road to the future, who will be the "windshield" and who will be the "bug"? Put another way: Just what does it take to turn discontinuities into opportunities? What it takes, we argue, is a deep capacity for *strategy innovation*—an ability to reinvent fundamentally the basis of competition within existing industries, and to invent entirely new industries. Business process reengineering tinkers at the margins. The real challenge is to become an author of industry revolution. In an increasingly nonlinear world, only nonlinear strategies will create substantial new wealth.

Consider the evidence.

Who has been creating the new wealth in the American grocery business? Though companies like Procter & Gamble, Kroger, and other traditional leaders have created a lot of new value in the past decade, it is industry revolutionaries such as Starbucks, Petco, ConAgra, and Wal-Mart that have created much of the new wealth. While the old guard has been focusing its efforts on rationalizing the supply chain and turning out thousands of almost trivial product-line extensions, the vanguard have been busy creating entirely new product and retailing concepts.

Take another example: between April 1995 and April 1996, the capitalization of Internet-related companies rose from near zero to almost $10 billion. Yahoo and Netscape are just two of the new Internet-exploiting value generators. DEC, Unisys, Computer Sciences Corporation, Hewlett Packard, and other traditional computer industry players have so far captured little Internet-related value.

Let us throw out a proposition: in the quest to create wealth, we have reached the end of incrementalism. Quality, cost, time-to-market, process improvement—these are important, but we are reaching the point of diminishing returns along many of these improvement trajectories.

Ford may be able to take another hour or two out of vehicle assembly time; its Japanese competitors may force it to do so. But if new companies totally reinvent the retailing and service of new and used automobiles, Ford's incremental improvements will not count for much. Neither will share buybacks, demergers, process reengineering, or downsizing lead to new wealth creation. At best, they will prolong the life of geriatric strategies and anachronistic companies.

The point is incontestable: in a discontinuous world, strategy innovation is the key to wealth creation. And if one redefines the metric of corporate success as *share of new wealth creation* within a broad opportunity domain, the innovation imperative becomes inescapable.

For start-ups and global giants alike, the challenge is strategy innovation. It is the only way for new companies to succeed in the face of enormous resource disadvantages, and the only way for incumbents to renew their lease on success. No company is immune from the challenge, however successful it may be today, but few companies seem able or willing to look beyond their current success formula. An interesting exception is Nokia of Finland. Their experience provides an example of some of the practical steps that can be taken to create a new future.

The Nokia Story

Imagine this: you are the CEO of a 130-year-old European company, which you have turned from a little known, loss-making conglomerate into a highly profitable world leader in an emerging industry that your company has helped to create. This has been achieved in little more than three years. Your young, talented, and energetic management team (average age forty-four) is working hard to tackle the challenges of explosive growth: increasing volume production 100 percent per year, entering new geographic markets, and building an organizational infrastructure in which 30 percent of the people were newcomers during the previous year. What, if anything, should you worry about? By any standards the level of achievement has already been remarkable, and with the day-to-day pressures of growth, you could be forgiven for feeling that you are onto a pretty good formula. Simply focusing on excellent operational implementation might seem a reasonable thing to do.

Not for Jorma Ollila, chief executive of the Finnish company Nokia. At forty-one, Ollila, along with his team, took the helm of the ailing Nokia in 1992. They quickly decided to rationalize the disparate portfolio of businesses, which included paper, aluminum, power generation, tires, and electronics, into a highly focused telecommunications business. Building on competencies that already existed, they catapulted the company into world-leader status in mobile telephony with a 20 percent world share of mobile handsets. So successful was Nokia's strategy that sales volume more than doubled from 1992 to 1995, making Nokia an $8 billion company. Gains in productivity (with higher sales per employee than key competitors Motorola and Ericsson) and profitability (a 20 percent growth of pretax profit to nearly $850 million between 1993 and 1994, for example) were also spectacular.

Nokia's performance is all the more remarkable when one considers that as a Finnish company its home market is little more than 5 million people. Of necessity Nokia has had to learn how to build more than 90 percent of its business outside of its home country, something few companies in the world have learned to do so quickly.

Why Change a Winning Formula?

In the light of this success, what was the motivation for Nokia to rethink fundamentally its strategy? And how did it do so in a way that captured the ideas, energy, and involvement of managers across the whole company? Even though Ollila and his team had every right to feel proud of Nokia's worldwide success, they displayed a humility uncharacteristic of most Western senior executives. They were deeply aware of the dangers they faced in becoming trapped by their own conventions. They were worried that success would set strategy in cement, that unbridled success in recent years might lead to the kind of complacency and laziness they had observed holding back other well-established companies.

Consider the warning signs they saw:

- The rate of change in the telecommunications industry was increasing. Liberalization, technology, increasing competition, and the emergence of new markets were among the factors rapidly changing Nokia's environment.

- Larger rivals could far outspend Nokia in research and development—challenging the company's ability to bring new products to market faster than competitors. Ollila and his team were keen to tap the growing pool of talent available to Nokia across the world, to somehow push creativity and innovation into important new domains.

- Worldwide growth threatened the organizational cohesion, values, and behaviors at the very core of Nokia's Finnish culture. Nokia is flatter and more fluid than most companies of its size, with highly autonomous subunits. Pekka Ala-Pietila, president of Nokia Mobile Phones, characterizes this structure as "keeping a fine balance between anarchy and bureaucracy." The challenge was to enlist all parts of the rapidly growing organization in innovative strategy creation, without undermining their independence—to generate diversity of thought and unity of action.

Planting the Seeds of Strategy Revolution

Getting started is the toughest step in any successful revolution. So it is with strategy. Beyond a set of general concerns, three elements coincided to provide the catalyst for Nokia's efforts. First, there was concern about how long growth rates in excess of 50 percent could be maintained. Managers in Nokia Mobile Phones (NMP) were concerned that no one in the industry could forecast growth rates accurately—thus the uncertainty about what the future would hold. Also, as mobile phones became more of a commodity, the company could expect increasing pressure on profit margins. The possibility that cellular telephones would one day become a low-profit business like color television engendered a shared sense of urgency about the need to look beyond today's business. Strategy could not be built around only the cellular handset as a product.

Second, Nokia's leaders recognized that they could not count on serendipity in the future; they would have to make their own luck. Neither was current success an indicator of great ability in strategic planning. In fact, Ollila was honest enough to tell his managers that all of Nokia's top management team, including himself, had significantly underestimated the scale and growth of the telecommunications opportunity. He saw a real need to develop greater foresight across the company.

Finally, Pekka Ala-Pietila initiated a new approach to strategy in NMP. During 1994 he brought together about twenty managers to examine NMP's core competencies and explore industry discontinuities. The dialogue this created among the senior team members generated a collective commitment to reconceive Nokia and its future.

A Process for Strategy Innovation

Building on NMP's experience, Nokia's first large-scale, cross-company strategic initiative was jointly designed by Nokia and two Strategos partners. The process embodied six characteristics that are particularly important in Nokia's context:

1. *The process was not a traditional top-down, forecast-laden, strategic-planning exercise. It was a learning experience.* The goal was to come up with not a *plan* but a *process* of creating strategy in a way that involves the whole company—a process that creates ambition, new insight, and implementable growth initiatives. We call this process of strategy innovation *strategizing*. It was not a calendar-

driven, form-filling exercise. There was still pressure from the corporate planning office for the businesses to complete annual plan returns, but in NMP's case they simply took the previous year's plan and amended it to free up time for strategizing.

2. *The process was iterative,* working through a set of interlinked modules intended to develop a deep understanding of current and potential future core competencies, major discontinuities in current or prospective business, and major opportunities beyond the boundaries of current businesses. The result would be a "strategic architecture" that would provide ongoing guidance for daily operational and strategic decisions across the company.

3. *The strategic process drew resources from all parts of the company.* The work was performed by about sixty managers, who committed between 25 and 100 percent of their time to the task. Largely a volunteer force, they represented all levels, functions, businesses, and geographies in the company and included newcomers, who had been with the company for only a matter of weeks, as well as longtime Nokia people. The diversity of experience and perspectives created a new richness of debate. Some of the most provocative insights came from the least expected quarters, such as young people with little experience of "the industry."

4. *The effort was broad-based.* In addition to the core group of sixty, several hundred managers made significant contributions to the work, especially on core competencies and discontinuities. And communications involving several thousand employees encouraged even wider involvement.

5. *Top management's role and contribution were multifaceted.* Senior executives provided resources and encouragement to get started. They provided their business experience as participants. They provided a sounding board as challenges and problems arose. And just as important, they provided their own time and attention, as a group, to developing a leadership agenda for the future. In a sense, by giving up any perceived monopoly on strategy making, they were able to concentrate on how they could enhance their

collective added value. The top team became students rather than teachers.

6. *The hope was to generate a companywide perspective on truly unconventional strategic options.* This was an attempt not to predict the future but to gain ideas on how to shape it. What these options might be and how they would be acted on were not clear at the outset but were to emerge through the process itself. That said, the top management group was very clear about the ambitious outcomes they expected from the process, particularly in terms of identifying major opportunities and how to act on them; about the kind of deliverables expected from each phase; and about the criteria by which people's efforts would be judged. These expectations provided a simple framework for the dialogue that occurred throughout the process. Apart from encouraging the exploration of new ideas, this framework enabled innovators to emerge and be heard.

From Strategizing to Organizing for the Future

Does Nokia believe it has achieved anything from five months of intensive strategizing? Ollila believes so. In his words, "We've created something very important, a process through which we can renew ourselves." Another senior manager added, "We have access to the best ideas and the best people, therefore the best opportunity to succeed." Five important outcomes from Nokia's strategic process encouraged managers to be optimistic about the future and their ability to shape it:

1. The most tangible outcome is *a set of new venture opportunities to create fundamentally new businesses*. Rather than being presented as plans for approval, the opportunities were shared with more than fifty senior managers from across the company at a New Ventures Fair, at which teams presented their ideas. Some of the opportunities can be worked on immediately, others are being advanced as seedcorn initiatives.

2. *Managers throughout the company report some important learnings:* a deep and widely shared understanding of the discontinuities

that could reshape Nokia's future, a new perspective on Nokia's core competencies and the ways they can be developed and leveraged to create new opportunities, and an appreciation of ways to tap the broad pool of talent and experience in different parts of the company.

3. The strategic process has provided *an opportunity for hundreds of managers, including Ollila's top team, to practice new behaviors across the business units as well as within them*. Learning how to operate more effectively across the businesses provides a working example of how to raise the collective added value. This could be regarded as a microcosm or working model of the way the "new" Nokia will need to operate as it acts on emerging opportunities.

4. *New mechanisms have been developed in the strategic process that will bring opportunities identified "off-line" (as in the strategic process) back "on-line" for implementation*. The mechanisms provide a means for Nokia to generate new business ideas continuously across the whole organization and link them to top management for support and action.

5. *Nokia has created a band of activists, who emerged from the process deeply committed to making their ideas a reality*. These activists are championing opportunities because they understand them, believe in them, and want to pursue them. They are not "assigned" by top management as "champions" (as is so often the case); they are truly committed. As a result, Nokia's leadership is not faced with the typical problem of how to get people who are unwilling or confused to implement ideas. Instead, it has the more interesting challenge of how to deal with the inevitability of implementation without sacrificing the performance of current operations.

Understanding the Roots of Strategy Innovation

Our experience in helping companies improve their capacity for strategizing suggests that there are five preconditions for the emergence of innovative strategy:

New Voices

Companies miss the future not because they are lazy but because they are "genetically" blind. Land is a mystery to fish—fish are not equipped to understand it. (And by the time a fish learns about land, it is usually too late!) Many companies are unequipped to see where the future is coming from. A lack of "genetic diversity" makes it difficult for companies to first encompass and then exploit the various trends and discontinuities that could be leveraged to create new wealth.

New voices—that is, new genetic material—must be brought into the strategic process. If you want to see a diverse team, look at what Microsoft assembled to reboot Microsoft Network—not many of this team's members look like the stereotypical "nerdy" programmer.

We have long argued that top management must give up its monopoly on creating strategy and that previously underrepresented constituencies must be given a larger share of voice in the strategy process. Specifically, we believe that young people, newcomers, and those at the geographic periphery of the organization deserve a larger voice. It is in these constituencies that diversity may be found. Creating strategy must be a pluralistic process, a deeply participative undertaking.

Strategizing requires light from outside the organization as well—light that can illuminate the huge areas of darkness lying just beyond the company's current perceptual boundaries.

New Conversations

The emergence of strategy depends not only on a diversity of voices but also on the connections between those voices. Insight comes when previously compartmentalized knowledge sets are juxtaposed in new ways. For strategy to emerge, we need new conversations that cross the boundaries of function, technology, hierarchy, business, and geography. One thing is certain: if for five or six years in a row the same ten or fifteen people in a company have the same conversations about strategy in the same way, new insights will be unlikely.

Not all talking and listening amounts to deep conversation. For both sides to find meaning in the interchange, the participants must create a common context; they must, to a degree, "invade each other's world." This takes time. Meaningful conversations cannot be shoehorned into the typical planning process or into a two-day strategy retreat at a posh hotel.

We often lament that it takes so long for new strategic insights to rise through the layers of a bureaucratic organization to a level where resources can be allocated. At one time or another many companies have set up "orphanages"—typically labeled "new venture divisions"—for such ideas. But imagine what happens when you put the resource holders—senior management—directly alongside the new, typically disenfranchised voices and then engage them all in deep conversations about opportunity and destiny. The route from insight to commitment does not have to be as painful and ponderous as most companies make it.

New Perspectives

One cannot raise an individual's IQ, but it is possible to help people see the world in new ways by shifting their vantage point. Remember when you took your first economics course? You may not have enjoyed it, but it suddenly made visible to you a set of phenomena that had previously been invisible. Suddenly you understood how interest rates get determined, how supply and demand work to set prices, and what things influence exchange rates. You became aware.

Strategy innovation requires new ways of seeing. Reconceiving a company in terms of core competencies constitutes a new way of seeing. Looking at today's products and separating form from function is a way of looking afresh at the essence of products and services. For example, Oracle Corporation hopes to reconceive the personal computer, to deliver an "information utility" without the expensive box. Indeed, the concept of strategy as revolution rather than incremental repositioning is for many individuals a new lens.

To increase the probability of strategy innovation, strategists must become the merchants of new perspective. They must search constantly for new lenses that help companies reconceive themselves, their customers, and their competitors, and thereby their opportunities.

New Passions

We have too often ignored the emotional side of strategy. If strategy is at least partly about collective purpose and a sense of shared destiny, should we not recognize this explicitly in the way we go about creating strategy? For example, has anyone studied the way commitment accumulates around a new strategy—not the commitment of financial resources by senior executives but the emotional commitment of individuals at the bottom of the organization who are being asked to devote their lives to the accomplishment of a strategy?

A bad strategy will always be a bad strategy, but does commitment automatically accumulate around good strategies? Can one accelerate the commitment process and thereby reduce the time between strategic insight and action? We believe that one way of raising commitment is to get individuals throughout the organization deeply involved in the process of creating strategy. Individuals, we believe, should have a say in determining the destiny of the organizations to which they devote their efforts.

Inside almost every individual is a deep passion for discovery and novelty. It is amazing to see the passions that are unleashed when an organization goes to its members and invites them to participate in charting their collective destiny. It might be argued that giving a broad range of individuals a voice in the strategy process will lead to many conflicting strategic agendas. But if it is possible to get thousands of people passionately involved with quality, and yet maintain coherence, why can't the same be accomplished with strategy? Our experience suggests that it can.

We must give employees an emotional stake in the future. You can be assured that it is possible to wrap meaning and purpose around even prosaic products. Listen to David Pottruck, CEO of Charles Schwab: "Our employees see themselves as 'the custodians of our customers' financial dreams.'" Wow! When was the last time your local bank teller had such a thought? So to all you strategists and corporate leaders eager to create value: get a soul!

Experimentation

There is a limit to foresight. Even when foresight is nearly perfect, a distinction remains between the clarity of the vision and the proximity of the goal. The end target may be clearly visible—"I want to climb that mountain"—but much of the route may be invisible from the starting point. The only way you are going to see the path ahead is to start moving. Thus strategy must be as much about experimentation as it is about foresight. One must guard against overdetermining strategy; it is dangerous to pretend that we know more than we do about how the future will turn out.

In many organizations the quest for efficiency drives out experimentation. One question we often ask folks in a company is, "Can you point to ten or twenty small experiments going on that you believe could fundamentally remake your company?" In most cases, the answer is no.

In the new economy, we are attempting to explore vast spaces of possibility: how genetics will remake medicine, how biotechnology will change the chemical industry, and how interactive technology will change the very idea of a university. IBM asks the question, "How will the Internet remake industry structures?" It doesn't matter how many gurus, consultants, and dollars IBM throws at this question, the answer is likely to remain uncertain. For even a glimmer of the future, IBM needs to experiment on a broad front.

Strategy is adaptive. It is a process of foresight, action, and feedback. The goal is to maximize the ratio of learning over investment. As Apple learned to its sorrow with the Newton, chutzpa isn't a substitute for carefully staged market learning.

Kent Foster, a senior executive at GTE, puts the problem of unknowability thus: "We are talking about products that are still evolving, delivered to a market that is still emerging, via a technology that is still changing on a daily basis." This must sound familiar to any executive trying to chart a course through the chaotic frenzy that is the new economy. Clearly, experimentation is a must in this environment.

The more a company experiments, the faster it can accumulate insight on which strategies are likely to work. We must pay more attention to the preconditions for innovative strategy creation. The goal is not to develop "perfect" strategies but to develop strategies that are directionally correct, and then progressively refine them through rapid experimentation and adjustment. This is the real work of the leader.

11 DOUGLAS K. SMITH

MAKING CHANGE STICK

Douglas K. Smith is a management consultant specializing in strategy, performance, and change. He is author of Taking Charge of Change *and coauthor of* The Wisdom of Teams. *His most recent book,* Make Success Measurable, *provides the tools to set and achieve the outcome-based goals required for successful change.*

As a society, we've spent a fortune—and considerable pain—trying to implement changes, using such methods as TQM, self-directed teams, and reengineering. Yet studies show that at least two-thirds of our change initiatives fail to achieve their intended results.

Why? The answer is simple, even if the remedy is not. We have assumed that if you can articulate where you're trying to go, and differentiate it from where you are now, then change will happen. Simply pointing the way from A to B has worked in the past. But it doesn't work when the changes in question are deeply behavioral in nature.

For forty years or more, most organizational change has been a matter of executing decisions—to enter a new market, adopt a new marketing strategy, forge an alliance, or reallocate a set of resources. None of these things is necessarily easy. But for the most part they involve traditional management approaches, for which tough-minded decision making, delegation, monitoring, and adjustment are good enough.

But many of the changes that today's organizations undertake require more than that. Typically you are working with staff and managers who are good at what they do. But to perform in a changing world, they now have to learn new ways of doing things, and new things to do. It is the most difficult management challenge we face today. A decision to pursue process reengineering, for instance, regardless of how well it has been communicated, is not enough to get people to take responsibility for learning the new skills and behaviors that are necessary to reach the performance goal.

Sensing that the changes they envision are profoundly different from those of the past, too many people—management gurus included—approach change as all or nothing, either-or. They demonize the old ways and sanctify the new. But language is critical to change, and the most pernicious statements include *either-or* and *we-they*. Productive and motivating words are *both-and* and *we*—for instance, reduce cost *and* improve service, or increase speed *and* improve yield, or even reduce cost, improve speed, *and* improve yield. Furthermore, only *we* can meet these goals. Such ambitious, inclusive goals are in creative tension with one another. And in the complex, interrelated processes that underlie most organizational tasks, such goals can drive people (we) to do whatever is necessary—such as reduce the number of steps in a process, add value to steps, or whatever might make a real difference.

But by condemning so-called traditional management practices out of hand—though these practices have taken us from 1776, when we first thought of the division of labor, to the end of the twentieth century—we are dismissing a system that has produced awesome social wealth. What's critical is that the decision-driven practices of the past aren't enough when people have to learn new behavior.

As a leader, you face both decision-driven and behavior-driven change. You have to understand which kind of change you are facing at any given moment, because you can't manage both of them the same way. To distinguish between decision-driven and behavior-driven challenges, ask yourself if you have the people with the capabilities to accomplish the desired outcome. If you do, you're looking at a decision-driven change. You identify your goal, commit the resources, communicate well, and just get on with it. The most frequent challenges that organizations face are probably still of that type.

Three years ago, for example, a large charitable organization, originally established to help immigrants to this country, became concerned with homelessness. Its board launched two major initiatives—first, to improve direct marketing and fundraising; second, to get frontline service people to be more responsive to the varied needs of the homeless. The latter involved everything from understanding mental illness, drug abuse, and family problems to learning how to work as a team and to refer clients to counseling or government agencies. On further analysis, the group's leaders realized that they didn't have to teach lots of existing employees direct marketing skills. They simply had to hire a couple of direct marketers and give them the budget to make it happen. That's decision-driven change. However, the shift in required frontline skills was brutally behavior-driven. That discovery led the organization to narrow its agenda and not bite off so much at once.

The Purpose of Change

It's not enough to manage change; you also have to manage *through* change—to continue to lead the organization itself while you're steering it in new directions. That's why the first of ten management principles is, *keep performance as the primary objective of change* (see box).

Too often, change efforts produce a bifurcated reality: you've got the business and you've got the change. Well, guess which one gets short shrift? The change. *Only when you challenge people to deliver performance outcomes that are relevant to their mission can you engage them in the change process.* Say, for example, that you want people to embrace continuous improvement. There are techniques to support that change—total quality processes, customer orientation, benchmarking, and so on. But these are techniques that have value only to the extent that they help achieve a performance outcome. To achieve results, you first have to make a continuing series of demands that require people to achieve continuous improvements in specific aspects of the business—such as cost, cycle time, or product development. Your goals have to focus on tangible performance, not just activity. So it's not a matter of sending people to training

---

Ten Principles for Leading Change

Most change efforts fall far short of their potential. Usually that's because leaders fail to address the deep behavioral changes they are seeking. The following management principles are at the heart of any successful change effort:

1. Keep performance results the primary objective of behavior and skill change.

2. Continually increase the number of individuals taking responsibility for their own change.

3. Make sure that each person always knows why his or her performance and change matters to the purpose and results of the whole organization.

4. Put people in a position to learn by doing and provide them with the information and support they need just in time to perform.

sessions on continuous improvement, having them read books on continuous improvement, or benchmarking your competitors. You have to let people learn by doing and performing, and then provide the help they need to perform.

Most organizations do the reverse—announce a big change program, train everybody, and raise awareness to get buy-in. But intellectual buy-in is not enough. After people have been trained in total quality or continuous improvement, they usually revert to what they've always done because they don't see the connection to their real work, that is, the specific performance contribution they make to the enterprise. To manage through a period of change, you have to get people to take responsibility for their own change and performance—an awareness program is never enough. You have to figure out three things:

5. Embrace improvisation as the best path to both performance and change.
6. Use team performance to drive change whenever demanded.
7. Concentrate organizational designs on the work that people do, not on the decision-making authority they have.
8. Create and focus energy and meaningful language because these are the scarcest resources during periods of change.
9. Stimulate and sustain behavior-driven change by harmonizing initiatives throughout the organization.
10. Practice leadership based on the courage to live the change you wish to bring about.

- What *performance outcomes* will push the enterprise ahead

- How to get people to make personal commitments to these performance outcomes

- How to provide people with the help they need just in time to perform

As a leader, you have to break down the purposeful level of performance into concrete actions. Say, for example, you want to be the fastest to develop new products. Well, that's a good goal, but it's not good enough. You have to set specific objectives, such as slash your new product development process from twenty-eight months to two months, and do it within three months. That's a concrete performance outcome. It motivates people and gives you a chance to monitor how you're doing. By contrast, if you just say, "Be the fastest," how do you monitor it?

Live the Change Yourself

The majority of leaders of organizations today face an unprecedented challenge. Ten years ago, if I came to you with a capital budgeting problem, you probably understood the problem—even if you weren't a financial specialist. You'd been there before. Likewise, if I came to you with a problem about maintaining morale or developing a particular individual's career, both of us could rely on our wisdom obtained from experience.

Today, if I come to you and say, "I'm having trouble coordinating the efforts of three self-directed work teams. What do I do about it?" or "I think my department needs a more horizontal, process-based structure," you probably haven't been there before. None of us has. Understanding and managing teams, in particular, is a new problem. Most leaders today don't understand and distinguish team discipline from individual discipline. Therefore, you're apt to rely on experiences that are irrelevant to the challenges you're facing.

Only by practicing the team discipline, by going into the field and listening to customers, by living the change, are you going to ground yourself in a genuine authority that I, as a subordinate, am going to respect. And only then will both of us—you and I—have confidence in the advice you are giving.

In short, every organization facing profound change needs better team performance by its leaders—especially if the organization's goal is to generate team performance down the line. Effective leaders roll up their sleeves, as a team, and say, "We, personally, are going to deliver. We're not just going to sit back and ask you to change your behavior. We are going to go out and win a key customer or deliver the reengineering process—not just delegate it to others."

Meaningful change is not a matter of throwing a senior vice president into a frontline worker team just for the sake of experience. It's finding the team performance opportunities that matter most *at your own level*—and you absolutely can find them. Leaders who take the same risks they ask of others—changing their own behavior and giving up a measure of comfort and control—truly inspire and energize others. When leaders are learning and growing, everything about them communicates the same opportunity to other people. They're excited, they do things differently. One of the most profound—and unusual—experiences people can have on the job is to see their leaders grow.

Win Over People Who Want to Be Convinced

All sorts of evidence—anecdotal, statistical, even biological—suggests that about 15 percent of any population seek out and embrace change; another 15 percent resist it, no matter what. That leaves the great middle, 70 percent, who are simply reluctant. So don't make the mistake of confusing reluctance with resistance. Managing reluctance (as opposed to resistance) means giving people a chance to try something in a real-life context. The nature of the reluctance that people feel before experiencing a change is far more abstract, ornate, and difficult to respond to than what they feel afterward. Once they've experienced a change, people tend to talk in particulars: well, this seemed to work; this didn't seem to work; we can improve response times by two days but not by two weeks. For the most part, you'll hear very specific concerns stated. Then the trick is to increase continually the number of people who attempt the change in a performance context that matters.

But when confronted with a pure resister, first ask yourself if there is an opportunity for that person to learn and continue to play a valuable, meaningful role in the organization. If there is, find it—everybody deserves that. If a person has had a performance-based opportunity to learn and just hasn't taken it, then try to find another role. And if that doesn't work, say good-bye. Having someone—at whatever level—undermine your efforts is poison.

Wean Yourself from Overplanning

It's impossible to know exactly how you're going to achieve the change you're after—trying to script a behavior-driven change precisely is pure folly. But it's essential to have in mind a clear mission, purpose, or vision of where you're heading. If you have that, change is a matter of embracing improvisation—which is another core principle of managing change. Make adjustments, vary your timing, incorporate what you learn along the way. But never lose sight of your goal.

Developing your improvisational skills will also help break the terrible habit of annual planning. Rather than spend months investing in the comforting fiction of an annual plan, move to another approach. Choose a single, overriding objective. Then articulate the three to five most critical performance outcomes that, if achieved in the next six to fifteen months, would make a meaningful difference in meeting your goal. Then, for each of these outcomes, identify three to five even more specific outcomes you would need to accomplish (see Figure 11.1). I've found that if you force yourself and others to think in terms of no more than three levels

Figure 11.1. A Performance Map for Change.

To map a strategy for sustaining change, translate your overall objective into a series of smaller, specific—and measurable—goals.

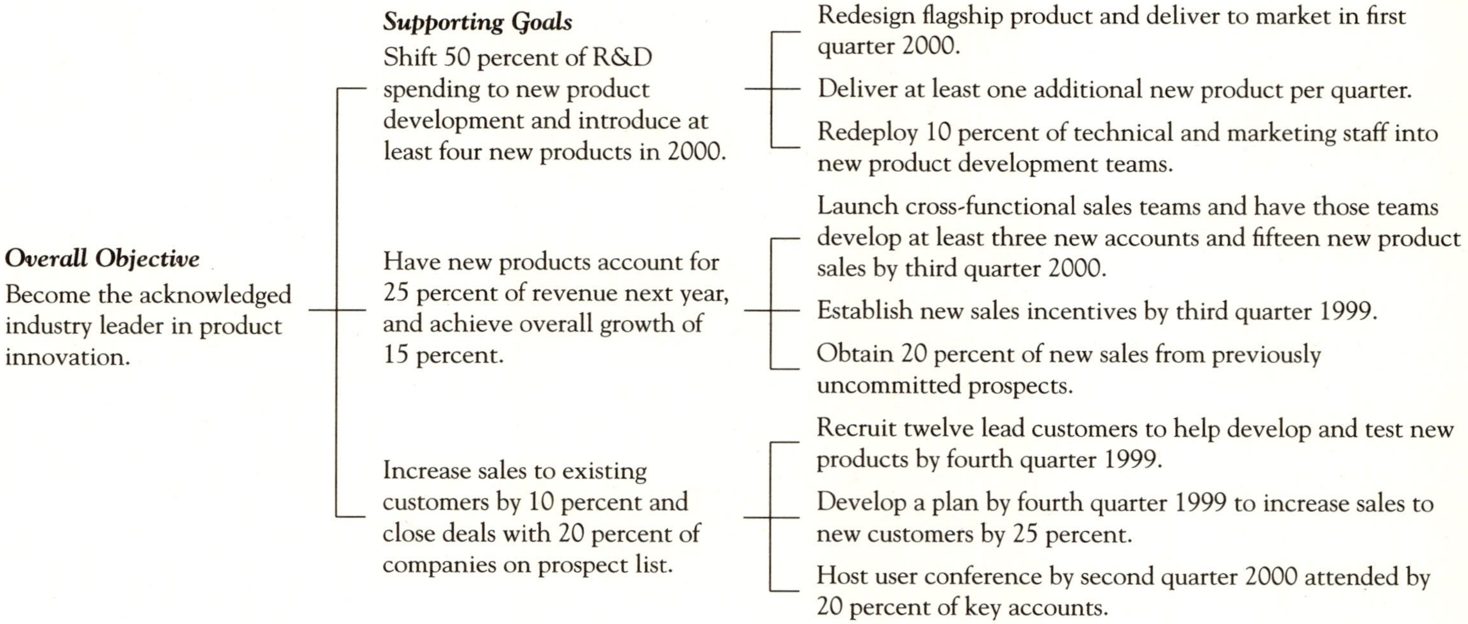

Overall Objective
Become the acknowledged industry leader in product innovation.

Supporting Goals

Shift 50 percent of R&D spending to new product development and introduce at least four new products in 2000.
- Redesign flagship product and deliver to market in first quarter 2000.
- Deliver at least one additional new product per quarter.
- Redeploy 10 percent of technical and marketing staff into new product development teams.

Have new products account for 25 percent of revenue next year, and achieve overall growth of 15 percent.
- Launch cross-functional sales teams and have those teams develop at least three new accounts and fifteen new product sales by third quarter 2000.
- Establish new sales incentives by third quarter 1999.
- Obtain 20 percent of new sales from previously uncommitted prospects.

Increase sales to existing customers by 10 percent and close deals with 20 percent of companies on prospect list.
- Recruit twelve lead customers to help develop and test new products by fourth quarter 1999.
- Develop a plan by fourth quarter 1999 to increase sales to new customers by 25 percent.
- Host user conference by second quarter 2000 attended by 20 percent of key accounts.

of specificity, more than 70 percent of the items at the third level will be concrete performance *outcomes* (rather than overly broad *activities* that aren't measurable).

This process gives you a performance map. It forces you to make tough choices. It's very hard to convert things from the level of purpose—we want to be the most responsive in our field—to the level of concrete, accessible performance goal—we want design engineers to team up with salespeople and visit six customers. The mapping process forces people to make choices about their specific priorities. And as you achieve your goals, you can develop new goals as needed at the moment. It's a much more dynamic, problem-solving approach than the annual budgeting process permits.

Once you've identified a change agenda, you have to ask the "so what" questions. That is, What's the performance outcome of the project? What are we trying to accomplish by changing? How would we (or anyone) know if we have succeeded? What would the change mean to the performance outcomes of this organization or this department or your work? The answers to those questions might not be obvious, but the inquiry that's set up by the questions is essential.

The Keys to Change Never Change

The principles of effective change do not depend on what sector you work in. There are always three constituencies that support one another—investors or funders, the people in the organization, and customers or constituents. Companies need shareholders who provide opportunities for people to provide value to customers to provide returns to shareholders, and so on. Charities and foundations need donors to provide opportunities to people to serve beneficiaries who inspire donors to provide more opportunities. Governments need constituents to provide opportunities to employees to enhance the health, security, or quality of life of the community. They're all organizations that, to be effective, need to become working, thriving communities of purpose and performance.

The biggest mistakes that leaders make in trying to manage change are not focusing on performance and not living the change. These are the first and last principles of change. Living the change is more than "walking the talk." It's showing up every day and saying "OK, I'm asking people to be more responsive. Am I doing that? Are we running the initiative in a responsive way? Let's spend a day with vendors getting ideas on speeding up our processes. How quickly are we going to act on that idea?"

In short, if you expect others to change their behavior, you have to change yours. It's as simple and as hard as that.

Part III

LEADERSHIP IN THE NEW INFORMATION ECONOMY

12 PETER F. DRUCKER

THE SHAPE OF THINGS TO COME

Peter F. Drucker has been a teacher, writer, and adviser to senior executives for more than fifty years. Author of thirty books, he is honorary chairman of the Drucker Foundation and Clarke Professor of Social Sciences at the Claremont Graduate University in Claremont, California.

Since writing *The End of Economic Man* in 1938, Peter F. Drucker has continued to demonstrate his gift for articulating the emerging issues of the day—and making them meaningful to the here-and-now work of managers. In 1996, for the premier issue of *Leader to Leader*, he spent several hours talking with managing editor Paul Cohen about what is changing—and what is not—in the world of work, society, and organizations.

PAUL COHEN: *Peter, let me ask you first what changes you see on the horizon that will have the most impact on our working lives?*

PETER F. DRUCKER: Recently I spent the day with the human resources people of twenty large Japanese corporations. I had reviewed a list of questions they sent me, and I began by saying there is one important question you have not asked: How will you run a company in fifteen years when the retirement age will be seventy-five? This shocked them out of their socks because most Japanese companies have yet to raise the retirement age to sixty. Japan has been the youngest of the developed countries; ten years from now it's going to be the oldest. And there is no way it can possibly support all those retired people; even loyal, faithful, obedient Japanese citizens will balk at handing over half their pay to people in reasonably good physical and mental shape.

In this country, we are talking about balancing the budget by the year 2003. That is sheer nonsense. No matter what Congress agrees on, by the year 2003 or so, with our present retirement age of sixty-five, let alone an enormous number of early retirements, we will be totally bankrupt. If our present trends continue, we will have about 3.3 people in the labor force for every retired person above sixty-five. We cannot expect a larger proportion of adults in the labor force—we already have the highest proportion in recorded history. We are not going to go back to sending eleven-year-old kids to work (though I do hope they spend fewer years in graduate school when they get older. I'm still an optimist on that point).

But for the last twenty years, in all developed countries the most privileged segment of the population has been older people in retirement. And it is by no means a new observation that older people become self-centered.

So we have a tremendous challenge. We have never had a demographic revolution as fast and as thorough as that of the last one hundred years. In 1900 or so, fewer than one in twenty people in the entire world did not do manual work. And fewer than one in twenty lived in a city with a population over 100,000. Today, in developed countries the proportion of people who do manual work is down to between one in four or one in five people in the work population. Half the people in the world live in cities with populations over 100,000. From an average work life span of about twenty-five years only a century ago, we now need to keep people working fifty years, so they can support themselves and we can maintain a growing economy. So, barring another world war, the great political issue in every developed country will be the age issue.

And it is not only a political issue. That people even in well-paid jobs choose ever earlier retirement is a severe indictment of our organizations—not just business, but government service, the universities. These people don't find their jobs interesting. Like a neighbor of mine, an engineer with a fairly responsible position in a major company: he took early retirement at about age fifty-four and is now spending his time playing golf, fishing, and driving around in an RV.

PC: *But don't companies provide an incentive for early retirement?*

PFD: Yes—and he took it. How boring that job must have been for him to prefer pulling an RV! No, fiscally it is simply inevitable that full retirement with pay will be given at a later and later age. It's a matter of simple arithmetic. But this means rethinking job structure. On the one hand, people need to work longer. On the other, believe me, people at sixty should step out of decision-making positions by and large. Why? Partly to keep opportunities for younger people open.

One of the challenges ahead is how to continue to use older, professional contributors. Among older workers—fifty-five years or more—a substantial minority wants to keep on working. So you will see a tremendous amount of experimentation. But this is going to create political and social conflict in every developed country. And nobody really sees it. People see it as an economic issue, and that's the least of it.

PC: *How does an aging workforce play out as a management issue?*

PFD: The fellow who works in a steel plant and takes early retirement at age fifty-five, after thirty-five years, is physically worn out from very heavy physical work. And he is willing to sit for twenty years on a pier in St. Petersburg and dangle a fishing line in the water—maybe. But the sales manager who works thirty-five years is not physically worn out. We are not facing up to the demand to make knowledge jobs interesting, challenging. Somehow we make them dumb—in large part because we put so much emphasis on promotion. And by definition, promotion is for one out of ten. So you disappoint a great many.

This emphasis on promotion is a post–World War II phenomenon resulting from earlier demographic changes. For example, between 1950 and 1975, in the major New York banks, twenty-seven years went from being the length of time you served before being eligible to become a vice president to being the age at which you could become vice president. When I first came to this country as a newspaper writer in the 1930s, you did not become a vice president of a New York bank until you were fifty, just as you did not become a full professor until that age—except perhaps in mathematics or physics. Now, of course, banks and major corporations have armies of vice presidents.

PC: *Are you suggesting that many high-level managers are not adding value to the organization?*

PFD: It's more than that. We have put too much emphasis on promotion and have not challenged people. But, look, it can be done. Let me give you an example. I know a young man, twenty-five, about to become first trumpeter in a major symphony orchestra. He is not going to be a conductor, not going to be first violinist. And nothing makes him happier than the idea of playing the trumpet for the next fifty years. What does the symphony orchestra do to satisfy people who will never get promoted that General Motors does not do for its engineers or its other professionals?

And it's not just business. I've been around academia for a long time and only a small minority of the really good people don't get tired of it. At age forty-three the rest retire on the job, go into midlife crisis, and either take to the bottle, have a torrid affair with a nineteen-year-old, or go into psychoanalysis. Of the three cures, psychoanalysis costs the most and takes the longest; otherwise, the results are pretty much the same. And yet there is that small minority who have inner resources, who still keep on. Many of the others wanted to, but the university system wouldn't allow them to; they had to become overspecialized. We have come to organize knowledge work very much on the model of industrial mass production.

PC: *Is it the manager's job not only to see that the work gets done but also to see that it's challenging?*

PFD: I think we are going to have to learn to develop more kinds of working options. For example, a friend of mine was the chief financial officer of a very substantial company. When he was fifty-eight, they offered him the chief executive job, and he said, "No, that has to go to a younger man." He is now working with fifteen small companies. Twice a month he discusses their management problems with their chief executive officers and their financial people. When they have a financial problem, he comes in and, of course, charges them; otherwise they wouldn't listen to him. And he turns that money over to charity. He's blissfully happy. He took the initiative himself. But one can learn from that. These are the kinds of challenges we need. And we need to provide them much earlier so that people will want to stay involved but can also be mobile.

PC: *Are you saying that older managers should leave their organizations and set themselves up as freelancers?*

PFD: Let me put it differently. For 150 years, from 1850 on, society moved inexorably toward being a society of organizations. In 1900, nobody worked in an "organization." It's a 1950s term. Lots of people were employed—hired hands on the farm, domestic servants, journeymen in their shop—but they worked for a master, not an organization. And the work was very personal.

Since then, the organization has become the organizer—though not necessarily the employer. Now we have all kinds of dangerous liaisons. One of the things to understand about outsourcing is that the woman who works for the hospital cleaning floors is very bored by the job. But if she works for ServiceMaster, an outsourcing company, she's very excited by it because people listen to her, people challenge her. She is expected to improve the job and gets paid for doing it—whereas before no one would listen. These days, her supervisor had a broom in her hands only five years ago. So the outsourcing people have a great strength in making what we might call a dead-end job much more challenging, because they take it seriously.

PC: *What will the organization of tomorrow and the executive of tomorrow look like?*

PFD: Perhaps this is not one question but two, for the simple reason that the executive may change more than the organization does. Charles Handy predicts that by the year 2000, practically nobody in the United States or the United Kingdom will be an employee. I think that's overreaching slightly. But the trend is clear: the employee society of organizations is mutating.

I met with a very big company not long ago—around eighty or so on the Fortune 500 list. They expect to be number five on that list in ten years, and I shocked them by saying I don't think that list will exist, so the goal is meaningless. That list basically assumes that everything you do is under your roof and is owned by you and run by you. But already in many companies most work is done through alliances, joint ventures, minority participation, and very informal agreements that no lawyer could possibly handle. They are on the order of "Joe, you are better on this than I am; you do it." Or "Joe, neither you nor I should do that; let's get Mary."

This company's CEO is a well-known amateur science historian, and I told him, "You'd better stop studying the history of science and start studying the history of tribes, because that's what you're going to be. You're going to be the elder chieftain of the Cherokees." And they have no authority other than that arising from wisdom and competence and accomplishment.

So you will have to learn not to run a business but to build a business. That means you will have far fewer employees but God knows how many people who work with you. And that's the organization. The young biochemist probably doesn't want to become a manager; seven years from now he wants to be back at the university. And yet during those seven years nobody's going to tell him what to do. Either he knows what to do or you'd better get rid of him. And you have no promotion opportunities for that fellow, but you have to reward and recognize and pay him properly. So you'd better stop talking about managers and talk about executives. "Manager" still implies to most of us somebody who has people working for him or her.

PC: *How does one learn to manage partnerships, joint ventures, and outside contributors? These things aren't taught in business school, are they?*

PFD: Far from it. The present people in organizations are still stuck in the nineteenth-century model of the organization. When big business first emerged throughout the industrial world around 1870, it did not emerge out of the small businesses of 1850—it emerged independently. The only model available, the most successful organization of the nineteenth century, was the Prussian Army, which had just been reorganized and had learned from the inability of the Americans in the Civil War to organize, transport, and communicate with masses of people. It was the first modern organization. It defeated the Austrians in 1866, who had a much larger and better-armed army, and then, four years later, defeated the French, who were even better armed. The Prussians succeeded because they had created an organization. They were the first ones to use modern technology effectively, which in those days meant railroad and telegraph. Business copied the command-and-control structure of the Prussian army, in which rank equaled authority. We are now evolving toward structures in which rank means responsibility but not authority. And in which your job is not to command but to persuade.

A friend of mine in his late forties or early fifties runs the worldwide leasing operations for one of the world's big banks. He visited me on his way to a conference in which he was presenting his business to the top brass. And he told me, "You know, I have thought through this business, and the way the bank wants to go about it is the wrong way. I'm going to present the way I am going to go. They can fire me, but they can't order me to do it their way. As long as I run it, I have to run it the way I know is right." And he was not being arrogant; he was simply being factual. His authority is based on expertise and on the respect and responsibility that go with it, not on his ability to pull rank.

PC: *Doesn't managing these new relationships assume a large degree of trust on the part of an organization—that it's working with people who know more about some aspects of the business than it does?*

PFD: First, it assumes a different attitude. You start out not with what's best for you but with what's best for them. You see yourself not as the boss but as the conductor. Good orchestra conductors are exceedingly autocratic. But they do not see themselves as the boss. They see themselves as the servant of the score. I've talked to a good many conductors and they all say, "My job is to make the orchestra hear the score the way I hear it." Partly because no conductor knows how to get a single note out of a clarinet. Only the clarinetist knows that. All a conductor can say is, "First clarinet, I would like to have this a little louder, or a little slower, or a little softer." That authority is a command authority, but it rests on the ability of the conductor to share, to communicate.

Then comes trust. Trust has to be built on the conviction that this conductor, this coordinator, this executive creates a partnership—and then you have trust. Trust very largely means there are no surprises. My best story about trust is from World War II. I did a fair amount of work with one of the world's nastiest human beings. He was a first-rate inventor and about as horrible and miserable a person as I've ever encountered. He was unspeakable. This was 1946, right after the end of the war, and the start of sensitivity training—which I persuaded him to go to. I thought I had made a contribution to humanity. And he came back totally convinced, overflowing with human kindness and caring, and I felt very good. Three weeks later I ran into his chief engineer and said, "Joe, how is so-and-so doing?" He said, "It is impossible, I don't think we can stand it any longer. He comes into the office in the morning and says 'Good Morning,' and we spend the rest of the day worrying about whether he meant it or not." Three weeks later I ran into the same chief engineer again and asked if things had gotten any better. He said, "Thank God, he is back to being the old, unbearable SOB and we know what to expect. We can trust him again."

PC: *You mentioned the conductor's artistic vision. Certainly social sector organizations organize themselves around a vision or mission. How important is it for other organizations to do that consciously?*

PFD: We know that knowledge people have to be managed as if they were volunteers. They have expectations, self-confidence, and above all, a network. And that gives them mobility, which is probably the greatest change in the human condition. A very short time ago, if you were the son of a peasant, you were going to be a peasant. Even in this country, social mobility was almost unknown. Now, every one of the young people I know has his or her resume in the bottom drawer, which no blue-collar worker ever did.

So accept the fact that we have to treat almost anybody as a volunteer. They carry their tools in their heads and can go anywhere. And we know what attracts and holds volunteers. The first thing is a clear mission. People need to know what their organization stands for and is trying to accomplish. The second thing is responsibility for results, which means appraisal and review. And the third thing is continuous learning. I learned those lessons from our friend

Frances Hesselbein. And business is going to have to learn them, too. A few are beginning to, but not many yet.

So what does mission mean? Don't expect a twenty-nine-year-old or thirty-three-year-old engineer to embrace a financial objective as a statement of mission. People want to know what their organization is here for and how they can contribute. It doesn't have to be anything very highfalutin, but it has to be concrete. I have known the Coca-Cola Company for a long time, and most of their people are totally dedicated. I know no other company that has such a strong feeling of community. Their mission is "Beat Pepsi." That's enough. But if you don't share that mission, you don't last long at Coca-Cola.

PC: *With all the changes you have seen in the last fifty years, and all the management practices that have come and gone, what do you see that remains true? What management practices will always apply?*

PFD: Of the little we know, most of it will apply. The question is, will we reach a point where we apply it? We don't, yet. But the first constant in the job of management is to make human strength effective and human weaknesses irrelevant. That's the purpose of any organization, the one thing an organization does that individuals can't do better.

The second constant is that managers are accountable for results, period. They are not being paid to be philosophers; they are not even being paid for their knowledge. They are paid for results. Management is not a branch of philosophy but a practice. Which is very hard to get across in the university. The management schools try to be academically respectable. But they face a very tough ten years, largely because they will have to rethink what they are trying to do and why. But what remains is that managers and management must deliver results, and results are not quite as easy to define in an organization. The balance between short term and long term, for instance, will remain a constant challenge.

And the last thing to say about what remains constant—actually, it will become even more relevant—is that people in developed societies will become increasingly dependent on access to an organization. Because they are specialists, they need access to the specialized knowledge of others in order to do a job.

PC: *How will people's dependence on an organization affect the organization itself?*

PFD: All institutions, including governments, churches, universities, and so on, will become more interdependent, more market- and customer-driven. Today it is a world of infinite choices. With churches, it used to be that you were born into a denomination and stayed there. In the fast-growing pastoral churches, which are the most significant social development in this country, 90 percent of the members were not born into the denomination. So competition in all realms is acute.

And yet there are new monopolies that we haven't yet taken into account. For example, we let one institution control access to careers and livelihood in a way no earlier society would have—the college and university are major gatekeepers. That's why you have all those fights about admission. Because, for better or worse, and I think it's for worse, the Bank of America isn't going to hire anybody for a training position who doesn't have a college degree. It's asinine, but that's beside the point; it's a fact.

PC: *People always seem to be responding to change after it has happened. What advice do you give on how to anticipate change?*

PFD: Look out the window. Literally. You know how painters are traditionally taught painting? The teacher places a flower vase, which looks deceptively simple to paint, on the table and tells the youngster to paint the vase. The teacher comes and looks at it and says turn around, bend down, look at what you have painted upside down through your legs. That is the traditional way to teach to see.

So look at our assumptions about technology or markets—suppose the opposite were true. Is there any evidence? Challenge your assumptions. This is basically looking at the vase upside down. Make yourself capable of doing this by building organized abandonment into your system. By asking yourself every few years, If we weren't doing what we now do, would we want to start doing it? And if the answer is "probably not," then maybe it isn't the right thing to do anymore. This is not very difficult. It's a habit more than a skill. But it's a habit you have to practice.

13 CHARLES HANDY

THE SEARCH FOR MEANING

Social philosopher, management scholar, best-selling author, and radio commentator Charles Handy is an influential voice worldwide. He has written some of the most influential articles and books of the past decade, including The Age of Unreason *and* The Age of Paradox. *After working for Shell International as a marketing executive, economist, and management educator, Handy helped to start the London Business School in 1967. He has worked closely with leaders of business, nonprofit, and government organizations.*

One of the first to predict the massive downsizing of organizations and the emergence of self-employed professionals, Charles Handy has a gift for looking twenty years ahead at ways that society and its institutions are changing. The Irish-born, London-based author spoke with Paul Cohen, managing editor of *Leader to Leader*, during a 1997 visit to the United States.

PAUL COHEN: *Charles, how do you view the business-guru system—of which you're a part—in the United States?*

CHARLES HANDY: It's interesting because we don't have that in Europe. The people who are respected in Europe are the captains of organizations—people like Percy Barnevik or Richard Branson—rather than what you might call the commentators. I am very unusual in Europe, and a lot of people think I'm American. The two continents are extreme in their different ways. In America you give too much importance to the commentators, because they have a tendency to oversimplify the world—that's what you have to do if you're making a one-hour presentation or writing a wildly popular book. In Europe, on the other hand, if you're actually running an organization, all you can usually do is talk about that organization or others like it. That's what you know. We actually need in Europe to have more people who can stand back and generalize. You need both traditions. I think we overdo it in Europe, not having the commentators, and I think you overdo it in America, paying too much attention to them.

PC: *How can we achieve more balance between the two traditions?*

CH: I would like to see American CEOs taking a higher public profile on the social and economic issues of the day. Bill Gates and Jack Welch should not be the only leaders anyone hears from.

PC: *You propose a model of corporate governance that gives shareholders far less management influence. That certainly challenges conventional wisdom in this country. Explain your thinking.*

CH: It seems to me rather obvious that the current system of capitalism is not going to be sustained, and let me explain why. The assumption, in the Anglo-American context—and it's different in continental Europe, different in Japan, in China—is that the company is a piece of property, owned by the people who buy shares of it. They therefore have the right to sell that property. But what is that property? It increasingly is a collection of people. The tangible, fixed assets of these corporations are worth considerably less than their market value. If you take the pure knowledge organizations—

advertising agencies, banks, software companies—the market value may be twenty, thirty, forty times the fixed assets. I think the rhetoric of the stock market is concealing from us the fact that what we're actually talking about is owning other people.

Now, when we think about it, this is both strange and, in the end, unworkable, because organizations, as we know, are whittling down to the core, outsourcing everything they can. They are going to employ a relatively small proportion of all the people they need. These core people, therefore, are going to be rather competent. And they are going to resent being owned by other people. They're going to say, "No, you can't just sell us over our heads or dictate our strategy. Furthermore, if you don't like it, we will leave." So what is the point of saying that you own something when actually that something can walk out the door?

The stock market is just a casino. When you buy shares in Microsoft, for instance, you are taking a gamble. It's not just a gamble on the profitability of Microsoft; it's more than that. You are gambling that Bill Gates can continue to motivate young people to work like fiends for the company. Therefore, I argue, stockholders will revert to their true role as investors and not owners. They will not have the right to combine and sell the company over the heads of its people.

PC: *What do you say to those who argue that it is the shareholders who take the risk, who give the organization its capital? And how do you raise the capital in your model?*

CH: I'm not saying we shouldn't have any shareholders. I'm saying go back to the old system of A shares and B shares. A shares are voting shares, and you only have A shares if you're a member of the company or have seriously invested in the company. We can assume that anyone who has, say, a 1 percent stake in a company is there for the long term. If the big stockholders who are proper members of the company think that the company is doing badly and want to change the management—well, they have votes, they can intervene. But they'd have to discuss it with other members. They couldn't just do it from the outside.

Then you have the other category of investors, the B shares, who are what you might call the parasites. These are the bettors, the traders, or the people in the secondary market who say, "Well, my stockbroker tells me that the next three months are going to look good for GM." They don't really have any responsibility or commitment to GM. They're not even putting any money into the business. The money that's churning around in the secondary market—which is most of the stock market—is going nowhere near the company. Most big companies do not raise new money in the stock market. They either raise it from the banks or from retained earnings. It's mostly new companies that raise new money from the stock market. The reason that the stock market is so important is not because it raises money; it's because it is putting a price on your property. Somebody else can buy you. When your stock price goes down, you're worried, not because you can't raise more money—you weren't doing that anyway. But suddenly it's as if your house is valued at half the price of the house next door.

Now, clearly we need entrepreneurs, we need people who take big risks and get big money from it. I'm not saying that that shouldn't happen at all. We need investors, we just don't need them to control the company's destiny.

PC: *Is anything like this system happening?*

CH: You begin to see it in the small businesses. I'm developing a concept that I call the citizen company. The inhabitants, if you like, are citizens. They have rights. They have the right of free speech, to express their preferences. They have the right of residence. Now we may have to put some boundaries on the right of residence—ten-year or fifteen-year rights—but they know they have a place in this community.

In new businesses, the start-up group—which may be ten, twenty, fifty people—has a psychological stake and often a financial stake in the business. These people use what I describe as the twin hierarchy approach. That is, there is the hierarchy of status—though not more than three or four levels. You find this in professional organizations, with senior partners, ordinary partners, and associates who would like to become partners. But you also have a totally different hierarchy, the task hierarchy, where you group people, irrespective of their status, into operational teams around projects. You can actually have a partner or even a nonpartner leading a project group with senior partners being part-time members of that group.

These citizen companies will also have probationary citizens: you have to show that you can speak the language, that you subscribe to the values. Finally they will have the outsiders, whom I call the mercenaries. That is not a bad word, necessarily. It's simply saying that you are hired for a particular task. You're not a member of the community. You are a very useful adjunct. My worry about companies at the moment is that we're all mercenaries. We're all there temporarily, but when it's time to move along, the theory of employability goes, you will be a better mercenary somewhere else.

I'm saying we need all three categories: full citizens, probationary citizens, and mercenaries. Deciding which is which and what the proportions are, and how you actually manage them, is the task of leaders and citizens both. But unless you have the citizen category, everybody is going to think like a mercenary. And that's dangerous. Mercenaries owe loyalty to no one except themselves and their careers. They tend to go to the highest bidder. Keeping their commitment, therefore, becomes increasingly expensive.

PC: *The search for meaning—in the workplace, in the community, and in public life—has become a growth industry. What do you think that signifies to leaders?*

CH: My next book, *The Hungry Spirit*, is an attempt to answer that. I think the search for meaning applies to individuals and to institutions. We're all looking for why we do the work we do. It was easy in the past—we were doing it because we needed the money to live. Now it's clear that money—for many people and institutions—is more symbolic than real. We generate more wealth than we really need to live on. And money becomes a rather crude measure of success. We're looking for something more.

There is, in my view, no God-given explanation for each of us as to what success might be. I do believe that we are each unique. We each—institutions as well as individuals—have something to contribute to the world, and the search for meaning is finding out what that is before we die. Until then, we have only tentative answers.

The first half of life is certainly a struggle to prove that you can survive and then can achieve some special capacity. But the interesting thing for me is that given that you can survive, that you are successful, what is it you can contribute? The companies that survive longest are the ones that work out what they uniquely can give to the world—not just growth or money but their excellence, their respect for others, or their ability to make people happy. Some call those things a soul.

PC: *How can leaders help their organizations discover their unique purpose before they die?*

CH: Organizations are significantly different from individuals in that individuals die and organizations can live forever. Very few do. The Catholic Church is perhaps the longest living, but Mitsui of Japan and Stora of Sweden are more than 600 years old. My Oxford College is 650 years old. The interesting thing about organizations is that they can make the assumption that they're never going to die. And the reason that you stay immortal is you have discovered what's unique about you. The job of the leader is to work that out, to express it. Very few leaders succeed in doing this. I ask a lot of leaders of organizations what it's all about. They usually say survival. I say that's only the first stage. If you're no use to anyone, you can't survive. What is it that you, uniquely, as an organization can contribute to the world?

Most don't know the answer. Why then would you want to devote your life to an organization that can't give something special to the world? No reason except that you get money or get a kick out of it yourself. But after getting those, you'll probably leave the organization. Businesses have an enormous amount to learn from nonprofit organizations. Successful nonprofits have had to be very clear about their unique contribution and the difference they make to the world.

PC: *You talk about society organizing itself around the affiliations or clubs that people choose for themselves. What will be the primary affiliations in the future?*

CH: I think there will be two. First, a work affiliation. If you're a citizen, in my language of organizations you're strongly affiliated with that organization. If you're a mercenary, it will probably be a professional club of some sort. In London, people who have a multiplicity of clients and occupations, who don't really have a professional liaison, have formed private groups they call "hives." They meet to share some of their problems, but also for friendship, because they're working on their own. They don't identify themselves with a particular profession; their profession is being self-employed. It's partly social, partly work related, and mostly female. We need to create more of these because I think everybody needs to have a work club. People also need a social club. Not in the sense of recreational club, but a bit of society to which they feel they belong. That, I'm arguing, is not the nation-state. It's the city and probably below the city, the district or social group.

PC: *How will this change our social institutions?*

CH: I think that Europe, for instance, is going to be organized around cities rather than nations. Cities are something we can relate to much more easily. Increasingly, national governments in Europe will become less powerful. You'll have supernational governments like the European Union, and you will have more powerful local, regional, city governments. And nothing much in between—which is why of course there's such a fuss going on in Europe at the moment. This is in essence what is going to happen in America. Some of the states will have to delegate more power to cities. Federal government will still be important for international affairs and broad national policies, but city government will become key.

Central government has done many things. And I'm not arguing that this *should* change, I'm just arguing that it *will* change. It seems to me that people want more control over their lives and what goes on around them. And all the evidence is that as you get richer you demand these things. So one of the strange things is that there are no rich dictatorships. When dictatorships are successful economically, the pressures for democracy become too great. I'm arguing that as countries get richer, even under democracy, they become more participatory.

PC: *Are you suggesting that there will be revolution in China in twenty years?*

CH: Probably not revolution, but I would say dissolution. I find it hard to think that China—which is developing at an incredible rate in some bits, and almost nothing in other bits—is going to hold together. So I can see China falling into twenty different bits, reverting to its history as a nation of regional warlords.

PC: *You were very optimistic in* The Age of Unreason *about the prospects for flexible organizations, healthy communities, and more fully integrated individuals. Your later work takes a more sober view of the future. How hopeful are you?*

CH: I remain pessimistic in the short term but optimistic in the long term. I do think that we humans are creative people. We will find solutions. In the short term it seems to me that we've become very selfish. I'm worried about capitalism, that it's distorted our purposes in life. The argument against *The Age of Unreason* eight years ago was that I was describing a world that was very well suited for a person like myself; that it was easy to have a good, independent life if you had education, professional skills, and a good partner. I took that criticism onboard; I think it was true. Now my argument is not that we should change the world but that we should try to make more people like me, if you will; people who have the skills and competencies to live in this more free-form world. I believe we will succeed, but it's going to take at least a generation. I believe in capitalism and competition, but we have got to equip everybody to cope with these two forces, and we have got to keep things in perspective. Simply making money, big flashy vacations, are not what it's all about.

PC: *Clearly, education is key to equipping people for the world. What do you see as the future of our school systems?*

CH: I think that one trend that's coming is that every child should understand at an early age his or her intelligence profile. This follows psychologist Howard Gardner's idea that there are several different kinds of intelligences—analytical, interpersonal, practical, physical, musical, and so on. People simply have different aptitudes. Once we have identified these, we can design an individual curriculum which, for at least half of the school time, concentrates on developing these particular intelligences, irrespective of the core base of the teaching.

It's already beginning to happen. Middle-class parents now say, "We want more emphasis on music, want more emphasis on sporting abilities—and we will pay for that outside of school." The school day should be split in two. The first half is what you might call a required, common curriculum, taught by schools. The second half is an individual curriculum in which many outside organizations take part—work organizations, community organizations. These activities may be organized by the school, but they may or may not take place in school. The school becomes a kind of broker for learning.

When it works properly, every young person will leave school with a personal portfolio of competence, including many more items than the classroom captures.

PC: *With all the changes you see, what do you think are the keys to sustaining positive change in an organization or in a community?*

CH: Change is always difficult. There are many people for whom the present is comfortable, who would rather not change at all. You've got to have confidence in the future. That's partly something you get from the community, from the institution, and from the leaders who say things are going to be better. It's also something that comes from inside you. You need an inner belief that you are in some sense meant to be here, that you can leave the world a little different in a small way. If you think that you're an accident of biology and that everything you do is because of your genes, or your early upbringing, or things that the government has done—if you see yourself as a victim—then I think that you will regard everything that happens to you as outside your control, an imposition. You would not be prepared to change unless you could see a direct, immediate payoff.

Leaders of institutions have to believe and declare that there is a future for their institution, some hope of glory, whatever that might be. Second, they have to make clear to the individuals that they are special to that dream of glory. That they are there because they can make a contribution and so can believe that there is a reason for their existence. Yes, we do inherit things from our parents, and yes, our upbringing affects us. But the great challenge of life is to override these things and to do better than them. We can do that. This is our unique human capacity. We can override our inheritance. I want leaders who can make people feel that this is true. Within limits, we can be what we want to be. We can, with great leaders, create something glorious.

PC: *Beyond giving people hope about the future, don't leaders have to put all the pieces in place for getting there?*

CH: The leader's first job is to be a missionary, to remind people what is special about them and their institutions. Second it is to set up the infrastructure for that to happen—not the superstructure, not to make the actual decisions, but to set the support systems, the people in place. The two go together; it's no good having a brilliant strategy and structure and great people unless there is some reason for it. And it doesn't get you very far to go around saying how wonderful things will be in the future without knowing how you might get there. This combination is rare.

PC: *You've worked with outstanding leaders from many types of organizations. What do you see as the key attributes that make them successful?*

CH: Passion. They really have to believe in what they do. Ironically, this means they can occasionally believe in very bad things. Most effective leaders therefore also have a moral compass. They've also got to be quite tough in order to deliver their passion. The effective leaders that I've met are a strange combination of passionate human beings who can communicate that passion to others and who, at the same time, are forceful, take big risks. If you don't measure up, they get rid of you. If you can do both of these two things, you get commitment from people. It is winning that commitment that makes effective leaders. Finally, the leader must be prepared to admit that he or she does not have all the answers. This is a very rare combination: someone who is passionate, very tough, and at the same time able to doubt.

PC: *Are you saying that leaders are born, not made?*

CH: I don't think you can teach the skills, or learn them from others, but often it is a matter of finding yourself in the right place. You may be hopeless in trying to run IBM, but put in charge of a school, you may make all the difference. In other words, you may say you're not a passionate person, but if you find something you're passionate about, then you've got one of the three elements of being a true leader. You may say, I say myself, I'm not able to be tough. But if I was engaged in running something I was passionate about, I think I could be tough.

Then one says if you're passionate, how do you have any decent doubt? I think you can be pulled up short by life. A friend or loved one dies, which suddenly gives you a jolt. You sense that you are not all-powerful. Maybe you say, "I've got it wrong. Maybe building this business, about which I'm passionate, isn't the right thing." So while these skills cannot be taught, they can be brought out under the right circumstances. One of the things that you can do in life is look for the right circumstances. I often say that life is like an apple—it falls into your hands. But it won't fall into your hands unless you stand under the tree. You have to find the orchard, find the tree, and then something may happen.

14 SALLY HELGESEN

WOMEN AND THE NEW ECONOMY

Sally Helgesen is a writer, speaker, and consultant who specializes in organizational innovation and employee participation. She is author of the bestsellers The Female Advantage: Women's Ways of Leadership, The Web of Inclusion: A New Architecture for Building Great Organizations, *and* Everyday Revolutionaries: Working Women and the Transformation of American Life.

In barely one generation, our culture has experienced two momentous changes in tandem. Rigid work structures that provided relative stability and prosperity for 150 years have given way to a more fluid postindustrial economy, driven by new technology and global competition. At the same time, women are for the first time assuming positions of influence in business and in public life. The confluence of these two transformations, one economic and one social, has enormous implications for the future.

The new economy is rewarding companies that decentralize the means of production, which today include knowledge, expertise, and human talent. It simply has become less expensive to organize work in dispersed, local settings—down to the private home—than in massive offices or factories. As Peter Drucker reminds us, value creation is shifting to the individual rather than to the organization as a result of these changes. For many, however, this concept presents difficulties. People frequently perceive themselves as powerless because of the pace of organizational change and the erosion of employment security. This is thus a time of great insecurity. Nevertheless, millions of professionals—women in particular—are learning to invent their own positions rather than waiting for a new system to provide them. Women are often most affected by the breakdown of barriers between work and home, and by the changing relationship between organizations and employees. They are initiators of the social revolution that has allowed half of humanity to begin taking its place in the larger society. So the study of women's lives at this particular moment offers us the opportunity to assess the impact that the social and economic revolutions are having in at least three realms of public life: career development and training, commercial and social entrepreneurship, and the new physical, social, and spiritual communities that are reshaping American culture.

The New Meaning of Careers

One common misconception is the conflict portrayed in the popular press between women who work outside the home and women who don't. In fact, most women today are, have been, or will be part of the paid workforce. They may take two or five or even ten years away from their jobs to raise children, to work part-time, or to volunteer for community organizations, but most eventually return to full-time work. In a rigid industrial system where one gets an education, works for thirty-five years, and then retires, taking several years off is destructive to one's work life. But today we need additional education and training throughout the course of our careers, whether or not we take time off from full-time work. And as men and women increasingly change careers and move in and out of the workplace, our institutions are starting to rethink the meaning of career development.

Women's traditional pattern of taking time away from work can give them an edge in adapting to difficult but increasingly common career transitions. Women who have chosen to make a career change after taking a few years off often use that period to reexamine the nature of their work in light of more mature personal and professional goals. When they return to the workplace, they have a better sense of who they are and what they want to do. And they often serve as a model for younger women and for the men in their lives who, because of workplace insecurity, must learn to repot themselves professionally.

The New Market for Training

The demand for continuing education programs by already well-educated adults is growing fast. Community colleges in the United States now provide an increasing amount of that vocational and professional training, either through their own programs or in partnership with local businesses. The interactions between businesses and colleges and universities are now pervasive, and are driving our educational institutions to become more responsive to the needs of the businesses and individuals that are paying most of the freight. Thus we see many schools and training programs competing on the basis of practical results, in some cases complete with the student's satisfaction guaranteed.

The revolution in adult education has led many educators and policymakers to question the future of our four-year colleges and universities. They have reason to wonder. There will always be a need for the traditional liberal arts training that universities and four-year colleges provide; the demand for well-rounded, thinking individuals will only increase. But clearly these institutions will have to reconsider their relationship to the rest of society. To the extent that they see themselves as full-time places for eighteen-to-twenty-one-year-olds, and eschew the kind of business and community partnerships pioneered by more innovative institutions, they will be less relevant to people's needs. As the demand for the continual upgrading of skills grows, education will become more integrated into peoples' lives.

Although men receive most of the dollars spent on corporate training, according to the Department of Labor, women are the largest consumers of outside training, whether public seminars, college courses, or personal development programs. Women more actively seek out such training opportunities and are more willing to spend their own money on these efforts. They are thus taking responsibility for their own training.

Cities on the Edge

The profound changes in how we live and work are closely tied to where we live and work. Forty years ago, William Whyte's book *The Organization Man* offered a groundbreaking view of American society. Whyte looked at the changes in postwar America through the lens of a relatively homogeneous community: Park Forest, Illinois, a bedroom suburb of Chicago. In Whyte's day, such communities represented mainstream American life. Today, the massive commercial, office, and residential developments in outlying areas—dubbed "edge cities" by writer Joel Garreau—dominate the landscape. These communities are much more complex and self-contained than the suburbs of the 1950s and provide a new stage for the twin revolutions of gender participation and technological and economic transformation.

To get a sense of how these changes are playing out in people's lives, I spent part of two years in Naperville, an edge-city community of just over 100,000 people thirty miles west of Chicago and eighteen miles northwest of Park Forest. In Whyte's Park Forest, everyone commuted by train into Chicago; virtually all the men (and these commuters were virtually all men) worked for large organizations. They took the 8:01 and were home by 5:30. The situation in Naperville today is entirely different. The jobs have moved to the western suburbs, and most local residents work in DuPage or one of the adjoining suburban counties rather than in Chicago. Some of the most sophisticated corporations in the world—such as Motorola, Lucent Technologies, Hewlett Packard, Nextel Communications, Amoco, McDonald's—have headquarters or major facilities in the area, as do more traditional industries—material distributors, trucking companies, and hotel, retail, and service businesses.

The population in the Naperville area is well educated and not necessarily U.S.-born. Immigrant Russians, Argentineans, Chinese, Pakistanis, Indians, and Iranians live in prosperous new developments, and a substantial Hispanic population lives and works in adjoining Aurora. Thus the region is far more diverse than Whyte's Park Forest.

Edge cities such as Naperville are often criticized for their lack of cultural institutions, public gathering places, and historic character. The physical layout of these suburban outposts creates further barriers to community. One can rarely walk to the corner store, florist, or restaurant that is part of the everyday urban landscape; instead, one must often drive miles to such places. Nevertheless, new kinds of institutions have evolved, particularly among women, who have actively created both formal and informal networks of support.

One important institution in Naperville is the College of DuPage (COD), a substantial number of whose students are adults returning to school for new training as a result of career shifts. The largest single-campus community college in the world, COD is expanding its role in the community by targeting business and professional programs for development. The school also offers programs for women who are returning to the workforce. It provides people with a forum in which to connect broadly with others—creating the kinds of stable social and professional bonds that once occurred in business organizations. The college is also important to the life of the community; it is home to a jazz band, an orchestra, a theater, and an art center—the kind of cultural organizations that would otherwise have no place in town to operate. As in most of suburbia, the tax structure of Naperville and DuPage County makes it difficult for these kinds of institutions to find public support outside of educational institutions.

Unlike traditional urban communities, today's suburban enclaves are organized not so much around neighborhoods as around self-identified social or religious affiliations. This situation mirrors the plug-in quality of the edge-city suburbs, a characteristic of our technology in general. One major effect of the technology revolution has been to deemphasize the importance of location and centralization, creating more atomized communities as a result. Americans, however, have always found new ways to come together. An example is the development of nondenominational megachurches, which enable large numbers of people to build communities of interest and service. In nearby Barrington, Willow Creek, one of the nation's largest institutions of faith, draws heavily from the region around Naperville. Its nondenominational nature attracts people broadly across ethnic, racial, and class lines, and with scant reference to historical religious traditions. Congregants are sorted into smaller groups according to circumstances, such as singles in their twenties, new fathers, and "empty nesters." The attention to social niche is not unlike the market strategy of Starbucks or the Gap. The emphasis is thus on personal choice and customization, both characteristic of our postindustrial environment.

New Forms of Affiliation

As people develop new ways of working, society needs to draw from increasingly broad bases of talent and perspective. In the society into which we're moving, leadership in organizations and communities will come from people who aren't necessarily in positions of power. Yet as organizational leaders struggle to be more inclusive, they are often burdened with rigid models of where a person should be at each stage of life. Many partnership firms, in particular, are still often marked by an unforgiving "up or out" mentality that denies many people the opportunity to contribute in other ways and robs the firm of superb talent. Correlating age to position is increasingly pointless—especially in regard to professional women, who are particularly likely to move in and out of the workforce. Technical specialists also find themselves suddenly overspecialized and having to change direction. Accomplished people throughout the economy are beginning to say, "Because there's no job security, I need to know what satisfies me. I want to find a way to make a living that suits me, rather than fitting into some slot."

All this turns the traditional notion of career attainment on its ear. Organizations in the years ahead are going to have to accommodate people who want to have fluid careers that are both self-directed and self-conceived. As people take more control of their work lives, they will use organizations in an almost instrumental way to create and mold their changing professional identities. Many people are already approaching their current jobs as an opportunity to lay the foundation for a second or third career. People who rely for their sense of pride, enjoyment, and personal mastery on their work are not going to want to bow out at seventy.

One outlet for displaced employees—and for women in particular—is entrepreneurship. More than one-third of all small businesses are now owned by women. (And small businesses, not coincidentally, tend to operate with fewer preconceptions about what people should be doing at a certain point in life.) These start-ups—in computer programming, graphic design, accounting, health services, and professional training, for example—are typically knowledge-based and are our greatest source of innovation and job growth. They are a manifestation of what Charles Handy calls the "work portfolio," encompassing the many jobs we will hold in our lives, as well as the family, community, and educational commitments we will pursue. Often these social and commercial ventures are done part-time, in the home, as people cobble together diverse "casserole careers" that suit their own needs and interests. Again, women are leading this social shift, in part because working women have traditionally conceived of their identity as more broadly determined than simply what position they hold in the workplace. This attitude is beginning to spread as the line between work and home is fading.

Community and Nonprofits

Volunteer work, like most undertakings, is beginning to assume a more professionalized character. This is particularly evident, for instance, among women who manage the health problems of a child or family member—for example, a thirty-two-year-old woman who has spent ten years in the workforce has a child who is diagnosed with a serious learning disability or health problem. She is accustomed to taking a professional approach to everything; she probably owns a computer and uses the Internet. She begins doing an extraordinary amount of research on her child's condition, becomes very informed, and seeks out world-class experts on the subject. Often she contributes her time and experience to a facility or organization dedicated to her cause. The result is an unparalleled growth in the influence and sophistication of volunteer enterprises. Educated, dedicated volunteers and professionals are an enormous resource for social policy change, not only in health care but also more broadly. The Americans with Disabilities Act, for example, was passed with the assistance of parents of disabled children, who actually worked on the language of many of its provisions.

The challenge for organizations, of course, is to engage the hearts and minds of their people at this level, to draw the same kind of commitment and energy that people devote to their voluntary activities. Yet many corporations are actually afraid to recreate the lost sense of community that people long for, because they don't want to be obligated to their employees or to the community. This lack of commitment is exacerbated by the increasing suburbanization of the workplace. As organizations have moved more frequently, and to ever more remote places, we have seen less identification of organizations with their geographic location and a decline in the kind of corporate patronage that has benefited cities and towns in the past.

Work is part of people's identity, but that identity is lifelong and changing, less tied to a particular organization than in the past. Increasingly, people's loyalty is to their profession, their colleagues, and their community of interest, rather than to their employer. William Whyte feared in the 1950s that the conformity engendered by close personal identification with large organizations would lead to the demise of entrepreneurship and individualism. Clearly that is no longer a serious worry. When is the last time you heard people agonizing about conformism and the emergence of "mass man"? In the 1950s we believed that technology would prove a force for centralized control; instead it has fragmented us into ever smaller units. The greater danger now is increased atomization and an environment too fluid for the development of stable families and communities. For organizational leaders, the challenge is to bring people together and create a sense of commitment and affiliation in spite of an uncertain and shifting environment. What leaders have going for them is that people want to be affiliated with and proud of their organizations. The organizations that thrive will be those that can help people balance their personal goals and aspirations with those of the larger institution.

The Intentional Community

Ironically, even with increased mobility and dislocation, people are becoming less willing to move out of communities that they believe serve their long-term needs. They are more apt to look for new opportunities where they are, even when their corporate division plans to move. This is very different from William Whyte's world, where people followed their employer freely and without question. It is thus going to become increasingly difficult for companies contemplating a move to bring their talent bases with them. One sees it all the time. People move to Boise, Idaho, or Madison, Wisconsin, for the quality of life—educational and health care services, recreational and cultural life, safe and affordable neighborhoods. They may not even have a job, but figure they'll be able to trade on their skills. They are drawn to a vibrant center where they feel they will be able to put together some kind of life, with or without the long-term commitment of an employer. It is further evidence that we live in a world of infinite choices and that, amid the insecurity, many people are exhibiting confidence in their ability to control their destiny in the new economy.

The dual revolutions in social and economic behavior are having a clear impact on individuals and organizations. As never before, people are defining their own vocations—sometimes two or three at a time—as well as their organizational affiliations. Increasingly, the most accomplished people in our society see themselves as part of a self-selected network, yet also as being larger than that network. For organizations, such once-peripheral issues as flextime, child care, family leave, employee training and development, community service, and work redesign are emerging as important competitive tools. That these were largely dismissed as "women's issues" just a few years ago is indicative of the extent to which women are leading today's workplace revolution.

Because they have rarely fitted easily into corporate molds that were not designed for them, women have been forced to pioneer policies and strategies that are turning out to be exactly suited to the conditions of the new knowledge-based economy. In the end, women's greatest contribution to our changing world may be their insistence on breaking the mold rather than just fitting in. Doing so has forced them to devise new strategies and improvisations that are collectively reshaping our world.

15 ESTHER DYSON

ALIGNING CORPORATE CULTURE TO MAXIMIZE HIGH TECHNOLOGY

Consultant, futurist, venture capitalist, and social entrepreneur Esther Dyson is president and owner of EDventure Holdings, publishers of the high-tech newsletter Release 1.0 *and sponsor of two major conferences on technology. She is author of the book* Release 2.0. *She also manages a venture capital fund investing in software and information start-ups in Russia and Eastern Europe, is director of several nonprofit organizations, and is a frequent speaker at industry and economic forums around the world.*

Esther Dyson is one of the most influential figures in high-tech business and culture. She took time out from work to speak with Paul Cohen, managing editor of *Leader to Leader*, about the technological and social changes affecting all organizations.

PAUL COHEN: *What do you see as the major organizational or cultural impact of the Internet and other information technology?*

ESTHER DYSON: It's a fallacy to believe that the technology is automatically going to change the culture. Some companies spend an awful lot of money on technology that does little good and wastes time, while others are actually making the social and cultural changes that will be effective. Information-age technology won't fly if it is hobbled by industrial-age organizational cultures. Technology will accentuate changes that are already under way, and it certainly allows the flattening of organizations. But it doesn't do it by itself.

Organizational leaders must have the will to make cultural changes, and then technology makes it easier. It's unlikely, for instance, that you will create a more flexible, responsive organization if you don't first reduce hierarchical barriers. And a better computer network won't buy you instant collaboration if there is not a culture of sharing knowledge. If people believe that their power depends on hoarding their knowledge, they won't suddenly start giving it away. Senior management has to be careful to provide incentives for people to make use of the beneficial capabilities of technology.

PC: *Is this good news for senior managers who don't have much technological savvy? Can they simply rely on their organizational skills?*

ED: Not really. Put it this way: if your organization is going to be using e-mail to improve accessibility and communication, and if the chairman is not on e-mail, he's going to miss an awful lot. He's going to say, "We want to be a flat organization with lots of communication," but he has his secretary read his e-mail. That is not a formula for effective leadership. But I see that a lot, even in a few high-tech companies.

PC: *What can organizations do to become more adaptable and responsive to change?*

ED: Companies must understand that no matter what business they're in, they're going to become much more information-intensive.

The marketplace is going to become even more fluid and fast moving than it is today. It's going to be much harder to maintain a competitive advantage. If you don't know how to move fast, somebody else in the industry will beat you. Those at the top need to be willing to listen to the market and to employees who are closer to the market. And ironically those at the top need to encourage decentralized change originating from below. That's the challenge. It means listening to your employees, giving them a voice. Either the CEO has the will to do it or the board has to find a new CEO.

Again, it takes a culture that rewards openness and cooperation. Technology makes it very cheap and easy to retrieve information, but it still takes time. And somebody has to input or record the information in the first place. But salespeople, for instance, don't get a lot of incentives for doing that—they get rewarded for making sales. But for a company to use technology effectively, salespeople have to record their client contacts, for example, or share what they learned competitively when they were out on the sales call. Such behavior needs to be recognized as valuable to the organization and rewarded somehow, even if no one gets a commission for it.

PC: *How can organizations create an atmosphere in which people are more open to learning and collaboration?*

ED: This is really like the question about losing weight—the answer is, eat less and exercise more. Fundamentally, you just have to do it. And yes, some people and companies have a metabolism or culture that makes that almost impossible to do. Yet people and companies do have to start behaving differently. There's no magic technology that will improve people. You can't put the Bible under your head when you go to sleep and wake up being good.

PC: *There's a lot of frustration with the nature of technological change—the requirement to learn new systems, adopt new standards, invest in the latest stuff, which quickly becomes obsolete anyway.*

ED: Your goal shouldn't be to have the latest stuff but to make the best use of the stuff you have. Your goal should be to make your organization more productive and effective. Sometimes the technology can be a year or two old but it works fine. It's the information you put into it and how you use it, not the system itself, that's valuable.

PC: *You have said that intellectual property will have less monetary value as a result of electronic distribution on the Internet. How will this affect our information economy?*

ED: Intellectual property will have less value *as copies*. It will still be extremely valuable as a brand name or as a way to attract attention and sell advertising. But you will probably get less money selling it as copies to the end users. That means that publishers, consultants, all information providers are going to be putting a greater premium on performance and less on product. Content providers will have to be able to think and add value to the content. A company's methodology by itself is worth nothing; the performance of a consultant implementing the methodology for a particular client is worth a lot. Companies need to learn that they're better off sharing information and using it as advertising or promotion rather than trying to keep it proprietary. Again, it's the intellectual process, not the intellectual property, that counts.

PC: *You're recommending the Netscape model of giving away your product to create a market for your add-ons?*

ED: Among other things. It's why I'm talking to you now—not because you are paying me for my wisdom but because I figure it is useful for my name to appear in print, for me to look like a source of wisdom, rather than saying, "Oh I can't tell you all the things I know because they're worth so much." They are not worth that much if I keep them secret.

PC: *How will the diminishing value of intellectual property change the way knowledge workers are paid and employed?*

ED: That and other changes mean that their work arrangements will be more flexible, mainly because the market for their services will be much more open. They will be more visible, and they will be valued for their ability to add performance value to otherwise static content—methodologies, software, brand names. It'll be easier for them to find new work if they're not treated well. So the best people will go with the best companies, and the less-than-best companies will find it harder and harder to compete for talent.

Knowledge people by and large are well paid, and they do care about the quality of the people with whom they associate. Companies will have to attract them with the presence of exciting coworkers, good reputations, interesting work—often mere money will not be enough. There will probably be less long-term loyalty on either side, but at the same time most people don't like being totally free agents. They want to be part of a community. They'll be hired to do some work for a client, or to do consulting, or to produce something around which advertising will appear. They will be paid for performance.

PC: *Do you worry about the new information economy leaving millions of people behind?*

ED: Yes. Therefore, it's very important for governments all over the world to spend a lot of effort educating the population because global competitiveness is no longer only about the distribution of assets or tax structure. It's about education. Does your population have the skills to be knowledge workers in the economy? This technology is going to make it easier for the elite in every country to be part of the same global economy—and, I'm afraid, to leave the less-educated people behind. And that doesn't bode well for social stability throughout the world.

PC: *You do a lot of philanthropic work, as well as entrepreneurial work, in Eastern Europe. What has that experience taught you?*

ED: First, don't be so insular. Not everyone in the world speaks English. There's a huge market outside the United States, and you need to understand it as well as sell to it. Many Americans are blind to the opportunities outside the United States.

The second thing is that the people who need to be shaken up the most are probably the Western Europeans. It is a generalization, but Americans are open to change and to new technology. Eastern Europeans have lots of smart and literate people and are embracing the new technology as a vehicle for joining the world economy. They see it as a way to get back into the mainstream after being stuck behind the wall all those years. But Western Europeans think that they're doing fine, thank you, and that they don't need all this newfangled stuff.

PC: *Based on your experience, do nonprofit or nongovernmental organizations (NGOs) have particular advantages in adapting to change?*

ED: They are generally more able to adapt, primarily because they're smaller. They have less encrusted ways of doing things. I wouldn't say that being nonprofit makes you necessarily more open to change, but being small usually does. The other advantage is, information technology is very cost-effective, and the NGO community is jumping onto it. A lot of what NGOs do is in many ways primarily information-oriented. It's putting people in touch with one another. It's helping interest groups coalesce, often over large distances. So these organizations are a natural fit for information technology.

PC: *Speaking of small versus large organizations, we're seeing a huge consolidation in health care, media, and communications businesses. Is that a good thing, and will it continue?*

ED: Some organizations are going to continue to be large, and big ones will always be swallowing up smaller ones, but the critical mass of creativity is going to be in the small, decentralized units. People will have better-defined relationships and alliances so they can work together better, but I think the world's going to be organized into smaller units. At least I hope so.

PC: *Your book* Release 2.0 *was originally subtitled* Second Thoughts on the Digital Age. *Are you having doubts about the electronic revolution?*

ED: I'm concerned about some of the issues I mentioned earlier. The Internet is a wonderful tool for advancement for those who are able to use it, but there are those who are not able to use it. There are also important questions about how the Internet will be governed. My first thoughts were, Gee, this is great. Worldwide global communications. My second thoughts are, OK, what are the implications for society, for governance? What are the conflicts? How do you deal with privacy versus openness? Security versus law enforcement, that kind of thing. There are no magical answers. The problem is not the technology; it's the human being. The new communication tools accentuate the problems of free will; we can use them for good or evil. Basically I'm optimistic about the technology because I'm optimistic about people.

16 MARGARET WHEATLEY

GOOD-BYE, COMMAND AND CONTROL

Margaret Wheatley is a consultant, speaker, and best-selling author. Her books include Leadership and the New Science *and, with Myron Kellner-Rogers,* A Simpler Way. *She is a partner in the consulting firm Kellner-Rogers & Wheatley and a cofounder of the Berkana Institute, a nonprofit research foundation supporting organizational change.*

Old ways die hard. Amid all the evidence that our world is radically changing, we cling to what has worked in the past. We still think of organizations in mechanistic terms, as collections of replaceable parts capable of being reengineered. We act as if even people were machines, redesigning their jobs as we would prepare an engineering diagram, expecting them to perform to specifications with machinelike obedience. Over the years, our ideas of leadership have supported this metaphoric myth. We have sought prediction and control, and have also charged leaders with providing everything that was absent from the machine: vision, inspiration, intelligence, and courage. They alone had to provide the energy and direction to move their rusting vehicles of organization into the future.

But in the late 1990s, we are surrounded by too many organizational failures to stay with this thinking. We know, for example, that in many recent surveys senior leaders report that more than two-thirds of their organizational change efforts fail. They and their employees report deep cynicism at the endless programs and fads; nearly everyone suffers from increased stress from the organizational lives we have created together. Survey after survey registers our loss of hope and increased uncertainty for every major institutional form in our society. Do we know how to organize anything anymore so that people want to engage in productive and contributing work?

But there is good news as well. We have known for nearly half a century that self-managed teams are far more productive than any other form of organizing. There is a clear correlation between participation and productivity; in fact, productivity gains in truly self-managed work environments are at minimum 35 percent higher than in traditionally managed organizations. And in all forms of institutions, Americans are asking for more local autonomy, insisting that they, at their own level, can do it better than the huge structures of organizations now in place. There is both a desire to participate more and strong evidence that such participation leads to the effectiveness and productivity we crave.

With so much evidence supporting participation, why isn't everyone working in a self-managed environment right now? This is a very bothersome question because it points to the fact that over the years leaders have consistently chosen control rather than productivity. Rather than rethinking our fundamental assumptions about organizational effectiveness, we have stayed preoccupied with charts and plans and designs. We have hoped they would yield the results we needed—but when they have failed consistently, we still haven't stopped to question whether such charts and plans are the real route to productive work. We just continue to adjust and tweak the various control measures, still hoping to find the one plan or design that will give us what we need.

Organizations of all kinds are cluttered with control mechanisms that paralyze employees and leaders alike. Where have all these policies, procedures, protocols, laws, and regulations come from? And why is it so difficult to avoid creating more, even as we suffer from the terrible confines of overcontrol? These mechanisms seem to derive from our fear—our fear of one another, of a harsh competitive world, and of the natural processes of growth and change that confront us daily. Years of such fear have resulted in these byzantine systems. We never effectively control people with these systems, but we certainly stop a lot of good work from getting done.

In the midst of so much fear it's important to remember something we all know: people organize together to accomplish more, not less. Behind every organizing impulse is a realization that by joining with others we can accomplish something important that we could not accomplish alone. And this impulse to organize so as to accomplish more is not only true of humans but is also found in all living systems. Every living thing seeks to create a world in which it can thrive. It does this by creating systems of relationships where all members of the system benefit from their connections. This movement toward organization, called self-organization in the sciences, is everywhere, from microbes to galaxies. Patterns of relationships form into effective systems of organization. Organization is a naturally occurring phenomenon. The world seeks organization, seeks its own effectiveness. And so do the people in our organizations.

As a living system self-organizes, it develops a shared understanding of what's important, what's acceptable behavior, what actions are required, and how these actions will get done. It develops channels of communication, networks of workers, and complex physical structures. And as the system develops, new capacities emerge from living and working together. Looking at this list of what a self-organizing system creates leads to the realization that the system can do for itself most of what leaders have felt was necessary to do to the systems they control.

Whenever we look at organizations as machines and deny the great self-organizing capacity in our midst, we as leaders attempt to change these systems from the outside in. We hope to change our organization by tinkering with the incentives, reshuffling the pieces, replacing a part, or retraining a colleague or group. But these efforts are doomed to fail, and nothing will make them work. What is required is a shift in how we think about organizing. Where does organization come from? Organization occurs from the inside out, as people see what needs to happen, apply their experience and perceptions to the issue, find those who can help them, and use their own creativity to invent solutions. This process is going on right now, all over our organizations, in spite of our efforts at control. People are exercising initiative from a deeper desire to contribute, displaying the creativity that is common to all living things. Can we recognize the self-organizing behaviors of those in our organizations? Can we learn to support them and forgo our fear-based approaches to leadership?

Belief in the System

To lead in a self-organizing system, we have to ask ourselves, How much trust do I really have in the people who work here? Have they demonstrated any of these self-organizing behaviors already? The question of trust leads to a moment of deep reflection for any leader. Those leaders who have embraced a more participative, self-organizing approach tell of their astonishment. They are overwhelmed by the capacity, energy, creativity, commitment, and even love that they receive from the people in their organization. In the past they had simply assumed that most people were there for the money, that they didn't care about the welfare of the whole enterprise, that they were self-serving and narrowly focused. No leader would voice these assumptions, but most leader behaviors reveal these beliefs. Does the leader believe that his or her vision is required to energize the whole company? Does the leadership team keep searching for new incentives to motivate employees as if they have no intrinsic motivation? Does the organization keep imposing new designs and plans on people and avoid real participation like the plague?

Every so often we open ourselves to a moment of truth and realize the conflict between our behaviors and our deeper knowledge. As one manager of a Fortune 100 company said to me: "I know in my heart that when people are driving in to work they're not thinking, How can I mess things up today? How can I give my boss a hard time? No one is driving here with that intent, but we then act as if we believed that. We're afraid to give them any slack."

Most of us know that as people drive to work they're wondering how they can get something done for the organization despite the organization—despite the political craziness, the bureaucratic nightmares, the mindless procedures piled up in their way. Those leaders who have opened to participation and self-organization have witnessed the inherent desire that most people have to contribute to their organizations. The commitment and energy resident in their organizations takes leaders by surprise. But in honoring and trusting the people who work with them, they have unleashed startlingly high levels of productivity and creativity.

Strategies for Change

If we think of organizations as living systems capable of self-organizing, then how do we think about change in these systems? The strategy for change becomes simpler and more localized. We need to encourage the creativity that lives throughout the organization, but keep local solutions localized. Most change efforts fail when leaders take an innovation that has worked well in one area of the organization and attempt to roll it out to the entire organization. This desire to replicate success actually destroys local initiative. It denies the creativity of everyone except a small group. All living systems change all the time, in new and surprising ways, discovering greater effectiveness, better solutions. They are not acting from some master plan. They are tinkering in their local environments, based on their intimate experience with conditions there—and their tinkering shows up as effective innovation. But only for them. Information about what has worked elsewhere can be very helpful. However, these solutions cannot be imposed; they have to remain local.

This highly localized change activity does not mean that the organization spins off wildly in all directions. If people are clear about the purpose and true values of their organization—if they understand what their organization stands for and who it shows itself to be through its actions—their individual tinkering will result in systemwide coherence. In organizations that know who they are and mean what they announce, people are free to create and contribute. A plurality of effective solutions emerges, each expressing a deeper coherence, an understanding of what this organization is trying to become.

Mort Meyerson, chairman of Perot Systems, said that the primary task of being a leader is to make sure that the organization knows itself. That is, we must realize that our task is to call people together often, so that everyone gains clarity about who we are, who we've just become, who we still want to be. This includes the interpretations available from our customers, our markets, our history, our mistakes. If the organization can stay in a continuous conversation about who it is and who it is becoming, then leaders don't have to undertake the impossible task of trying to hold it all together. Organizations that are clear at their core hold themselves together because of their deep congruence. People are then free to explore new avenues of activity, new ventures and customers, in ways that make sense for the organization. It is a strange and promising paradox of living systems: clarity about who we are as a group creates freedom for individual contributions. People exercise that freedom in the service of the organization, and their capacity to respond and change becomes a capability of the whole organization.

If we as leaders can ensure that our organization knows itself, that it's clear at its core, we must also tolerate unprecedented levels of "messiness" at the edges. This constant tinkering, this localized hunt for solutions does not look neat. There is no conformity possible unless we want to kill local initiative. Freedom and creativity create diverse responses. We have to be prepared to support such diversity, to welcome the surprises people will invent, and to stop wasting time trying to impose solutions developed elsewhere.

People always want to talk about what they do, what they see, how they can improve things, what they know about their customers. Supporting these conversations is an essential task of leaders. It's not about you, "the leader," developing the mission statement or employing experts to do a detailed analysis of your market strategy. These exercises, because they exclude more people than they include, never work as planned. Only when everyone in our organization understands who we are, and has contributed to this deep understanding, do we gain the levels of commitment and capacity we so desperately need. As a leader supports the processes that help the organization know itself, the organization flourishes.

It's also notable that when we engage in meaningful conversations as an organization, and when we engage our customers, suppliers, community, and regulators in these conversations, everything changes. People develop new levels of trust for one another that show up as more cooperation and more forgiveness. People stop being so arbitrarily demanding when they are part of the process, when they no longer are looking in from the outside trying to get someone's attention.

Moving to Action

Leaders put a premium on action. Organizations that have learned how to think together and that know themselves are filled with action. People are constantly taking initiative and making changes, often without asking or telling. Their individual freedom and creativity become critical resources to the organization. Their local responsiveness translates into a much faster and more adaptable organization overall.

But leaders need to know how to support these self-organizing responses. People do not need the intricate directions, time lines, plans, and organization charts that we thought we had to give them. These are not how people accomplish good work; they are what impede contributions. But people do need a lot from their leaders. They need information, access, resources, trust, and follow-through. Leaders are necessary to foster experimentation, to help create connections across the organization, to feed the system with rich information from multiple sources—all while helping everyone stay clear on what we agreed we wanted to accomplish and who we wanted to be.

Most of us were raised in a culture that told us that the way to manage for excellence was to tell people exactly what they had to do and then make sure they did it. We learned to play master designer, assuming we could engineer people into perfect performance. But you can't direct people into perfection; you can only engage them enough so that they want to do perfect work. For example, a few chemical plants that operate with near-perfect safety records for years at a time achieve these results because their workers are committed to safety. It becomes a personal mission. The regulations, the EPA, and OSHA are all necessary parts of their system, but they can never spell out the route to perfect safety. That comes from hundreds and thousands of workers who understand their role in safety, who understand the whys of safety, who understand that it's up to them.

For all the unscripted events—an irate customer, a leak, a winter storm—we depend on individual initiative. Ultimately we have to rely not on the procedure manuals but on people's brains and their commitment to doing the right thing. If they are acting by rote or regimen, they actually have lost the capacity for excellence.

Imposed control breeds passivity. But people do have to know what right means. They have to know what safety really means. If they know what's right, then we have engaged their intelligence and heart on behalf of the organization.

No More Quick Fixes

Self-organization is a long-term exploration requiring enormous self-awareness and support. This is true partially because it represents such a fundamentally different way of thinking about organization and partially because all changes in organization take much longer than we want to acknowledge. If we've learned anything in the past twenty years it's that there are no quick fixes. For most organizations, meaningful change is at least a three-to-five-year process—although this seems impossibly long for many managers. Yet multiyear strategic change efforts are the hard reality we must face. These things take time. How long, for instance, has your organization been struggling with total quality? At Motorola, it's been more than a decade. How many years have you been working with the concept of teams? (Jack Welch, for one, understood that it would take at least ten years to develop the capacities of GE's people. In the crazed world of the late 1980s, that was a radical insight and a shocking commitment.)

Most CEOs aren't trying simply to squeeze their organizations for short-term profitability or shortsighted outcomes that don't endure. Most leaders would never say, "I just want this organization to perform well for a few quarters." More and more, leaders talk about their legacy. They talk about a deep desire for their work to have meant something. This has been a difficult time in which to be a leader. Leaders are not immune to the terrible destruction we've visited on many organizations. A senior executive of a major industrial firm, speaking for many, said in a meeting: "I've just destroyed what I spent twenty years creating." Who among us wants to end a career with that realization?

But if we are to develop organizations of greater and enduring capacity, we have to turn to the people of our organization. We have to learn how to encourage the creativity and commitment that they wanted to express when they first joined the organization. We have to learn how to get past the distress and cynicism that's been created in the past several years and use our best talents to figure out how to reengage people in the important work of organizing.

The Leader's Journey

Whenever we're trying to change a deeply structured belief system, everything in life is called into question—our relationships with loved ones, children, and colleagues; our relationships with authority and major institutions. One group of senior leaders, reflecting on the changes they've gone through, commented that the higher you are in the organization, the more change is required of you personally. Those who have led their organizations into new ways of organizing often say that the most important change was what occurred in themselves. Nothing would have changed in their organizations if they hadn't changed.

All this seems true to me, but I think the story is more complex. Leaders managing difficult personal transitions are usually simultaneously opening new avenues for people in the organization. They are moving toward true team structures, opening to more and more participative processes, introducing new ways of thinking. They are setting a great many things in motion inside the organization. These ripple through the system; some work, some don't, but the climate for experimentation is evident. A change here elicits a response there, which calls for a new idea, which elicits yet another response. It's an intricate exchange and coevolution, and it's nearly impossible to look back and name any one change as the cause of all the others. Organizational change is a dance, not a forced march.

Leaders experience their own personal change most intensely, so I think they report on this as the key process. But what I observe is far more complex. In the end, you can't define a list of activities that were responsible for the organization shifting, and you certainly can't replicate anyone else's exact process for success. But you can encourage the experimentation and tinkering, the constant feedback and learning, and the wonderful sense of camaraderie that emerges as everyone gets engaged in making the organization work better than ever before, even in the most difficult of circumstances.

Sustainability, Not Employability

I believe there is one principle that should be embraced by all organizations as they move into the future, and that is sustainability. How can we endure over time? What about us is worth sustaining long term? This focus flies in the face of current fashion. Our infatuation with fleeting "virtual" organizations misses an important truth: we cannot create an organization that means something to its people if that organization has no life beyond the next project or contract. We cannot promise people, for instance, only three years of employment—with vague assurances of their future employability—and expect the kind of energy and commitment that I've described.

Employability in lieu of mutual commitment is a cop-out. We seem to focus on it as a response to the grave uncertainty we feel about the future. Because we can't predict markets, products, customers, governments, or anything, we decide not to promise anything to anyone. Too many leaders are saying, in effect, "We don't know what the future will be or how to manage this uncertainty, so let's think of our employees as negotiable commodities." What they've really said is, "Let's buy flexibility by giving up loyalty."

Commitment and loyalty are essential in human relationships. So how can we pretend we don't need them at work? The real issue is that we don't know yet how to engage people's loyalty while maintaining the flexibility we require. But leaders should be searching for creative answers to this dilemma, not ignoring it by settling on the nonsolution of so-called employability. Employability is a far more destructive practice than we have imagined. The organizations that people love to be in are ones that have a sense of history and identity and purpose. These are things that people want to work for. The belief that a company has stood for something in the past is a reason to want to move it into the future.

The Real Criteria for Measuring Change

You know when you walk in the door of an organization whether people want to be there or not. The sense of belonging (or not) is palpable. Yet few change efforts take that into account—and far too many end up killing the organization's capacity for more change. To measure whether a change effort has been successful, we need to ask, Are people in the organization more committed to being here now than they were at the beginning of this effort? In terms of sustainability, we need to ask if, at the end of this change effort, people feel more prepared for the next wave of change. Did we develop capacity or just stage an event? Do people feel that their creativity and expertise contributed to the changes?

If we're focused on these questions as indicators, we can create organizations that know how to respond continuously to shifts in markets and environments, organizations that have learned how to access the intelligence that lives everywhere in the system. We will have supported people's innate capacity to deal with changing conditions because we will have learned how to engage people. We will have honored their innate capacity for self-organization. And they will respond with the initiative and creativity that is found only in life, never in machines.

17 KEVIN KELLY

THE SOUL OF THE NETWORK ECONOMY

> *Kevin Kelly is executive editor of* Wired, *the award-winning magazine of the digital revolution. He was previously editor and publisher of the influential* Whole Earth Review *and is author of* Out of Control: The New Biology of Machines, Social Systems, and the Economic World *and* New Rules for the New Economy.

The forces now transforming our business and social institutions—the acceleration of knowledge and technological change, the emergence of global competitors, and the breakdown of traditional hierarchical systems—find their full expression in the new network economy. That economy is marked by two simple attributes. It is, by definition, a system of many points connected to many other points. It is also the product of a world in which there will soon be a tiny silicon chip in everything we manufacture.

Five years ago, when Rodney Brooks at the MIT Media Lab suggested that microchips would soon become so cheap that they

---

Source: Adapted from Kevin Kelly, *New Rules for the New Economy*, New York: Viking Penguin, 1998. Copyright © Kevin Kelly.

would be found in every door, the idea seemed laughable. But sure enough, when you stay at a hotel today you probably have a key card that fits into a computer in your door. You can find shoes, lamps, desks, and bathtubs comparably equipped. And Bill Gates's Xanadu-like dream house, which can recognize guests and pipe their favorite music into whatever room they enter, gives new meaning to the term *home electronics*. The transformation of everyday goods and services is happening very quickly.

As the number and variety of products on the market increase, we are beginning to connect those products electronically. At some point soon, the two growth curves will intersect and everything we manufacture will be wired into the network. The paradox is that the things being connected aren't very smart—and don't have to be. They are communicating via wireless or infrared signals, with very simple messages. They're saying, "I'm here," or "I'm on," or "I was last used two days ago."

The great force that's operating in the network economy is called *dumb power*—the ability to take lots of dumb things and connect them to create something very smart. That is also the force of evolution, of ecology; it is the force in our brains—a lot of dumb neurons that cannot construct a thought individually but when linked can think. In other words, smart is many dumb things interconnected. That's where we're headed in the network economy. We're giving the manufactured world the ability to converse, and those conversations—between us and our machines and among the machines themselves—are adding new value to the economy.

Communication, Not Computation

Ironically, the rise of the network economy means that the age of computers is over. All the effects that we're likely to see in our society due to a stand-alone computer on a desk have already happened. Computers have sped up our lives a bit, they have made symbol and image processing easier, but those changes have fundamentally run their course. What we're now seeing is a communications revolution, and communication is the foundation of culture. So forget about computers; we're now shaking the underpinnings of society because we're reinventing the ways we communicate with one another and with the world around us.

When people talk about the Internet ("the Net") on which the network economy is based, they often think of something like America Online or CompuServe, or the tangled mass of the World Wide Web—people sitting in front of keyboards typing away at one other. But that's not what the Net really is. The Net is every cash register in the world, every weather satellite, every medical-record instrument, all sending data to a mainframe computer, or to another machine. It's all the objects we manufacture talking to each other. That is the network side of the network economy; the crucial, economic side is that anything that can hold an electronic charge can hold a fiscal charge. We have constructed a new matrix in which economic and financial information is flowing through essentially everything.

Think of a grocery store where every item is bar coded, and attached to or embedded in each item is a silicon chip. Imagine a head of lettuce with a bar-coded tag. A small readout on the shelf shows the price of that lettuce—and the number changes while you watch. Companies could adjust the price of their products in real time, depending on the day's, the moment's demand. That's called *yield management* and it is already an art (some say a black art) in the airline industry, for instance, with carriers manipulating the price of a seat depending on how close to flight time that seat is being sold. Prices vary to maximize capacity because an unsold seat is worth nothing.

The pervasive flow of economic and financial information will make this commonplace. All goods and services will be tied to a ubiquitous electronic currency—what I call *e-money*. The world is swimming with information, and money is basically a form of information. Consumers and producers are constantly bidding on resources, and every transaction is captured in a computational cycle. Network economics—that system of relationships and interconnections—is the driving force of our times. And with networks, five new dynamics will shape the future of every organization—exponential technological growth, increasing returns, compounded value, fax effects, and wealth from the free. Together they are upending our most basic social and economic assumptions.

Exponential Growth

Linear growth was the model for the machine age—small change, small effect; large change, large effect. That is how clocks, gears, and assembly lines work. Exponential growth is the model for biology and population growth. Change moves very quickly in these worlds—and in the network economy. There's little correlation between disturbances and results. Organizations have never worked this way, but people have an intuitive sense about such workings because of the world of nature and our own biology.

Increasing Returns

The law of increasing returns, or positive feedback loops, is a fashionable topic in economics today. It applies the snowball effect to commerce; it says, simply, "them that's got gets more." For example, Silicon Valley keeps attracting more start-up companies, and the more that come, the more that will come. Early leads are a significant factor in compounding that advantage. So rather than operating in a world of scarcity, the network economy makes possible a world of plenitude and abundance.

Compound Value

Everybody knows the power of compound interest; it is the beauty of savings and investment. Compound value is a similar force in the microchip world. The smaller things get, the smaller they can get. One example we may soon see in our streets is the hypercar—a supercompact vehicle expected to get hundreds of miles per gallon, made primarily with composite fibers. It is designed around the fact that most of the energy consumed by a car is used to move the car, not the passenger. By decreasing the mass of the car, you can make the engine smaller. And since most of the mass of the car is the engine, if you make that smaller, you need less energy to drive it, which means you can make the engine smaller still. The more you take away, the less you need. You quickly gain efficiency based on the compounded value of decreasing size. The same thing happens with microchips; the smaller the device, the greater its power.

The Fax Effect

For the millions of dollars that the Japanese used to develop fax technology, the first fax machine that rolled off the assembly line was worth nothing. The second fax machine was worth something because it could communicate with the first one. And each additional fax machine sold increases the value of all the fax machines before it. Likewise, the first e-mail account had zero value, but each new e-mail account raises the value of all the other accounts. People who have e-mail know that—that's why they're always asking for your e-mail address. This is a hallmark of the network economy. We become evangelists for the technology because things increase in value the more plentiful they are.

The fax effect is also subject to exponential growth, however; things in the network economy increase in value by the square of their plenitude. In the industrial economy, if I'm a window manufacturer with four customers and I grow to seven customers, I'll not quite double my business. But in the network economy, if I'm in the telecommunications business with four telephone customers and I grow to seven customers, they'll generate more than three times as much business as four customers did. And that exponential difference increases tremendously as the numbers get even larger. That is what makes the network economy such a powerful creator of wealth.

Wealth from the Free

If things increase in value the more plentiful they are, then the way to make something really valuable is to give it away. We see some notable examples of businesses doing exactly that—Netscape, Microsoft, and Yahoo all offered free Internet software to build a customer base, a market value, a reputation, and a technical standard. That strategy is so well established in the new network economy that there's now a need to be not just first to market but also free first to market. It's a way to develop a company's presence and identity.

The Limits of Efficiency

As we have seen in the network economy, goods and services initially given for free can become extremely valuable. That has huge implications for other sectors of the economy as well. Think about who does free well: young people and nonprofit organizations. I have a theory about why the young are always coming up with the good ideas: it's because they waste time. They follow their passion and do something, not looking for a payoff, just doing what's interesting. For instance, if you really want to learn how to use the Internet for research, it takes fifty hours of wasting time, clicking through worthless Web sites, before you can become expert at using the Web. The same is true for mastering video games or multimedia; they are tremendous wasters of time, but they are also a powerful source of innovation and new ideas.

I call the pursuit of such activities *afficiency*. It's not that they're inefficient but that efficiency is not an important measure of their value. Sometimes the young are efficient, sometimes not. Sometimes nonprofit organizations are efficient, sometimes not. This is not the criterion by which they should be judged. In biology, again, there's a useful evolutionary model called the *adaptive landscape*. Simply put, this model pictures a theoretical pyramid with the fittest organism at the top and the least adapted organism at the bottom. Over time an organism or an organization traces an upward path as it climbs the peak toward increased fitness.

In the industrial world it was relatively easy to plan your ascent. If you were a steel company you could see where you should be heading. You could move toward increased efficiency and begin to climb that peak. The new network economy, however, presents a different topography, called a rugged landscape. The problem is that the highest peak—maximum adaptation—is not clearly evident; you may be climbing a local peak surrounded by many higher peaks. In fact, the landscape is not only rugged but also constantly changing. New peaks arise very quickly. The mountain you are climbing—or sitting atop—can suddenly become a molehill.

New Paths to Fitness

The new turbulent landscape changes every aspect of work. Peter Drucker has said that in the industrial economy, your chief task as a worker was to do the job right, to do it efficiently, and to find out how to do it better. The chief task in the network economy, however, is not to do the job right but to do the right job—to make sure you're climbing the right peak. Searching the landscape, discovering your position, is the job of the young, the visionary, and those not concerned about efficiency as such.

It's one thing, for instance, to imagine a new destination, and it's often easy to think it will be a quick trip. Yet invariably it becomes a long and difficult crossing. The problem for most organizations is that if you are stuck on a local peak and have determined that a higher peak looms just over the horizon, the only way to get there is to devolve, let go of what you are doing well, and head down your little mountain. And there is almost no organization that can do that well. The entire organization is built around the idea of pushing things uphill, becoming efficient and adapting to a particular terrain. For the organization to go backward almost defies the genetic code.

Voluntary organizations can be models of such adaptability for business. Without the weight of the profit motive, they can more readily go back down, search out, experiment, and let go of their old model. So we will see more and more for-profits associating in a symbiotic way with nonprofits to help them achieve greater afficiency. For-profit organizations will need such help because they are by nature honed to be efficient; afficiency is not something they do well. Yes, nonprofits can be run like businesses, when appropriate. However, organizational fitness in the network economy requires you to be messy, dynamic, afficient. Some may think their organization is like that already, but few really are. They are more often rigid and static. And in the network economy, the price of poor adaptation is, increasingly, extinction.

Tools for the New Economy

The network economy is creating new metaphors for organizational strategy, identity, and relationship to the marketplace. It is also transforming models of behavior inside the organization. For instance, the multiplayer games now being played on-line are becoming a metaphor for the social interactions of the new workplace. We have to think not of personal desktops but of shared space. In the new organization we find increasingly fragmented work environments. People work at the client's office, at home, in the car. Remote working and telecommuting are important strategies—though many organizations are finding that nobody wants to work either at home or at the office full-time. Thus we're seeing organizations trying to accommodate people who want to split their time between home and office.

Organizational behavior is changing in deeper ways as well. As companies become more diffuse and their relationships become more complicated, individual employees are assuming multiple identities. They represent their organization, their professional discipline, their personal aspirations. Their interactions with clients and colleagues are growing in complexity as their autonomy is increasing. All of which means that more than ever we have to hire for attitude and train for skills—attitude about learning, about exploring, about innovation.

By understanding the dynamics of the network economy, leaders can help their organizations set new rules, invent new tools, and respond to its new demands. Organizations in the network economy need to be run like an ecology of clans—diverse groups of employees, customers, and partners linked for a common purpose—just as the Internet operates as an ecology of interconnected agents. Too many leaders still think that these changes apply just to computers and communication, that they have little effect on the rest of the economy. That's a serious mistake. The network economy is rewriting the rules for all of us. Every organization will have to learn to play the game.

Part IV

COMPETITIVE STRATEGY IN A GLOBAL ECONOMY

18 ROSABETH MOSS KANTER

HOW LOCALS CAN WIN GLOBAL CONTESTS

Rosabeth Moss Kanter is the Class of 1960 Professor of Business Administration at Harvard Business School and cofounder of the consulting firm Goodmeasure Inc. She is author of twelve books, including World Class: Thriving Locally in the Global Economy *and* Rosabeth Moss Kanter on the Frontiers of Management.

Most leaders accept the premise that our organizations must become more knowledge intensive and value enhancing. Knowledge, we understand, creates wealth and opportunity. We are less sure about embracing the global marketplace; international competition generates fear and uncertainty. But just as knowledge and information have infused the most mundane products and services, globalism has infused almost all business and community activity. The heirs to the global economy—I call them cosmopolitans—may become the elite class of the knowledge society.

Cosmopolitanism is a state of mind. Every business now has theoretical access to the best products, services, and ideas from anywhere in the world, making all organizations de facto members of the global economy. New technology companies in particular are fundamentally born global. They design their products and distribution strategies with world standards and international customers in mind. But whatever an organization's mission, its leaders have to learn to think and act globally. That means, for instance, asking how a policy or strategy affects the company's ability to compete in the world marketplace.

Although global competition can be brutal, the benefits can be huge. International markets allow you to spread the costs of innovation over a wider customer base. For small companies that occupy niches, this can make a big difference. For example, Merlin Metalworks, a thirty-person manufacturer of titanium bicycles, makes a very expensive product and earns one-third of its revenues overseas. It's doubtful they could survive without a global market.

Competing in markets outside of your home country also gives you a hedge against an economic downturn in your home country; it's a way of smoothing fluctuations. And serving a range of customers, some of whom may be more demanding than those in your home market, forces additional organizational learning in quality and innovation. Finally, a global reach gives you access to a wider array of inputs—whether they be sources of tangible goods and services or of new ideas. Since no one country has a monopoly on good ideas, this access can have a major impact on your organization's future performance.

A Strategy for Communities

Information and communications technology make it easier for companies to serve the world from any place they choose. Overnight package-delivery services allow businesses to get parts from nearly anywhere within a day or two, so they don't necessarily need suppliers to be nearby. High-speed, low-cost communications systems link companies to offices anywhere in the world, giving even small or remote communities opportunities to compete. As a result, places like Omaha, Nebraska, have become backroom centers for telemarketers, travel agencies, and credit card processors.

So, just as the acquisition and application of knowledge will differentiate winners from losers in business, the adoption of a global outlook will mark those communities and individuals who thrive in the next century. The benefits to communities include the following:

- *Creation of new jobs.* Popular attention has focused on job loss, and to be sure the disappearance of relatively low-skill, low-wage jobs is real and painful. But the loss of those jobs is also inevitable. Hundreds of local communities have won high-skill jobs with a future by playing in the global marketplace.
- *Capital investment.* In addition to bringing jobs, any business moving into a community is also likely to bring new services, technologies, and equipment that can help a community grow.
- *New knowledge and experience.* Cosmopolitans who come to a community can help raise the standards of schools, government, and public services as well as those of businesses. For example, when Honda moved to Marysville, Ohio, it introduced its total quality techniques to the local school system and other agencies.

Three Key Assets for Local Development

Of course a community that cannot offer the brain power or skills that employers demand, and that is forced to compete with low-wage labor overseas, is in trouble. But communities can develop three key assets that will raise their competitive standing—concepts, competence, and connections. *Concept-driven* communities search for new ideas and have a knowledge-intensive workforce. *Competence-driven* communities develop centers of quality for manufacturing or other disciplines, using a combination of good infrastructure, customized job training, and commitment to world-class standards. *Connection-driven* communities combine cultural knowledge of the world with a healthy commercial infrastructure to become places where trade is centered or deals are made.

Each of these assets creates the basis for a globally linked local economy that attracts jobs, capital, and the flow of customers or visitors. Of course it doesn't happen overnight, and it doesn't happen by accident. Atlanta has been developing its position as a high-technology center for twenty-five years. Raleigh-Durham's Triangle Park is at least a generation in the making. Austin, Texas, began its growth as a high-tech mecca years ago and of course had the benefit of a major university. But even without a hometown university or a major transportation hub, communities can compete for global business. Three strategies have worked for a variety of communities:

- *Provide exceptional workforce training.* Public, private, and social sector organizations in Spartanburg and Greenville, South Carolina, have collaborated to develop one of the world's most skilled blue-collar labor pools. The communities provided short-term workforce training for high school graduates (and dropouts) in specific skills needed by automotive, textile, and other targeted industries—and have attracted more than 215 companies from eighteen countries.

- *Support entrepreneurs.* Giving people with promising ideas the tools and resources to go into business for themselves is ultimately the best way to create jobs. Local government, community, and business leaders all have a part to play in creating a more collaborative, innovative, and learning-oriented environment that is hospitable to entrepreneurs. As South Carolina discovered, the flexibility and "go for it" approach of American workers is a magnet for international companies.

- *Focus on quality of life.* Increasingly, what enables a company to attract and retain the right people are the amenities and livability of the community. Downtown Baltimore has become a convention and tourist destination thanks largely to its reinvigorated waterfront. Much of the public and social sector is oriented toward culture, education, and health care, and those can be important communal assets. Most companies expanding to new locations understand that, for instance, a symphony orchestra or a good museum makes a community more attractive.

Communities should compete not to be the cheapest place to do business but to be the best place—and help the company get what it needs to operate there. Cleveland has become a model nationally and internationally. Ten years ago, the city couldn't attract a skilled workforce, didn't support the formation of new businesses, and struggled to improve a deteriorating quality of life. But its private sector came together with the public sector and with major cultural and nonprofit institutions to create a shared vision of what the city should be. Civic leaders built on Cleveland's core competence in manufacturing, nurtured new capabilities in trade and tourism, and tended to a badly frayed social infrastructure by reaching out to neighborhood groups, churches, small business networks, and schools.

The lesson is clear: communities that neglect their social infrastructure, that fail to build a shared sense of their fate, that haven't developed networks of organizations that can reach consensus, will be hard pressed to attract good jobs.

Focusing on the Future

Aside from purely local services, any company that competes on the basis of low labor cost is eventually going to look for lower-cost places to operate. It is clear, for instance, that we will need fewer people in manufacturing plants. That's why the competition to attract those jobs is so intense; there are simply fewer of them. The problem is, people who have had those jobs aren't given the skills to move up the ladder but have to accept lower wages in their next jobs.

The only forward-looking strategy is to try to move as many people as possible up the skill ladder. That doesn't mean that everybody is going to be a rocket scientist; it does mean that everyone deserves an opportunity to learn new, marketable skills. Some people are still going to be housecleaners or truck drivers, but there are ways to add skills even to service jobs that appear low wage at the moment. For one thing, you can teach people how to run their own housecleaning or truck-driving business.

Remember, it is the industries of the past that keep consolidating. It's the industries of the future, such as software, biotechnology, and travel and tourism, that will grow and create employment in other sectors. Remember, too, that American companies are among the most international enterprises on the planet. And there is nothing that makes an American company any more loyal to local communities than a foreign company would be. International companies need to review continually where their operations are located, how many of them they have, and where they can grow. Capital flight did not start in the global economy; it started five or six decades ago when the New England textile industry moved south. The 1995 strike against Boeing, for instance, was prompted in part by the company's threat to pull jobs out of Seattle and put them in their plant in Wichita, where costs are lower.

Giant companies that used to be the source of security for communities are now more footloose. If you had a big corporate headquarters, a big bank, and a big utility, you had stability. These can still be tremendous assets if you have them. But increasingly the headquarters are moving, the banks are being swallowed up, and the utility is downsizing. So communities should put their resources into building workforce skills and entrepreneurship—instead of racing to give tax breaks to any company that asks.

Employees as Ambassadors

As companies become more focused in a highly competitive world, they increasingly look for strategic reasons to practice philanthropy and community service. Some have sound economic reasons—their very real interest in supporting a robust workforce and marketplace.

They also have the line on a corporate balance sheet called goodwill, and that tends to be customer relationships. But there are other kinds of goodwill that also enhance the value of a company. Many organizations are driven by their employees to participate in charitable work, and this activity is increasingly valued as an employee benefit. For example, Sun Microsystems funds local schools and food drives, matches employees' charitable contributions, and coordinates the efforts of employees who want to do volunteer work, largely because employees themselves pressed for company involvement. Within five years, the chance to do community service under the umbrella of one's employer may be a widespread employee benefit and motivational tool.

The strongest link between international companies and the local community is usually the employees, including top management, who live there. Companies, after all, are composed of people who have values, and values drive behavior. So one way to induce companies to be good citizens is for each of us to be good citizens ourselves, to participate in the life of the community and the organization. Another way is to create a climate in the community that companies value. This is where other community institutions play a role; the press, for instance, can recognize good corporate behavior as well as bad.

One of the most overlooked community assets may be its ethnic composition. Just as smart businesses are learning that a diverse workforce can help them build links to new markets, smart communities find that diversity can be a magnet for business. Miami is a fascinating example. Miami was a dying city before the Cuban exiles arrived. The fact that so many of its people speak Spanish helped it become a trade capital. Likewise, San Francisco's ethnic diversity and historic connections to Asia and Latin America have become huge economic assets. The presence of foreign language speakers, a varied culinary tradition, and strong ethnic cultural institutions helps cities attract international tourists, if nothing else.

And travel, tourism, and related industries account for an astonishing 20 percent of the U.S. gross domestic product. So even in an age of immigration backlash, a community's ethnic diversity can be mined for the benefit of all.

There's no doubt that wrenching changes are still ahead. But communities can compete using strategies that enhance their workforce skills, entrepreneurship, and quality of life. They really have no choice.

19 ANN WINBLAD

LEADERSHIP SECRETS OF A VENTURE CAPITALIST

> Ann Winblad is an influential entrepreneur and technology leader. She is partner in Hummer Winblad Venture Partners, a venture capital fund with $200 million under management, for investment exclusively in software companies. Prior to launching Hummer Winblad she founded and managed her own software company, and served as a strategic planning consultant.

In today's economy, the biggest obstacle to launching a successful product, service, or company is no longer attracting financial capital; it is attracting intellectual capital. This is true for any organization that relies on innovation, but it is most evident in high technology, where in 1997 unemployment was 3 percent or less. In the United States we had only 26,000 computer science graduates in 1996 and 190,000 unfilled jobs requiring such skills. The demand for high-tech talent will be voracious for years. Most hiring is done by raiding the stable of another company—often in response to raids on your own stable.

The stakes are huge. In 1997, worldwide revenues for commercial software companies alone surpassed $100 billion; that makes software the third-largest industry in the world, behind motor vehicles and electronic components. The deregulation of the telecommunications business, the consolidation of the defense industry, and the worldwide demand for information technology has created awesome opportunities for high-tech start-ups—and enormous challenges to all entrepreneurial leaders, who must attract, retain, and manage talent in every line of work.

Investing in Leadership

When we at Hummer Winblad decide whether or not to back a company, we look for three things—market opportunity, the capacity to deliver the product, and the ability of the entrepreneur to sustain excellence and grow new leaders. Five years ago, a venture capital firm or board of directors could fire an unsuccessful entrepreneur and simply hire new talent. That does not work today; instant leaders don't exist. So our job is simultaneously to build leaders and build companies around significant market opportunities.

As senior members of our companies' boards, we have to coach the firm's leaders on the basic strategic playbook. The game is so fast and competitive that the leaders sometimes have to plan their next move on the fly. Who does what on the team? How does the team play together? As investors, we get only a few minutes to huddle between plays, so we have to be good coaches. And on critical occasions we step up and say, let me make that introduction for you; let me help you recruit new talent.

To support the growth of a company's intellectual capital, we may even recruit other young entrepreneurs for the company's board. These people usually have just a few more years of experience than the company's CEO but remember well what it's like to be doing everything for the first time. We then have the entrepreneur, who is still learning the next phase of the job, coach an entrepreneur who is just a step behind.

Managing Talent

In my experience, leaders who are able to manage talent share four traits. First is the willingness to take risks—and even some entrepreneurs have trouble with that. Everyone fears failure, fears moving into new frontiers—and that fear only gets worse in bigger companies. But successful leaders have confidence. They know how to operate in a zone of discomfort. They aren't afraid to hire people who are smarter than themselves, especially to complement an acknowledged weakness. And they are able to dial out their business strategy to the edge of uncertainty and then—often with the help of their board—dial it back to reality. They learn to be fearless without being reckless.

Second, leaders have to be good communicators. That means that early on they must communicate their market position to everyone—the board, potential customers and employees, the press. If the leader lacks these presentation skills, we send him or her to the best trainers in the business.

Third, successful leaders are decisive. They are forced to make a lot of decisions quickly, but they learn the fine distinction between decisive and authoritarian—a skill in which the relative inexperience of the entrepreneurial leader is most telling. Thus a young organization needs a set of strategic assumptions—no more than ten—on which to base its business plan, its product strategy, its organizational strategy. These assumptions give the leader, when lost in the fog of decision making, a way to remember the fundamentals that drive the business.

Fourth and perhaps most important is intellectual honesty. From the minute we decide to invest in a company we say, "Here are our concerns with you, the CEO. We're going to be very frank in pointing out your weaknesses, not to demoralize you but to help you grow. We'll be your mirror until you are willing to do it yourself." Without open, ongoing exchange among investors, directors, senior managers, and employees, you get cheerleading, not leadership.

Why Culture Counts

Along with effective leadership, culture—a defining set of values and practices—is a powerful force in the software industry. In the networked world of high technology, everyone knows everything about everyone in the business. The casual, creative, collaborative settings of most software firms are key to effective work processes—and they provide a powerful magnet for talented contributors who demand both independence and engagement. Successful companies know that every person counts, that you cannot develop and market a product alone.

A capital-efficient, people-driven company is not an assembly line; it is a community of skilled craftspeople able to make decisions at every level and in every functional area. From customer support to software development to marketing to sales, everyone knows that they are selling tomorrow to their customers.

But working within such fluid cultures poses dangers as well; if you can't build a leadership style that works well for people in your company, the business implodes. You cannot, for instance, contain a morale problem within engineering, or marketing, or reception. Communication is horizontal, with no distinction between departmental or hierarchical boundaries. Until you grow to a thousand or more employees, organizational structures are largely irrelevant.

This more open "digital culture" has begun to permeate almost every institution in our society—partly because software itself is becoming such an integral part of society. There is, for instance, a software subculture within each company that maintains its own information system. And the attributes of that digital culture are increasingly prized by all organizations that seek to be more competitive, fast moving, innovative, and value oriented.

Software is a young industry, and will remain so for decades. Bill Gates is forty-three. The average age of the software CEO is thirty-eight. Microsoft was founded in 1976, but no one thinks of it as a twenty-one-year-old company. It is understood that if you feel safe, if you march in place or think that you have to be entrepreneurial only once, you'll fail. That demand for continued innovation offers lessons to other businesses.

Marrying Vision and Experience

The real challenge in our industry is not how to deal with maturity; it's understanding how to manage an industry that is likely to stay young for another twenty years. What happens when the competitive forces accelerate, rather than abate, over time? We don't yet know, because we haven't been there before.

Entrepreneurial leaders face a twin challenge—to develop raw talent so that people can assume early leadership roles, while at the same time knowing how to preserve part of that raw material. You want people always to believe "I can do anything," to run at the brick wall, to do things that have never been done before. You have to know how to lead and how to think. You need unending stamina. You need to replenish and renew yourself, personally and organizationally.

Investors, board members, and mentors have to remember that the entrepreneur is the visionary. He or she has identified the opportunity and understands intuitively how to get there—but probably has limited experience in building a company. We can attract talent by offering two kinds of opportunities: the opportunity to contribute to a vision for the future, and the opportunity to share in the rewards. We then have to surround that talent with the experience to make the opportunity possible.

20 KENICHI OHMAE

STRATEGY IN A WORLD WITHOUT BORDERS

> *Kenichi Ohmae is a leading authority on issues of competitive strategy and public policy. He has written more than seventy books, including* The Mind of the Strategist *and* The Borderless World. *He teaches at Stanford University and the University of California Los Angeles, and advises corporations and governments around the world. He was a partner at McKinsey & Company for twenty-three years and now leads his own consulting firm based in Tokyo. In 1992 he founded a citizens' political reform movement in Japan.*

The essence of business strategy is to offer better value to customers than the competition, in the most cost-effective and sustainable way. Today, however, thousands of competitors from every corner of the world are able to serve customers well. To develop effective strategy, we as leaders have to understand what's happening in the rest of the world, and reshape our organization to respond accordingly. No leader can hope to guide an enterprise into the future without understanding the commercial, political, and social impact of the global economy.

To be sure, walls between markets, organizations, and nations are coming down. Corporations and customers are moving more freely in and out of countries. Services and information, spanning the planet, have supplanted manufacturing as the primary sources of wealth. And whatever your business or mission, the name of the game is intelligence. But what we call the global economy is really the conjunction of at least five forces:

- Booming regional economies
- New media and information technology
- Universal consumer cultures
- Emerging global standards
- Opportunities for corporate cost-sharing

Booming Regional Economies

An economic tour of the planet shows a vast network of economic hot spots, such as Hong Kong, Kaoshung (Taiwan), Penang (Malaysia), Subic Bay (the Philippines), and Bangalore (India), each with little dependence on a central government. The tour takes you to the zebra-like economy of the United States, where most major metropolitan areas are still relatively weak while Silicon Valley, the Pacific Northwest, and parts of Texas and the mountain states are thriving—the economies of some cities in those regions are growing at 20 percent per year. The tour stops in small countries like Singapore, New Zealand, and Ireland, which are growing at 6 to 7 percent per year, much faster than the largest economies in their respective neighborhoods.

In addition, the emergence of global alliances such as the European Union, the North American Free Trade Agreement, the Association of Southeast Asian Nations (ASEAN), and Mercosur in South America mark the decline of national sovereignty. The solid-line national border is giving way to dotted lines, resulting in the migration of capital, information, products, and services. And the world's most prosperous regions have reversed the traditional role of government—from protecting weak domestic industries to inviting in strong global corporations that can serve the global marketplace from these host locations.

The rise of regional powers, within and across national borders, is changing the rules for business. How, for instance, does a company decide to do business in China? Is the risk universal across China's huge land mass? Probably not. Chances are that Dalian and Guangzhou will be hospitable regardless of what happens in Beijing. Likewise, as the borders disappear in the European Union, it's difficult to say whether Spain is a good place to invest. People have to start talking instead about Catalonia, Wales, Alsace-Lorraine, and other regions.

New Media and Information Technology

Digital media, information technology, and telecommunications are driving economic and social change worldwide. So powerful is this force that an entire nation—Malaysia—has based its economic development strategy on the growth of high technology. Malaysia is, in effect, creating a country within a country—the Multimedia Super Corridor (MSC), a ten-by-thirty-mile swatch of former palm oil plantations south of Kuala Lumpur. MSC will provide a twenty-first-century infrastructure designed to the specifications of the world's leading high-tech firms, and it will showcase eight "flagship applications," including distance learning, telemedicine, and electronic government. The single-minded vision of Prime Minister Mahathir Mohamad, MSC will include a new cyberuniversity, transportation system, paperless government center, research and development labs, and regional headquarters for more than forty global companies, including Microsoft, Intel, Oracle, Sun Microsystems, and Nippon Telegraph & Telephone. If the effort is successful,

Malaysia will become an advanced information value-added economy by 2020.

Building an information-technology economy requires not only high-speed phone lines and state-of-the-art facilities but also new laws, policies, and relationships among business, government, individuals, and communities. Most industrialized countries have not yet come to grips with that reality. In Japan, for example, the educational code says that teachers and students must be in the same premises—which makes distance learning difficult. Medical law today requires the doctor to be in the same room as the patient or no fee can be charged. And commercial law in effect bans a board of directors from meeting via teleconference.

Of course, information technology is challenging not only legal conventions but business practices as well. Amazon.com became the world's largest bookstore within a year, but it doesn't exist physically. Amazon handles three million titles and creates an interactive relationship with customers. As an author, for instance, I can find out what readers are saying about my books and respond to their feedback. Likewise, software and compact discs are now distributed electronically. Service organizations are also bypassing traditional distribution systems. On-line trading services such as E*trade and e.Schwab have become the fastest-growing part of the brokerage business in the United States. And catalogue companies such as L. L. Bean, Lands' End, and J. Crew make more than $100 million in sales in Japan without having a single retail outlet.

Entire professions—tax preparers, travel agents, even, God willing, lawyers—may succumb to information technology. Family Lawyer, a $95 CD-ROM by Intuit, can produce a detailed will, divorce settlement, or business contract in a matter of minutes. Personal finance software, such as Quicken, is used by thirteen million Americans; and major banks, brokerage houses, utilities, and even the IRS are now electronically linked to consumers. Services like E-Ticket locate the lowest possible airfares to any destination in the world, and deliver your ticket within days.

But the eight-hundred-pound gorilla of the information era is the digital satellite. DirectTV now has 2.5 million subscribers in the United States. In Australia and the Asia-Pacific region, more than ten million people watch Fox TV, Star Television, and other satellite broadcasts. In Japan, HDTV is received by thirteen million people—and by a half-million more in Taiwan and Korea, where consumers need only buy a small satellite dish to receive 350 Japanese channels. A satellite knows no national borders. Just as the Japanese satellite footprint covers parts of Taiwan, Korea, and China, other overseas broadcasts are bound to reach Japan, the United States, France, or Saudi Arabia. So-called pirate broadcasters can beam signals into any country without the bother of licensing or official approval, not to mention (in the case of Japan) the high costs of entertaining all those businessmen and bureaucrats.

Universal Consumer Cultures

Global media are causing a cultural revolution that is far different from the one Chairman Mao envisioned—the emergence of a worldwide class of mostly young consumers. With hundreds of channels available through CNN, Fox TV, Sky TV, and MTV, consumers everywhere now know exactly what products they want to buy—and those products usually carry names like Nike, Sony, Disney, Toyota, Coca-Cola, and McDonald's. These universal users—who increasingly emulate California teenagers in tastes, interests, and disposable income—create a volume opportunity for global marketeers. Few domestic markets can match the growth potential of the world's developing economies.

With the homogenization of consumer tastes comes the emergence of global technical standards. No longer do official bodies convene formal proceedings to set standards for fax transmissions, for instance. Rather, a few global corporations capture a market. Microsoft's Windows and Intel's microprocessors have created Wintel, the de facto standard for personal computing. Java is becoming a universal language for the World Wide Web. Housing codes are increasingly converging so that houses made in the United States or Canada can be exported to Japan, reducing the cost of housing construction by as much as half. Companies such as MasterCard, Visa, and American Express have set de facto standards for electronic cash and digital signatures. The global standard-setting process is often random and unplanned, but it lays the groundwork for enormous generation of wealth.

Corporate Cost Sharing

Most corporate strategists are concerned with minimizing costs and maximizing revenues, so it is no wonder they are turning their eyes to the rest of the world. The global economy gives corporations huge opportunities on both sides of the cost/revenue equation. They can increase revenue by filling the appetite of a billion new consumers; at the same time they can reduce their fixed costs (manufacturing, capital, R&D, and branding) and their variable costs (labor and materials). They do not necessarily have to pack up and move operations overseas. All manner of strategic alliances, mergers and acquisitions, global franchising, and outsourcing can translate into remarkable cost savings. As long as the global economy offers ways to improve the financial contribution to fixed costs, companies of all sizes will exploit it.

The twist on conventional business strategy is twofold: global competitiveness is ultimately a race for brains and know-how, not for cheap labor. And the borderless economy creates opportunities for savvy enterprises of any size. General Electric may insist on being number one or two in its markets, but there are benefits to being number seven or eight. Smallness at this point in history is a virtue. You have little to lose in reinventing yourself. You have the opportunity to become ten times or a hundred times bigger, instead of at best attaining 20 percent growth. Using multimedia technology and global networks, you have access to the same communications technology and marketing networks as large companies. Through alliances, cost-sharing, and creative collaboration, small companies can think big. They can exploit the common weakness of all big corporations—a vested interest in doing things the way they always have. In other words, a large company will have less flexibility to "do it right" in the twenty-first century.

The Role of Strategic Leaders

What all this means for leaders is that we have to build networks rather than pyramids. We have to learn to share, sort, and synthesize information, rather than simply direct the work of others. We have to rethink our basic approach to decision making, risk taking, and organizational strategy. And we have to create meaning and uphold values in flatter, more dispersed enterprises.

Globalization also forces us to reconsider the boundaries and definitions of a corporation, starting with the question, What is a company? We have to question old assumptions regarding make-or-buy policies, strategic alliances, joint ventures, and vertical integration. We have to anticipate—and invent—new shapes for the corporation, wherever it is based.

American companies, for instance, tend to have clear corporate borders. They are ownership driven, and their intent is to maximize shareholders' interests. Procurement policies, dealership networks, and community interests are peripheral concerns. Fifty-one percent ownership means total control. In the Japanese corporate model, the boundaries always have been blurred. They are relationship driven, with a family of companies often moving people from one company to another. This creates a more harmonious web of common interests. The participation of people rather than equity participation is the basis of corporate relationships. On the other hand, the German corporate model is driven by social contracts, and German companies are very cognizant of the social and environmental responsibility of the corporation.

These three corporate models reflect deep differences in governance and culture. Yet in a deeper sense they all share a linear, twentieth-century view of how to operate a business (See Figure 20.1). All three models will have to change. A business system created for industrial-era organizations around the world, with their fixed borders between R&D, engineering, manufacturing, sales, marketing, finance, and customer service, is being challenged by twenty-first-century information-era competitors with their fluid, extended networks (Figure 20.2). If you go to South Sioux Falls, South Dakota, for example, you will find Gateway Computer—a $6 billion computer company in the prairie. They have no retail outlets. Call a telephone sales representative—Gateway has 3,500 of them—and once he or she takes your order, that sales rep becomes your technical support person whenever you call in. The company has worldwide procurement and just-in-time delivery, with

Figure 20.1. The Twentieth-Century Company.

Rigid business systems with clearly defined functional, ownership, and organizational links are the norm.

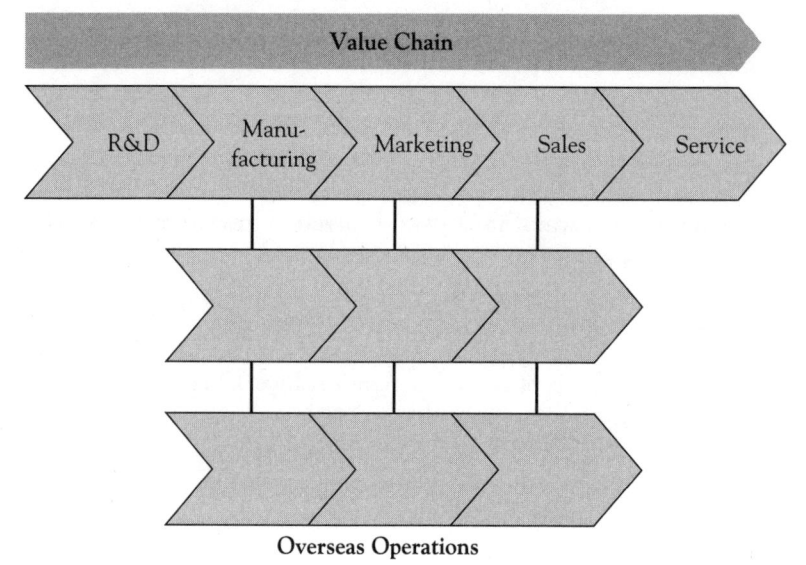

Value Chain

R&D → Manufacturing → Marketing → Sales → Service

Overseas Operations

a regional call center in South Dakota and another, for European operations, in Dublin. The computer itself may be shipped from South Sioux Falls, the software and manuals from California, and the monitors from Taiwan. United Parcel Service has built an electronic data interchange system so that all these things are delivered as a package within twenty-four hours to any household in North America.

That is the shape of the new global organization. It will look nothing like the organization of the past 150 years. Detailed engineering might be done in India, manufacturing in Vietnam or China. R&D could be in Silicon Valley or the Research Triangle, and sales and service could be handled in a dozen major markets. Many of

Figure 20.2. A Twenty-First-Century Company.

Fluid, networked systems with extensive outsourcing and flexible partnerships will eclipse today's business system.

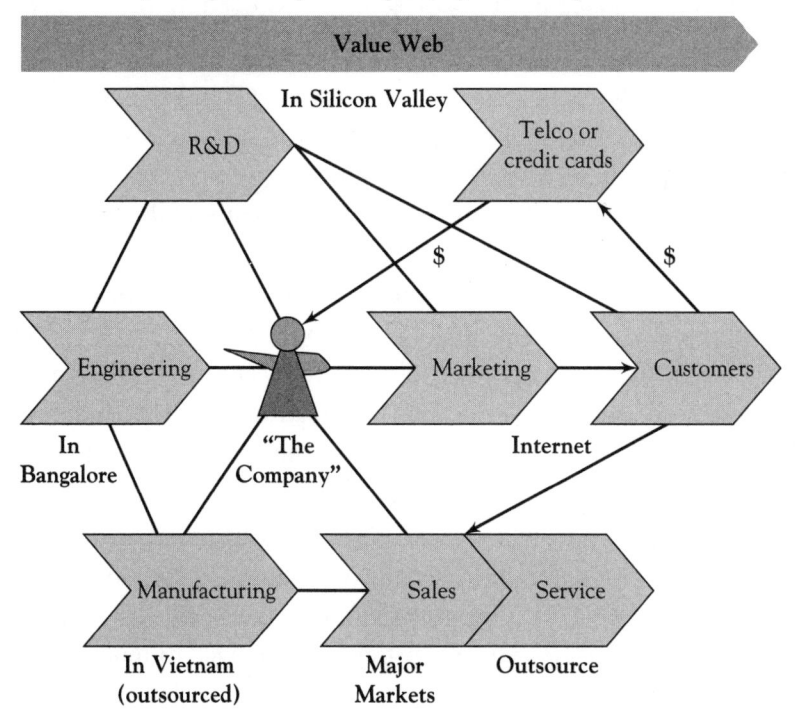

the basic networked functions will be outsourced. Thousands of managers and staff members will work from remote offices or their homes. The challenge will be to manage these scattered functions harmoniously. That, too, requires a new understanding of the global marketplace. Foreign markets are not only for selling but also for procuring skills and special expertise. The ability to manage a network will determine market success. Your role as a corporate-center leader is to make connections.

The shape of the twenty-first-century organization is flat, networked, and amorphous. Much of its activity is outsourced, not to cheap locations but to the best producers, the best R&D labs and designers. Core skills—such as marketing for Nike or logistics for FedEx—are retained in-house. Leaders become organizers of complex systems—brokers of performance and efficiency.

The hierarchical twentieth-century structures were characterized by static relationships and clearly defined value chains. Chief executives—who have reached the top of the pyramid by knowing the best practices of the day and charting successful strategies—may find their years of experience a liability, not an asset. Increasingly we will need to reexamine the world regularly and throw out what has worked in the past, not imitate it. These changes are going to create a crisis of leadership in companies that fail to create opportunities for fast-moving mavericks, entrepreneurs, and risk takers. Survival dictates that we review the composition of leadership, that we think about ways the chief executive can be assisted by change leaders inside and outside the organization.

The new era of intellectual value-added means that the boss may not know all the answers because all constituents, inside and outside the company, have an equal opportunity to contribute. Everyone has to become both a transmitter and a receiver of information. For that kind of exchange to take place, strategists, corporate planners, and senior decision makers have to become catalysts, as opposed to preserving their personal right to dictate what the company ought to do. Leaders will be constantly challenged to remove the boundaries between business functions, which may look perfectly balanced on the organization chart but seldom are that way in reality. A strong manufacturing base may exist at the expense of a neglected sales or marketing staff. Leaders must constantly evaluate the performance of key functions and look for gaps in their business system. Usually that means looking outside the walls of the business for help; few organizations can maintain world-class performance in all functional areas on their own.

In the new global enterprise, another leadership skill is the preservation of core skills and values. As organizations become increasingly diverse and amorphous, the notion of who you are and what binds you together becomes a matter of strategic importance. You cannot successfully enter China, Chile, or Chad unless you are a value-driven company. Simply setting up shop, even with a very good product or service, and telling the locals whatever they want to hear is likely to turn problems into disasters. Without core values driven by the customer's interest, you will find it even more difficult than it already is to sustain success.

The challenge for leaders over the next five to ten years will be to speed the transition from the static boxes of the twentieth-century value chains to the anarchic network of the twenty-first-century model. The leader's role will be not to master a narrow functional discipline but to develop a balanced expertise encompassing people, finance, marketing, and—most important of all—technology and geography. The ability to synthesize information and generate ideas, energy, and shared values over the globe becomes paramount. No one can do it alone. We need to have a network of advisers and allies. Via the network, we can be advised by the world's best all the time. And we can master the difficult balancing act of being equidistant to the top forty economic hot spots around the world.

So, what should the leader do in the face of this unprecedented discontinuity? You have to clear your memory—unlearn everything you know. Reset the way you do business and think about whether you have an opportunity to become an Amazon.com or a Nike. You have to act as if you are the CEO, regardless of your position, because the top of the ladder gives you the best view of what's coming.

21 DAVID A. NADLER
MARK NADLER

THE SUCCESS SYNDROME

David A. Nadler is chairman and CEO of the Delta Consulting Group. He specializes in organizational change, executive leadership, and team development. He formerly taught at Columbia University and has written, edited, or coauthored twelve books, including Champions of Change *and* Competing by Design. *Mark Nadler is chairman of the editorial board at Delta Consulting Group. He advises clients on communications strategies for organizational change and manages the firm's publishing efforts. Formerly he worked as an editor and newsroom executive for newspapers including the* Chicago Sun Times *and the* Wall Street Journal.

The mid- and late 1990s have been glorious days for business in the United States. Earnings, productivity, and financial markets have been high; unemployment rates are low and inflation seems like nothing but a bad memory. It's the best of times, a fin-de-siècle Golden Age.

Of course, we have been through this before, and not so long ago. U.S. businesses enjoyed a similar period during the 1960s, before hyperinflation, oil embargoes, and global competition revealed the underlying weaknesses in so many companies. By the time the boom had gone bust, we were starting to learn an important lesson: don't confuse a vigorous economic cycle with managerial brilliance.

Scores of leading companies learned that lesson the hard way. Compare the *Fortune* lists of biggest corporations for 1967 and 1997 and you'll see just how transient market leadership can be. Of the fifty biggest companies on the 1967 list, fewer than half show up anywhere in today's top one hundred. Some were swallowed up in mergers and acquisitions, others slipped to the lower rungs in the rankings, and a few simply ceased to exist. If you take a global perspective, the record is even bleaker: only ten of those top fifty U.S. corporate giants of 1967 are among today's global one hundred.

Indeed, there's an even more important lesson for business leaders to keep in mind as the buoyant economy envelops so many companies in the warm glow of success. You don't have to go back thirty years to see the warning signs. Just look at the executive purges in the early 1990s at such corporate stalwarts as IBM, General Motors, American Express, Westinghouse, Eastman Kodak, AlliedSignal, and Digital Equipment—and the late-1990s turmoil at AT&T.

The patterns are clear: in one industry after another, a company's sustained success inevitably carries the seeds of future disaster.

We have come to call this phenomenon the *Success Syndrome*—a progressive organizational pathology that strikes companies precisely when they seem to be most dominant. It is a condition that goes far deeper than mere complacency, though that's certainly an early symptom. Left untreated, the syndrome leads to a stultifying inward focus. Innovation diminishes as costs and bureaucracy grow. The organization loses its capacity to act, to learn, to adapt.

In reality, there is no way to eliminate the threat permanently. If your company enjoys success for any significant stretch, the risk of the Success Syndrome comes with the territory. What you can do as a leader is be aware of it, understand its causes and symptoms, and take specific steps to control it.

How Success Feeds Disaster

The origins of the Success Syndrome can be traced to the very way organizations operate. Four basic elements constitute the core of any organization: the work, or the tasks required to perform each function in the value chain; the people who carry out those tasks; the formal organization of structures, processes, and practices that specify how work is assigned and performed; and the informal organization, the patterns of behavior that shape the daily interactions of employees, supervisors, coworkers, and customers.

At any given time, each of the four components is in some degree of fit, or congruence, with the other three. The tighter the fit, the smaller the gap between strategic objectives and actual performance. But organizational systems are in a constant state of flux. The job of managers is constantly to make the decisions required to readjust the fit among work, people, formal structures, and the informal environment.

In the most successful companies, the internal fit seems almost automatic. At some point, everyone begins to understand the formula for success, and it becomes self-perpetuating. The problem is that the near-perfect internal fit is often accompanied by a deteriorating external fit. Organizations become so convinced that what they're doing is right that they stop paying attention to changes in the outside world—new competitors, new technologies, changing customer tastes.

Given that scenario, it's almost inevitable that symptoms of the Success Syndrome will eventually surface. They usually take the following forms:

- *Internal focus and insularity.* Convinced of its unassailable dominance, the organization assumes it has nothing to fear—or learn—from its competitors. It loses touch with changing customer tastes and demands. Benchmarking is unheard of. Managers focus more on corporate politics than on customers, new markets, and competitive challenges. They reject people, ideas, technology, and strategies that aren't "homegrown," assuming that by definition these must be second best.

Probably the best example is the U.S. auto industry. Frank Pipp, the now retired head of manufacturing at Xerox, tells of being a young plant manager at Ford Motor Company in the late 1970s when the Japanese threat was first becoming evident. Pipp recalls bringing a Toyota Corolla into the plant and having his people take it apart and put it back together. They were amazed by the level of "snap fit" the Japanese had attained: when you put the car back together, the pieces just snapped into place without the aid of the rubber mallet that was a fixture on U.S. assembly lines. When the incredible workmanship was pointed out to a Ford division manager, he wasn't worried. "The customer will never notice the difference," he said. "The customer won't care."

- *Codification.* Informal ways of doing things become associated with success and soon become formalized, inflexible policies and procedures. These can range from executive decision-making practices to scheduling processes to issues as mundane as the use of overhead projectors in meetings.

During the glory days of Digital Equipment, for example, CEO Kenneth Olson believed that customers would go out of their way to seek out Digital's products because of their innovative edge. In the beginning, he was right. But Olson's personal disdain for sales and marketing evolved into a corporate mantra that served the company poorly once customers could find adequate substitutes for Digital's products.

- *Complexity.* As more and more practices become codified, complexity increases dramatically. The growing demands for formalized control—compounded by the growing focus on internal power and politics—lead to more and more bureaucracy.

Few organizations could rival AT&T when it came to stultifying layers of policies, procedures, and permissions. Consider the old bible for employee training—the Bell System Training and Development Standards. This wasn't actually a training manual: it was a guide to the methodology for developing training. And people were employed to do nothing but update and publish this guide to producing guides.

- *Conservatism.* As constant success becomes the norm, risk is discouraged. With market leadership at stake, there's little stomach for the kind of early gambles that enabled the company to grow.

A late-1990s example is Apple Computer, which achieved early success as an innovative maverick. But success bred caution and conservatism. As the competitive world changed and other computer manufacturers consolidated their hold on the market, Apple couldn't bring itself to make any of the big bets. Caught up in a state of corporate denial, it refused to accept the realities of the changing environment and ended up paying the price.

- *Disabled learning and reduced innovation.* Complacency and conservatism lead to a form of institutionally disabled learning. The organization becomes incapable of experimenting, learning from failure, or gaining new insights. Promotions, financial incentives, and rewards in general are based on maintaining the status quo: there's rarely much percentage in trying anything new.

In the early 1980s, Xerox's Palo Alto Research Center (PARC) was a hotbed of innovation, producing one breakthrough after another (including the basis for what later became the Macintosh Operating System). Somehow, none of PARC's inventions became successful products. In the early 1990s, Xerox's management took a hard look at what was wrong. They found that the failures of the early 1980s—a lack of focus on customers and competitors during the early stages of development—were still plaguing the company a decade later.

Impact on Performance

Over time, these problems start affecting performance in at least three tangible ways:

- *Increased costs.* In the absence of benchmarking and attention to competitive pressure, bureaucracy and empire building drive ever-mounting costs. If the prevailing assumption is that "business as usual" is the way to stay on top, budgets continue to grow incrementally year after year.

- *Loss of speed.* Organizations that are oblivious to external pressure can become sluggish—a tendency they often justify with self-satisfied slogans such as "We don't have to be the first as long as we're the best." As competitors close the perceived gap in quality between their product and that of the leader, consumers become less willing to wait longer for a marginally better product. And complacency slows processes throughout the organization, from design and development to production and order fulfillment.

- *Impaired capacity to act.* Middle management gradually slips into a state of semiparalysis. Stifled by strict controls, starved for information, discouraged from taking risks, and fearful of the future, managers become reluctant to make difficult decisions. The tough issues keep getting kicked back upstairs, to the frustration of many, including customers.

The truth is that under certain conditions a company can suffer from the symptoms of the Success Syndrome and still appear to be successful. Xerox, for example, enjoyed a banner year, in terms of financial performance, in 1981—the year before the bottom dropped out. That's because financial results, the preeminent yardsticks of corporate achievement, are in reality lagging indicators of true performance. Managers ought to be spending a lot more time analyzing the leading indicators: customer defections, employee performance, the development pipeline, and competitive benchmarking. Too often, solid financial numbers mask serious underlying problems.

In fact, the numbers can hold up for years at a time, as long as the competitive environment remains essentially unchanged. But all industries experience stretches of gradual change punctuated by sudden, disruptive events—government deregulation, a technological breakthrough, or a war. Such changes can wipe out the basis for a company's market leadership.

As things begin to unravel, victims of the Success Syndrome respond with behavior that psychologists describe as "dominant response." Faced with a perceived threat, most people revert to their tried-and-true way of dealing with a crisis. Clearly an organization's reliance on just doing more of the same can be disastrous. Quite predictably, doing more of the same accelerates the decline in performance. It is a vicious and potentially terminal cycle.

You can usually tell when a company has begun this tailspin by watching the revolving door to the CEO's office. In just a few short years, for example, Apple had been through three CEOs and was starting on its fourth. Each was heralded upon his arrival as Apple's savior, and each left the company worse off than when he arrived. It is the board's job to recognize the onset of the Success Syndrome and to act before such successive—and apparently futile—executive purges become a way of life.

Avoiding the Success Syndrome

It's hard to imagine Microsoft or Intel suffering major organizational failure—but few people foresaw the problems that befell IBM or General Motors not long ago. Keep in mind that many of the new high-tech giants are still led by their first generation of entrepreneurial founders. The real test will come with successive generations of institutional leadership. Chances are that Bill Gates's personal management techniques will eventually become memorialized as "the Microsoft way," potentially handcuffing future generations of managers as they face strategic and organizational problems that Gates never imagined.

The good news is that self-destructive attitudes such as arrogance, insularity, and complacency don't assume their full form overnight. The bad news is that they can slowly creep up on an organization, becoming deeply entrenched before anyone is really aware of the change that has taken place. Astute leaders need to pay attention to the symptoms and root out those attitudes and practices when they appear. Leaders can take eight steps to prevent the Success Syndrome from taking hold:

1. *Create and sustain an external focus.* If there is a single, all-encompassing approach to avoiding the Success Syndrome, this is it. It's the job of senior management to set a tone—supporting it through constant personal example—that clearly demonstrates that what goes on outside corporate headquarters, and outside the company's boundaries, is most critical to the company's continued success. Management's unmistakable message is that the unwavering focus has to be on customers, competitors, new technology, and gathering market forces that hold the potential for important change.

This isn't a matter of plastering the walls with slogans about having "a passion for the customer." This is hard, everyday work that requires concrete action, ongoing attention, special initiatives, the careful use of symbolic acts, and carefully designed incentives that support an external focus and discourage those who are overly concerned with internal power and politics.

At Sun Microsystems, for example, CEO Scott McNealy's executive team meetings often start with informal discussions about competitors—who's up, who's down, who seems to have a new strategy. To hear McNealy describe it, there's something close to an obsession with outguessing the competition—a view, as he puts it, that "the whole world is our chessboard." When Xerox was struggling with quality problems ten years ago, CEO David Kearns ordered executives to work regularly in the customer service center and take calls from irate customers.

2. *Maintain a contrarian mind-set.* Top leaders—and CEOs in particular—have to operate on the assumption that no matter how

well things are going, they could be better. James R. Houghton, the retired CEO of Corning, referred to this approach as contrarian leadership. His job, he believed, was to be optimistic and supportive during the tough times, but to focus on keeping people from becoming overly self-satisfied during the good times. In various forms, this is a popular theme among successful CEOs. Andrew Grove of Intel summed it up in the title of his book, *Only the Paranoid Survive*. At Sun Microsystems, Scott McNealy says he never stops worrying about what will be "the next big thing" to challenge his company. Despite Sun's success, he never stops worrying, he told us, "because they don't pay me to feel good."

3. *Assume that the competition is both right and competent.* All too often the arrogance associated with the Success Syndrome lulls market leaders into dismissing their competitors' periodic successes as temporary aberrations. They reach a point where it becomes unthinkable that the small competitors nipping at their heels could actually have a better strategy, a more accurate view of the marketplace, or a more sophisticated product. To remain vigilant, you've got to assume that your competitors are smart, competent, motivated, and constantly looking for ways to eat into your market share or, even more seriously, figure out a way to leapfrog ahead of you using entirely new approaches.

4. *Anticipate change through systematic, periodic scans of the competitive environment.* There are several ways to categorize organizational change, and one of the most important has to do with timing. Without question, anticipatory change in advance of some major destabilizing event is far better than reactive change. The earlier you act, the greater the chance of success. Anticipatory change makes it possible to assess the situation, experiment with various approaches, and prepare for difficult change at a time when your resources and reputation are at their height.

Consequently, smart companies use very deliberate processes to look for early warnings of impending change. It was that kind of information sweep that led Citicorp to redefine itself fundamentally in the 1970s as a comprehensive financial institution rather than as a traditional bank. It is also what prompted Xerox to embrace digital technology as it prepared itself for the arrival of the electronic workplace of the 1990s.

Such environmental scans must be ongoing. The senior team should regularly hear from outside experts—academics, analysts, industry observers—and customers. They should be exposed to people who can offer new perspectives on broad issues—technology, public policy, social trends—that will affect their industry and their business.

5. *Think of yourself as your own biggest competitor.* The logical extension to scanning the environment for signs of radical change is being willing to do something about it. In some cases, that means being willing to cannibalize existing product lines or business processes in order to position yourself for the next level of competition. That's not easy to do: it means making sure you get to market first with the next major innovation, even if it takes business away from your favorite cash cow. That's exactly what Hewlett Packard (HP) did when it assaulted its best-selling product, the laser printer, by launching the lower-priced inkjet printer. The move seemed counterintuitive at the time. In retrospect, it was right on target, given the enormous success of the less expensive printer—a market niche that would have offered tremendous opportunities to HP's competitors.

6. *Don't wait until a crisis to bring in outsiders.* Corporate cultures are self-perpetuating organisms. The culture rewards those who thrive in a given environment; it nurtures them, promotes them, and cements their loyalty. The leaders of this generation go out and hire young copies of themselves and prepare them to become the next generation of leaders. Over time, people are continually reinforced in their belief that their way of doing things is not only the best way, it's the only way that makes sense.

That's why companies that have succumbed to the Success Syndrome nearly always go outside to find new leaders—because the homegrown leaders are so deeply entrenched in doing things the same way that they can't imagine any different approaches. Companies that avoid the Success Syndrome regularly hire senior managers from the outside—and often from outside their own industry—with the specific intention of bringing in new ideas, fresh perspectives, and a willingness to ask, "Why do we do things that way?"

7. *Pay close attention to the observations of frontline employees.* Salespeople, service technicians, customer service reps—the people who never set foot in an executive office—are often the first to sense that things are somehow going awry. On a daily basis, their interactions with customers and consumers give them a narrow but clear idea of what's going on in the marketplace. Yet all too often the rich store of information they possess goes unused. Some managers simply assume that frontline people love to gripe and that their horror stories should be discounted. Then, to the extent that those managers do pass along what they're hearing, they tend to soften the bad news. By the time the information makes its way to the top—if it ever does—it has been so heavily sanitized that any sense of urgency has long since dissipated. It's essential for CEOs and senior executives to get unvarnished information regularly and directly from those employees who know what customers are saying and doing.

8. *Institute formal learning processes.* When an organization repeats anything associated with its emergence as a leader—without understanding what it was that led to success—it becomes frozen in time, incapable of renewing itself through learning.

Organizational learning doesn't just happen—top leadership has to make it happen. There are informal ways to support learning that involve the way leaders treat risk takers who don't always succeed. But learning can also be formalized. Xerox uses a process called Presidential Reviews that brings people together at a crucial stage in a project—a new product launch, for example—to spend several days analyzing what worked and what didn't. The object isn't to criticize or lay blame; instead, senior executives—sometimes the CEO—make it clear from the outset that the only objective is to learn from experience, so lessons can be applied appropriately throughout the company.

The Leader's Role

Ultimately the best defense against the Success Syndrome is the view that success is a transitory, even dangerous, state. That mindset has to begin with the CEO. No one else in the organization wields the power and influence required to define an operating environment, or to combat arrogance, insularity, complacency, complexity, conservatism, and disabled organizational learning. Through words and symbols, the CEO can set a tone, send clear messages, and create constant dissatisfaction with the status quo. Through coaching and recruitment, the CEO can build a senior team that constantly seeks outside perspectives and aggressively attacks signs of smugness. The executive team can design processes and sponsor special events aimed at maintaining a sharp competitive edge. They can remind people that success ought never be taken for granted.

The late Roberto Goizueta, the tremendously successful CEO of Coca-Cola, told *Fortune* magazine in 1995 that he was often asked whether, given all the competition in his industry, he slept well at night. "I sleep like a baby," Goizueta would answer. "They say, 'That's wonderful.' I say, 'No, no, I wake up every two hours and cry.' Because it's true. You have to feel that restlessness."

Part V

LEADING FOR HIGH PERFORMANCE

22 STEPHEN R. COVEY

THE HABITS OF EFFECTIVE ORGANIZATIONS

Stephen R. Covey, for twenty years a professor of business management and organizational behavior at Brigham Young University, is the cochairman of Franklin Covey Co. and founder of the former Covey Leadership Center. He is the author of several best-selling books, including The Seven Habits of Highly Effective People, *which has sold more than ten million copies in thirty-two languages.*

One of the world's most influential business writers, speakers, and consultants, Stephen R. Covey offers an enduring message for organizations and individuals. In a time of packaged solutions and easy answers, he focuses instead on "principle-centered leadership," the belief that successful personal or organizational practices are based on universal laws and ethics.

Covey spoke with Editor-in-Chief Frances Hesselbein about such far-ranging topics as organizational culture, personal values, leadership, and change.

FRANCES HESSELBEIN: *We have all gained so much from your work on personal effectiveness. What are the habits, if you will, of effective organizations?*

STEPHEN R. COVEY: Organizational effectiveness is so interwoven with the personal side that they're almost inseparable. Organizational behavior is simply the collective outcome of individual behavior. But as you develop cultural norms and mores inside an organization, a spirit of *we* rather than a spirit of *me* can begin to emerge. So that is the fundamental habit.

I look at an organization as a high-wire trapeze act, and today there's no net. We're at a level of competition that exceeds anything we've known before. It takes a tremendous spirit of partnership, of synergy, of reading the nuances of each others' minds and hearts, to catch those moving bodies in midair. You need certain strengths and skills before you can begin to work without a net.

The Seven Habits

The habits of highly effective people articulated by Stephen R. Covey are

1. Be Proactive (Personal Vision)
2. Begin with the End in Mind (Personal Leadership)
3. Put First Things First (Personal Management)
4. Think Win/Win (Interpersonal Leadership)
5. Seek First to Understand, Then to Be Understood (Empathetic Communication)
6. Synergize (Creative Cooperation)
7. Sharpen the Saw (Self-Renewal)

Source: Reprinted with the permission of Simon & Schuster from *The Seven Habits of Highly Effective People* by Stephen R. Covey. Copyright © 1989 by Stephen R. Covey.

That's why I tie together the individual with the organizational; unless you have the character strength of individuals who have abundance in their soul, then whatever their skills, they're not going to have the emotional security to achieve the teamwork necessary for this high-wire act.

FH: *But you begin with leadership—a ringmaster, to use your analogy—that can instill the culture and develop the practices that serve as a net.*

SRC: You begin with the leaders and the creation of a culture that values personal integrity and empowerment. Without that culture, you may have formal leaders, but you won't have true leadership. A culture of values is the foundation that supports your tent, that keeps the trapeze artists moving in the right direction. In other words, if you say you value long-term thinking, then you reward it. If you say you value all stakeholders, you don't just gather financial data; you have 360-degree data on all stakeholders. That's essentially Habit 5—"Seek first to understand, then to be understood"—at the organizational level. But few organizations really integrate the practice of teamwork and cooperation. We're still relying on the old forms of the industrial age, as Peter Drucker said in the first issue of *Leader to Leader* (see Chapter Twelve). People have not yet made the leap to the new society of organizations he described.

FH: *You have hit on a major issue that leaders face: moving from a culture of control—the old hierarchy—to a culture of commitment and inclusion and alignment. How do we do it? Would we look at mission? Would we look within ourselves? What is the first step?*

SRC: I think the first step is deep reflection on what your own life is about. What are your values? Do you have a bone-deep belief in the potential of other people, and do you truly want to see that potential identified and released and recognized? Otherwise, you may talk a good game, but you are just using a new, more subtle form of control.

I had an opportunity to interview the leaders of several Malcolm Baldrige Award–winning organizations, and I asked each, "What was the toughest struggle you had?" To a person they all said, giving up control. They all feared the consequences of letting go. But ultimately they found their fears were groundless—they found an unimagined resource capability that emerged when there was a common vision and a common value system.

FH: *Stephen, are you saying that these leaders simply made a leap of faith to give up control and unleash the energy of the organization? Or was there some spadework they had to do before taking that step?*

SRC: There was some spadework. These leaders sought the participation of people throughout their organization and beyond. But it was an almost daily question of, "Wow, do we really want people that involved? Do we want them that informed? Do we want them to have that much freedom of action?" These executives struggled constantly, in a very personal way, to let go, step back, and change their role.

FH: *Great change is often precipitated by a crisis. Did you find there was some crisis point these leaders faced in making the changes you describe?*

SRC: They did have crises, triggered by different things in each case. But as the leaders got more deeply involved in the change process, a lot of them began to ask the same kinds of questions: Do we really want to go after this? Why? Do we want to do it because we'll get the recognition of winning the award, or is there deep integrity and sincerity behind the effort? The winners found that the award became a by-product of the empowerment and the tapping of people's talents and energies.

FH: *What you are describing is the reflection and transformation of not just a single leader but of an entire organization. Would that not require many leaders dispersed across the organization?*

SRC: It would, Frances, and as you go through organizational redesign, you also go through personal redesign, which in turn affects interpersonal design. You begin seeing people differently and treating them differently. You have to address four dimensions of change: personal, interpersonal, managerial, and organizational. It's one large ecosystem that is interrelated and interdependent. So you're always working on yourself, and working to improve your emotional bank account with others. You're creating a little more empowerment in your management. You're working on your structures and systems and processes so they are in alignment with and supportive of your values. And all the time you're going through a personal struggle, just muddling through, not sure exactly what's going to happen.

This struggle drives people back to their roots, to see if they have an abundance mentality or a scarcity mentality. I'm telling you, it really is an emotional uprooting and a tearing at people's core. You need enough internal security to afford the risks of thinking abundantly and being willing to share power and knowledge and recognition and to gain and profit with other people. That is a prerequisite for tapping a new synergistic source of wealth and excitement.

FH: *So we're looking at enormous change within the person who is trying to pull from his inner depths what he needs to move from the old control paradigms to a new culture of commitment and vision. But at the same time we have great ferment within the organization, with new structures and new expectations of people. Going back to your high trapeze, how do we find the strength, that inner security to deal on a twenty-four-hour basis with change in almost everything we've been doing and thinking?*

SRC: We're talking about a transition figure, really, that is in a sense changing the practices of prior generations of managerial leadership to reflect the new rules of the new marketplace. It is so much more open and synergistic and ecologically tied, so much more free and flexible and empowering. But transitions are tough work. I think the key to that work is what the chaos and complexity experts call the *strange attractor*, a force that seems to catalyze action. There has to be an internal sense of what you are about. This takes a person of vision and of tremendous courage and also of humility. Someone who understands how shared principles influence outcomes and who learns to draw security from integrity.

FH: *In my work, I've found that leadership is a matter of how to be, not how to do it. It seems to me you've been describing how to be. We're talking about quality and character, not technique.*

SRC: Yes, I believe leadership lies more in character than in technical competence, but these two are interwoven. As people grow in competence, they gain awareness of a new dimension of their character. Then, as they begin to develop that aspect of their character, they find that their competence also increases. For instance, when we teach the skill of empathic listening—in other words, Habit 5—people see that they'd always looked at things from their own frame of reference, and they start to explore the richness of other people's perspective. As they get better at listening, they gather more information, and realize they've always lived with an insufficiency of data. Applying that learning to their personal and professional lives is exciting. People say, "Now I really know *why* to listen, instead of just *how*." So these two—the why of character and the how of competence—feed one another.

FH: *Of course, the struggle does not end at the office. What about work-life balance? Is that a part of the growth and development you've been describing?*

SRC: I think it is. It is part of the same spirit of discovery. You say, "If my colleagues have capabilities I have not known, what have I ignored in myself?" I found this in my own life. Our organization now has about four thousand people working with ten thousand clients in thirty-three countries. And so I've had to personally experience the kinds of changes I'm talking about. I've developed a complementary team in which other people's strengths compensate for my weaknesses, and I can use my strengths in a productive way because of that. We're all performing at a level I wouldn't have considered possible ten years ago.

Now, the more you rely on a complementary team, the less you have to become work-obsessed. It enables you to lead a more balanced personal life, with good quantity as well as quality time for your family life, for your community life, for your friends, for new learning adventures. I call it "to live, to love, to learn, to leave a legacy"—the four basic needs that we all need to cultivate. To live has to do with physical well-being and the economic side of life; to love addresses the relationship side so you can have deep, meaningful communication with your loved ones; to learn means the expansion of your talents into new areas in a disciplined way throughout your life; to leave a legacy has to do with finding meaning in your life.

By the way, just this morning I had a tremendous conversation with Viktor Frankl. He's a very bright, very humble spirit, and his life has been an inspiration to me. His whole thrust is that meaning is found through healing and the ability to transcend the past. It's not something you invent like a lot of popular psychology focuses on; it's what you detect from your responsibilities and your life context. Our whole approach toward stress management, for instance, is too much a sideshow. I think the essence of stress management is to have a unified sense of purpose and meaning and integrity, rather than just doing biofeedback exercises and meditation. I'm not against those things, but what if a person's fundamental thrust in life lacks integrity? Or what if it doesn't add value to society? That kind of personal imbalance is an underlying weakening of the immune system and makes us vulnerable to the stresses of life. But being stress-hardy comes from a deep sense of purpose and meaning.

FH: *I can't tell you how inspiring it is to be talking with you, Stephen. You've described a remarkable transformation of self, of the enterprise, of the culture, of something I call "beyond the walls." We have to go beyond the walls of the corporation, the university, the government and look at the community and involve ourselves in that whole healing and unifying spirit. Do you see this as an imperative of the kind of organization* *that you're describing? Do you feel that there is an obligation to move beyond the walls?*

SRC: Absolutely. I think it transcends the old social responsibility issue of the industrial age because it reflects the deep awareness that we are so interconnected, so interdependent, so much a part of our context that it is imperative that we think systemically.

This new approach is far more inclusive. It comes out of a deep sense of stewardship about the totality of our lives and that we don't think so much of *me* and *mine*. Of course you have to be fiscally healthy and respect shareholder value because profit is the wage for capital. But you must also respect other stakeholders, not just your investors. You must not take advantage of suppliers. You must understand the needs of customers and of employees. In a very real sense, there are only two roles in organizational life: supplier and customer. Whether in business or the public sector or the voluntary sector, we all play both roles all the time. We are all givers and receivers. Everything is relationship.

And the efficiency approach of the industrial forms, with the clock as the organizing metaphor, is in my mind going to be eclipsed by the effectiveness approach, with the compass as the metaphor. We have to embrace a sense of direction and sense of natural laws that are universal.

FH: *And that must encompass a sense of responsibility for people who have great needs. I see communities across the country and the world with burgeoning needs, and I see shrinking resources that don't match the needs. What is our role there?*

SRC: We have to prepare for the next generation, which means dealing with education, with the environment. We have to deal with the social problems that are deepening and proliferating to such a point today that they could overwhelm our social and economic machinery. We have to affirm disadvantaged people in their basic worth and then train them in their competency to survive the realities of today's marketplace. Employers have to take a far-seeing approach toward downsizing and reengineering so that they enhance the skills of their present workforce, so they don't have a demoralized, mistrusting organization. There has to be a sense of honor among people. It's like Gandhi said, "A person cannot do right in one department of life while attempting to do wrong in another department. Life is one indivisible whole." I think integrity means that we're integrated, personally and organizationally.

The result of personal or organizational disintegration is that most people in the workforce are operating on only four cylinders. I like to ask audiences two questions: "How many of you agree that the vast majority of the workforce possesses a lot more intelligence and talent and creativity than the present jobs require or even allow?" About 99 percent raise their hands. Then I ask, "Of the four cylinders that are being used, what percent of that capacity is spent in adding value and what percent is spent in protecting turf, interpersonal conflict, playing political games, and hidden agendas?" And the overwhelming majority of audiences say people use 25 to 50 percent of their capacity in these dysfunctional, negative kinds of activities. Look at the energy and the talent that are being wasted!

FH: *Stephen, in your work do you see organizations that have gotten close to that point of personal integration and social responsibility, or are you describing a kind of nirvana that you have to strive for but you may never ultimately attain?*

SRC: There is no doubt that organizations are taking these issues seriously, which is a huge step. Last year I spoke at a Fortune 500 conference. There were close to three hundred Fortune 500 CEOs present. One session was called "How are you going to stay at the head of your game in five years?" A side issue came up having to do with the community. I'm telling you, it was absolutely overwhelming to the group, and they ignored the main topic. They wanted to talk about what they could do to help schools at risk, to help kids get literate, to help people off drugs, to help families have a father back home again. The spirit of these people was so focused and their commitment so genuine that it would really have inspired you.

FH: *We see the same enormous interest in our work across all three sectors. In our experience, the best-led, best-managed corporations are looking for social partnerships where they can truly make a difference and change lives. To have this validated by your observations is very exciting.*

SRC: I think they're looking for a local infrastructure and competency to make good things happen. It's what John Gardner talked about in the first issue of *Leader to Leader* (see Chapter Thirty-Five): most cities have enough talent among their citizens to run a country. But you need to develop new organizational forms and structures and capabilities in the community to turn good intentions into reality. Don't you think as the awareness grows of the seriousness of these problems that we're going to see this social competency increasing?

FH: *I do, and I think the kind of moral and ethical leadership you're providing makes a real difference. I'm hearing a message of hope and possibility all the way through our discussion, and I think people across the country are hungry for that. People mobilize around positive messages.*

SRC: I believe that hope is an absolute moral imperative, because if we don't have it we have become part of the problem ourselves, not part of the solution. I think another moral imperative is that we focus on principles that are universal and get more magnanimous about other people's contributions and more grateful for them.

I believe that the number one problem we have is not any particular problem, it's how we solve problems. We're too focused on a legalistic approach, which at best ends in compromise, rather than on the creation of new alternatives. So I'm out there teaching this, and someone comes up and asks if I can help him negotiate a solution with someone who is suing his company. I told him, "You missed my whole point. You can do that yourself. All you have to do is understand and follow those basic principles." And he did. He called up the president of the other company and asked if he'd be willing to have lunch and discuss their differences.

This fellow persuaded his very wary adversary simply to hear him out in person, and at that meeting he began to describe the other person's point of view to that person's satisfaction. The other man was so amazed at the level of understanding of the issues from his perspective, he started to open up. His attorney, who had accompanied him to the lunch, said to him, "Don't talk anymore, it may compromise our situation in court." And the man told his attorney, "No, we're going to settle this thing now." Hope was born in him; they settled their differences in about three hours.

FH: *That is fascinating. Underlying much of what you have been talking about is the essence of Habit 7, which is self-renewal. It's perhaps better understood on the personal level than on the organizational, but I'm wondering what works for organizations seeking to sustain and renew themselves in the ways you describe.*

SRC: I really believe that if there isn't a process of continual organizational renewal the most successful organization will soon decay. There needs to be continual reinvention of any organization—government, business, nonprofit, or even family. They must constantly revisit their mission to see if their structures and systems are in alignment with it. Structures and systems tend to get fossilized and bureaucratized so easily and gradually; the means becomes the end, and people in those organizations begin to lose a sense of what they're really about. That's why in our own home we have family meetings once a week where we go over our family mission statement and ask, Do we still believe that? Do we live it? Is this a place where we have the sounds of love? Do we nurture independence? Do we nurture interdependence? Do we still contribute, are we trying to serve and add value to our society?

Another key renewal source is a 360-degree sense of accountability and gathering information from all the stakeholders who are involved. You get it anonymously, at least once a year, so it's honest and open and you examine yourself against it to make sure you're not only in alignment with your own value system but you're in alignment with the marketplace and the people and organizations you're trying to serve. It's humbling to hear what customers and suppliers and dealers and distributors say about you, and to take stock of the level of trust and credibility of your own executive team.

I find those are the two main sources of renewal: revisiting the mission with deep sincerity and revisiting all the markets to which you're attempting to add value. It's kind of a self-examination but also a social report. I'm accountable to all these people, I'd better be open to their influence. Humility is the mother of all virtues. It takes a lot of humility to do this—and it takes a lot of courage to then take the action to reinvent yourself. But the fruit of that kind of effort is integrity and wisdom.

23 STEVEN KERR

GE'S COLLECTIVE GENIUS

Steven Kerr is chief learning officer for General Electric Company, with responsibility for GE's Crotonville leadership education center. He has taught at Ohio State University, the University of Michigan, and the University of Southern California, where he served as dean of the business school faculty.

To manage a large organization today is to manage a central paradox: how to develop strong leaders while decentralizing and delayering the operation. Developing such leaders is more an art than a science, and it doesn't lend itself to such simple formulas as "promote from within" or "recruit from outside."

The best companies, however, share a remarkable ability to understand their key opportunities, recognize their vulnerabilities, and match their executives to their needs. They also find ways to institutionalize and integrate the leadership development process with the real work of the organization.

Most people know that the experiences they have had—as opposed to formal training—are the major builders of management skill. Can these experiences be orchestrated? Job rotation is a strategy that many companies use. But General Electric, PepsiCo, and a handful of others have elevated it to new heights. GE moves people across businesses at the highest level—and its chairman, Jack Welch, takes a direct, personal interest in the process. In meetings with heads of GE's businesses, for instance, Welch might say, "What's with Jones? Didn't we agree a year ago that we wanted to move him?" Yes. "But didn't we agree he had no union experience and that we'd move him to a union plant? And now I see he isn't there yet." He could also tell you whether Jones has had experience with a short product cycle, a consumer business, or a global assignment.

We move potential leaders—the chief financial officer, head of human resources, or even the business head—into multibillion-dollar units in GE, and we're not always sure it's the right fit. It's a great way for the executive to grow, however, and a great way to evaluate his or her performance in the job. Job rotation is a deliberate, carefully tracked process of balancing people's life experiences. It's a process through which many people leave the company and many others move up.

Putting Your House in Order

Before you get very far into executive development strategies, however, you have to look at your reward systems and corporate culture. In the long run, these basics are more powerful than the most lavish leadership development program.

One answer to the riddle of executive incentives is, reward performance, not rank. You also need to balance short-term and long-term incentives. It's correctly said that corporations—particularly American corporations—overemphasize short-run performance. The chief advantage of stock options, profit sharing, or plans that vest after three or five years is that they give people reasons to care about the long run, balancing all the obvious pressures to care about the short run. This approach poses another problem, however, with incentives: line of sight. Ideally, all employees ought to understand that what they do influences their reward. Rewards tied to the price of stock are very powerful for the CEO, who has some influence over stock performance; but for an analyst or a programmer four levels down, it's like being a spectator at a movie. You do want people to have long-range incentives, but you'd also like to give people an incentive to produce. Profit sharing and stock options are not really incentives to produce quarterly results, because most employees can't influence those things. Still, these longer-term rewards do have value; they're incentives to care about the enterprise.

Finally, reward systems should be orchestrated to support organizational goals and desired behaviors. Most are not. For example, at a large high-tech firm a few years ago, one division head ran a videotaped speech about how the company had to be much more collaborative and team-oriented. At the same time he announced a new performance-ranking system that discouraged collaboration. So organizations should start with what they want in terms of employee actions and attitudes, then build a reward system around those things (see Chapter Twenty-Four). Few firms, however, take that approach.

Learning from Nonprofit Organizations

Some public agencies, universities, and nonprofits think that because they don't have stock options or profit sharing, they're less able to build a competent reward system. The fact is, most organizations that have lots of money waste it because they don't build competent reward systems. The unalterable truth about cash is this: nobody refuses it, and nobody returns it. After you give it, it's gone; but if you don't give it out competently, you haven't bought anything. While corporations may have the potential for better incentive systems than public and nonprofit agencies, they often squander the opportunity.

Often the most powerful rewards are nonfinancial—recognition, the opportunity to participate and be challenged, and the sense of doing important work. These rewards are at least as available in the public and social sector as in the private sector. In fact, very dedicated career people are often found in public sector organizations, even though they're seldom well paid. If it's clear that they're doing important work—in public policy, health, education, or housing—they find it's a lot easier to galvanize people around goals than if they're just making money for shareholders.

Defining Empowerment Correctly

To develop effective leaders is also to understand that leaders cannot act alone. As we move to more complex and collaborative structures, people become more interdependent. With downsizing there are likely to be fewer people in any one location; with globalization organizations are more spread out. You need more, not fewer, people to do a job—but they may not be on your payroll. Old norms, such as pay systems that reward managers for having more staff, will not work. So how do you manage these new-look organizations?

There is no one right answer; there are just more ways than ever of getting work done. Even in today's fast-changing, networked organization, the basic needs don't necessarily change. Somebody has to organize the enterprise, somebody has to plan it, somebody has to control it. Organizations still have to interact with the community. Leaders are connected; they make decisions more participatively. But even in collaborative senior executive teams, there will always be a leader and decisions that are his or hers to make.

At GE, today's realities led Welch to articulate a new corporate culture based on empowerment, accountability, and boundarylessness—in effect, to "order" a more empowered culture. The seeming paradox of "empowerment by executive edict" can incite cynicism and confuse constituents. It's an unnecessary confusion.

For instance, I have a seat on the corporate executive council. Do I feel empowered? Yes. Do I make major decisions on my own? Yes. Am I equal to the chairman? Of course not. Does this bother me? No. I accept the Japanese version of empowerment: "You outrank me, yet you have chosen to listen to my views. I am honored."

(The American version is, "If you aren't going to take my advice, why the hell did you ask me?")

Empowerment is simply having a voice: we expect the chairman to get our views; we don't expect to be his equal in corporate governance.

With that understanding, GE's managers must also learn to manage dialogue and conflict. In high-performance organizations you can never sell the soft stuff on its own merits. You have to make the connection to the bottom line. So we teach group facilitation skills as a productivity tool. Our executives learn the saying, "If you're not taking flak, you're not over the target." If you're serious about a quality revolution, or a customer service revolution, you have to go back to the history books. Do you know any revolution where nobody got upset? If everybody's on board, you're having a bad revolution. You have to teach that. You don't want total buy-in. The only way you'll ever get total buy-in is if nobody thinks he is going to have to change his behavior.

Conflict, however, just like any key business process, has to be managed. You can do that in three ways:

1. *Acknowledge its importance.* Don't worry that your people are upset with each other—they're supposed to be. That's what it's like to manage change.

2. *Do not tolerate personal attacks.* There are protocols for the expression of honest disagreement. Teach them.

3. *Provide support.* We have trained coaches and facilitators on staff, and our businesses seek out these people. They'll say, "We're planning a meeting; it could get hairy. Let's get a good process coach to lead us."

Building a Culture of Change

To be an effective leader, one must be an effective change agent. It's hard to imagine any change effort succeeding without those at the top providing the impetus and the support. They're the most visible people in an organization; they enjoy more authority and possess more resources to accomplish the task.

Every leader must understand the tools for managing change and give his or her people access to those tools. At GE, for example, one of Welch's first moves was to require that senior people in the company attend a seven-day executive development program. It was a crash course in theory and techniques for leading change, and it helped answer some critical questions: How do you mobilize people's commitment? How do you shape a vision? How do you monitor progress? How do you realign your reward and measurement systems to support change?

Required Reading for Leaders

Each year, hundreds of books are published on change, motivation, and leadership, but true management classics are hard to find. Following are a few titles by which to set your compass.

Beyond Certainty, by Charles Handy (Harvard Business Press, $19.95). A collection of brilliantly conceived, beautifully written essays. These thirty-five pieces comprise the essential ideas of one of the world's great thinkers.

The Boundaryless Organization, by Ron Ashkenas, Dave Ulrich, Todd Jick, and Steve Kerr (Jossey-Bass, $28.50). A thoughtful and practical guide to removing obstacles—up and down the hierarchy and across organizational and geographical boundaries.

Control Your Destiny or Someone Else Will, by Noel Tichy and Stratford Sherman (Harper Business, $13). The inside story of Jack Welch's celebrated makeover of General Electric. Tichy's appended "Handbook for Revolutionaries" provides useful assessment tools for applying a radical change.

The Leader of the Future, edited by Frances Hesselbein, Marshall Goldsmith, and Richard Beckhard (Jossey-Bass, $25). The first in the Future Series by the Drucker Foundation. Thirty-seven world-class authors, consultants, and executives offer unique perspectives on the challenges facing today's leaders.

There is a large body of resources that can help answer those questions, and leaders must be as conversant with it as they are with the theories of finance, marketing, and strategic development (see box).

Another essential tool for promoting personal leadership and organizational change is a tolerance for failure. The most powerful way that any culture communicates its attitudes is in how it treats mistakes. If you're making changes, you're sure to get some of them wrong. If you treat this as a major tragedy and never let anyone forget

---

Leadership Is an Art, by Max De Pree (Dell, $12.95). A deceptively simple and truly uplifting volume. De Pree offers probing, personal, and seldom-asked questions and their answers. "The first responsibility of a leader," he says, "is to define reality. The last is to say thank you. In between the two, the leader must become a servant and a debtor."

Out of Control, by Kevin Kelly (Addison-Wesley, $16). A genuinely original worldview from the executive editor of *Wired* magazine. As biological, organizational, and technological systems come to resemble one another more and more, loss of control counts as a blessing—given the creativity, energy, and adaptability that goes with it.

On Becoming a Leader, by Warren Bennis (Addison-Wesley, $13). A pioneering work based on profiles of more than two dozen leaders in business, media and the arts, and nonprofit organizations. Bennis concludes that everyone has the capacity to lead, and provides wise guidance on how to achieve that potential.

Taking Charge of Change, by Douglas K. Smith (Addison-Wesley, $25). The best book on change management in current release. Smith combines a sweeping view of organizational behavior with a concrete agenda for overcoming the obstacles that doom most change efforts.

it, you will have very change-resistant people. So, first you must give people the tools. Second, don't punish failure; learn from it and move on. And third, remember the saying, "People don't resist change; they resist being changed." If it's done to you, you're going resist it. If it's done by you, you won't. For leaders, that means giving people a sense of inclusion, helping them understand why change is necessary, and helping them shape the direction of change in their own businesses or departments.

Central to the values at GE is a mandate to relish change, to understand that the future is bound to be different from the present. In times past, GE was world-renowned as a model of centralized planning. But today GE does surprisingly little centralized planning for a company its size. The reason is that the future's coming so fast, we can't possibly predict it; we can only learn to respond quickly. So you have to find ways to measure responsiveness to change. If you're managing products, for example, there are hard measures of change, such as the "vitality index," which asks, What percentage of your product line was not in existence two or three years ago?

But you can also look at process change. That means examining not simply what you're making but also how you're making it. Businesses that are receptive to change will always be looking at new ways of doing things, not just measuring output. They are always monitoring, testing, and learning from the environment, and looking for indicators of change. Do you have networks? Do you have consortia? Do you routinely benchmark against other organizations to develop new measures of performance? Are you structured to operate more flexibly? These things are not necessarily proof that you are changing, but if you're not doing them, you're probably not changing.

Watching for Pitfalls

Any organization that is trying to build an effective leadership is likely to encounter three pitfalls. Pitfall No. 1 is failing to recognize that you are working with people who have already accomplished a lot, often on their own. High achievers tend to be mavericks. They're not patient people. Americans measure and reward individually—we underuse group measures just as the Japanese overuse them. So it's important to understand that achievers didn't necessarily get where they are by being patient, by being good team players, by being great listeners.

Given the nature of high performers, Pitfall No. 2 is not having tests to ensure that the people who get to the top are capable of managing in a collaborative way. At GE, it used to be that if you made your numbers, you got promoted. But in 1992 Welch said, if you don't have the right values, even if you make the numbers, you're not going to get promoted. To test for values, you can't leave performance measurement solely to the boss. It's important to do 360-degree appraisals, because colleagues usually know a lot about each other but seldom get a chance to tell.

Pitfall No. 3 is asking those around you to "be like me." People tend to gravitate toward those with whom they feel comfortable. Philip Wrigley, the longtime owner of the Chicago Cubs, once said that when two people in a business always agree, one of them is unnecessary. Rather than looking for people who always give assent, you have to look for what the situation requires. General Patton may be good at storming Berlin, but if you are smart you know that the person you need by your side on a daily basis is not a General Patton but someone who can make sure the food's coming, the supplies are coming, and the troops are being supported.

There's still a lot of work to be done in the training and development of our leaders. You have fewer managers in a downsized world, but the role of leadership doesn't go away. Training people to be leaders includes training people who don't have the formal title of manager. The old, elitist standards reserve leadership development for those already at or near the top. If you operate according to these outmoded standards, the people who might really be able to move the organization forward will not have been taught the skills they need to do so.

24 JIM COLLINS

ALIGNING ACTION AND VALUES

Jim Collins is a management educator, and coauthor with Jerry Porras of Built to Last: Successful Habits of Visionary Companies. *He has taught and consulted with more than one hundred corporations and nonprofit organizations.*

Executives spend too much time drafting, wordsmithing, and redrafting vision statements, mission statements, values statements, purpose statements, aspiration statements, and so on. They spend nowhere near enough time trying to align their organizations with the values and visions already in place.

Studying and working closely with some of the world's most visionary organizations has made it clear to me that these organizations concentrate primarily on the process of alignment, not on crafting the perfect statement. Not that it is a waste of time to think through fundamental questions like, What are our core values? What is our fundamental reason for existence? What do we aspire to achieve and become? Indeed, these are very important questions—questions that get at the "vision" of the organization.

Yet vision is one of the least understood—and most overused—terms in the language. Vision is simply a combination of three basic elements: (1) an organization's fundamental reason for existence beyond just making money (often called its mission or purpose); (2) its timeless, unchanging core values; and (3) huge and audacious—but ultimately achievable—aspirations for its own future (I like to call these BHAGs, for "big hairy audacious goals"). Of these elements, the most important to great, enduring organizations are their core values.

Okay, all fine and good to understand the basic concept of vision. But there is a big difference between being an organization with a vision statement and becoming a truly visionary organization. The difference lies in creating alignment—to preserve an organization's core values, to reinforce its purpose, and to stimulate continued progress toward its aspirations. When you have superb alignment, a visitor could drop into your organization from another planet and infer the vision without having to read it on paper.

In fact, the founders of great, enduring organizations like Hewlett Packard, 3M, and Johnson & Johnson often did not have a vision statement when they started out. They usually began with a set of strong personal core values and a relentless drive for progress, and had—most important—a remarkable ability to translate these into concrete mechanisms. 3M, for instance, has always had a sense of its core values—sponsoring innovation, protecting the creative individual, solving problems in a way that makes people's lives better. These values have defined the organization and given it a soul. But what has really set 3M apart has been the ability of its leadership over the years to create mechanisms that bring these principles to life and translate them into action. For example, 3M allows scientists to spend 15 percent of their time working on whatever interests them, requires divisions to generate 30 percent of their revenues from new products introduced in the past four years, has an active internal venture capital fund to support promising new ventures, preserves a dual-career track to encourage innovators to remain innovators rather than become managers, grants prestigious awards for innovations and entrepreneurial success, and so on. I don't even know if 3M has a formal "values statement" (if it does, we never came across it in all of our research into 3M), but because of its alignments, I know—with absolute clarity—3M's core values, as does anyone familiar with the organization and how it operates.

Creating alignment is a two-part process. The first part is identifying and correcting misalignments. The second part is creating new alignments, or what I call "mechanisms with teeth." I'm going to discuss the process as it applies primarily to core values, but the same basic process applies to creating alignment with purpose and BHAGs.

Identifying and Correcting Misalignments

Identifying misalignments means looking around the organization, talking to people, getting input, and asking, "If these are our core values and this is fundamentally why we exist, what are the obstacles that get in our way?" For instance, many organizations say they respect and trust their people to do the right thing, but they undermine that statement by doing X, Y, and Z. The misalignments exist not because the statements are false: these companies believe what they say. The misalignments occur because years of ad hoc policies and practices have become institutionalized and have obscured the firm's underlying values. For example, say an organization launches a new service without coordinating its internal processes, creating problems for customers. To make sure it doesn't happen again, managers institute a sign-off process for each new service that's introduced. The policy remains embedded in operations long after people have forgotten why it was created. At some point, people in the organization begin to grumble about the organization's elaborate sign-off process, recognizing its inconsistency with the notion of respect and trust for the individual. The first task for leaders, then, is to create an environment and a process that enable people to safely identify and eliminate these misalignments.

I recommend working collaboratively with people throughout the organization. Ask each individual to identify something in his or her daily work that is inconsistent with the organization's core values. Randomly sort the individuals into groups of three to six and ask each group to come up with the three most significant misalignments pertaining to each core value.

Let's say you had twenty-four people involved—four groups of six. Each of the four groups comes up with three misalignments for each core value. Lo and behold—what do you find? Typically each group has identified the same misalignments. This process allows your organization to identify quickly—without pointing fingers—the four or five most significant misalignments. Once you've agreed that the emperor has no clothes, you can begin to dress him.

Creating New Alignments

It's one thing to eliminate misalignments that exist but shouldn't. It's another to create something that doesn't yet exist but ought to. Just being consistent is not enough. True alignment means being creatively compulsive. It means going over the top. Consider, for example, Granite Rock Company, a small construction-materials outfit that won the Baldrige Award in 1992. The company espouses continuous improvement in customer satisfaction. They tell their customers, "If there's anything about an order you don't like, simply don't pay us for it. Deduct that amount from the invoice and send us a check for the balance." They call it shortpay; I call it a thorn in the laurel, or a mechanism with teeth. While many successful organizations rest on their laurels, Granite Rock does the opposite. They have devised a system that makes it difficult if not impossible to become complacent about continuously improving customer satisfaction. Would Granite Rock be inconsistent without shortpay? No, but telling customers, "If there's anything you don't like, don't pay for it," goes way beyond what other organizations normally do.

Likewise, 3M could simply say, "We don't get in the way of innovators." Fine. But that's very different from creating mechanisms—like requiring that 30 percent of revenues be generated by new products—that actually stimulate innovation. By instituting these reinforcement mechanisms, Granite Rock and 3M bring their values to life.

To take another example, it's easy to say, "We ought to do more training of new people when they come in the door so they'll learn our value system." But that's not creating alignment. Alignment would be to enact a process in which "within their first forty-eight hours on the job all new employees will go through an eight-hour orientation process to learn what this organization is about. They'll study its history and philosophy. They'll meet with a senior executive." That's concrete and specific—two requirements of an effective alignment mechanism. It also has teeth.

Suppose one of your core values is encouraging employee participation and creativity, and therefore you want to encourage input and ideas from people throughout your organization. So you create a suggestion box. Is that alignment? Yes, it is an alignment mechanism; but to make it an effective mechanism, you must take the concept much further. Instead of sticking a suggestion box off by itself in some hallway, consider putting suggestion boxes in every hallway, corridor, conference room, and lunch room—anywhere people might be when they get an idea. And don't stop there. Add the commitment that every submission, anonymous or signed, will be responded to publicly within forty-eight hours in the form of a statement specifying what will be done and who is responsible for getting it done. And beyond that, perhaps give recognition, prizes, or bonuses for the best ideas and suggestions, or even give "thanks for the input" prizes randomly to a subset of all suggestions, no matter how valuable. Now, that's alignment.

Identifying Core Values

In describing the alignment process, I have assumed that your organization's core values are already clearly defined—a big assumption. Let me make a few points about identifying core values, for without this stake firmly in the ground, there can be no effective alignment.

First, you cannot "set" organizational values, you can only discover them. Nor can you "install" new core values into people. Core values are not something people buy into. People must be predisposed to holding them. Executives often ask me, "How do we get people to share our core values?" You don't. Instead, the task is to find people who are already predisposed to sharing your core values. You must attract and then retain these people and let those who aren't predisposed to sharing your core values go elsewhere.

I've never encountered an organization, even a global organization composed of people from widely diverse cultures, that could not identify a set of shared values. The key is to start with the individual and proceed to the organization. One way to identify your organization's authentic core values is to form what I call the Mars group. Imagine you've been asked to recreate the very best attributes of your organization on another planet, but you only have seats on the rocketship for five to seven people. Who would you send? They are the people who probably have a gut-level understanding of your core values, who have the highest level of credibility with their peers, and who demonstrate the highest levels of competence. I'll often ask a group of fifty or sixty people to nominate a Mars group of five to seven individuals. Invariably they end up selecting a powerful, credible group that does a super job of articulating the core values precisely because they are exemplars of those values. One caveat: top management has to be confident enough to trust the Mars group to do its work. In my experience, those executives who are willing to take this risk find that the group identifies organic values that the executive was tempted to impose from above. This experience in itself strengthens the manager's belief in the core nature of the values.

The Mars group should wrestle with certain basic questions:

What core values do you bring to your work—values you hold to be so fundamental that you would hold them regardless of whether or not they were rewarded?

How would you describe to your loved ones the core values you stand for in your work and that you hope they stand for in their working lives?

If you awoke tomorrow morning with enough money to retire for the rest of your life, would you continue to hold on to these core values?

Perhaps most important, can you envision these values being as valid one hundred years from now as they are today?

Would you want the organization to continue to hold these values, even if at some point one or more of them became a competitive disadvantage?

If you were to start a new organization tomorrow in a different line of work, what core values would you build into the new organization regardless of its activities?

The last three questions are key because they help groups make a crucial distinction: core values are timeless and do not change, while practices and strategies should be changing all the time.

Distinguishing Between Values, Practices, and Strategies

Every institution—whether for-profit or not—has to wrestle with a vexing question: What should change and what should never change? It's a matter of distinguishing timeless core values from operating practices and cultural norms.

Timeless core values should never change; operating practices and cultural norms should never stop changing. A timeless core value in an academic institution, for instance, is freedom of intellectual inquiry. A practice adopted to support that core value is academic tenure. But there's a lot of evidence to suggest that the practice of tenure probably needs to be changed or discarded because it no longer serves the purposes for which it was created.

But if I suggest that academic institutions should seriously think about changing the tenure system, the average academic is likely to say, "Never! You're violating our core values." But that protest arises from a failure to distinguish between values and practices. The core value is freedom of inquiry; tenure is a practice. Frequently institutions cling doggedly to practices that are in truth nothing more than familiar habits. As a result, they fail to change things that ought to change. And by defending outmoded practices under the banner of core values, they might actually be betraying their true core values.

Your core values and purpose, if properly conceived, remain fixed. Everything else—your practices, strategies, structures, systems, policies, and procedures—should be open for change. The confusion between timeless and temporal concepts shows up in every walk of life. On a national level, for instance, the president of the United States says, "We can't touch Medicaid in its current form because that would be inconsistent with the core values of the nation." But if you pull out the Declaration of Independence and the Gettysburg Address—the two great statements of what we stand for and why we exist—you won't see anything about Medicaid in either of them. That kind of obfuscation—intentional or not and from either side of the aisle—inhibits debate, let alone change.

How to Spend Your Next Off-Site Retreat

More often than not, off-site retreats for the executive team or for large numbers of managers and staff are a wasted opportunity. Yes, you need time away from the office for many reasons. But most organizations spend it the wrong way.

To stop everything while you spend days drafting and revising a values statement is not the most effective use of time—especially if people come back the next year and do the whole process again. Instead, get together and ask, How are our alignments working? What progress are we making on eliminating our misalignments?

Do we need to adjust what we decided to do last year? It becomes an ongoing process. Your values are a fixed stake in the ground. You get it right once, and the rest of the work consists of tinkering with the organization.

Typically, executives devote a tiny percentage of their time and effort to gaining understanding, a tiny percentage to creating alignment, and the vast majority to documenting and writing a statement. In fact, the distribution of time and effort should be nearly the opposite (see Figure 24.1). You should spend a significant percentage of time actually trying to gain understanding, a tiny percentage documenting that understanding, and the vast majority of your time creating alignment. In short, worry about what you do as an organization, not about what you say.

Figure 24.1. Allocation of Time for Creating Alignment.

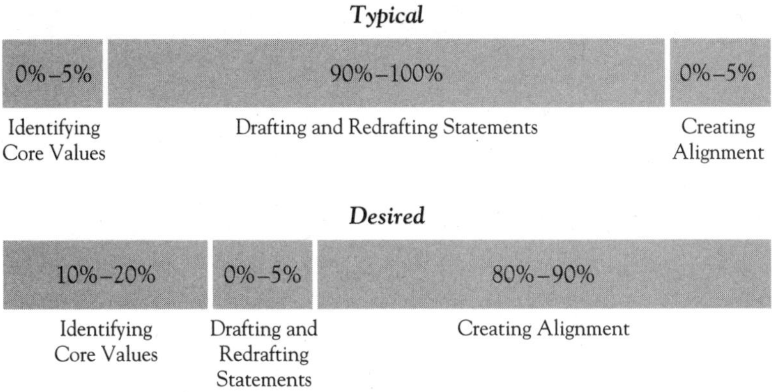

Typical

0%–5%	90%–100%	0%–5%
Identifying Core Values	Drafting and Redrafting Statements	Creating Alignment

Desired

10%–20%	0%–5%	80%–90%
Identifying Core Values	Drafting and Redrafting Statements	Creating Alignment

25 CHARLOTTE BEERS

BUILDING COMPANIES WORTHY OF DEVOTION

Charlotte Beers is chairman emeritus of Ogilvy & Mather. Since she joined the advertising agency as chairman and CEO in 1992, its billings have grown to $7.6 billion from $5.5 billion, and the firm has regained its luster as one of the premier ad agencies in the world. Beers has led a successful reorganization of O&M and has overseen the development of landmark ad campaigns for such clients as IBM, American Express, Sears, Shell, and Ford.

Just a few years ago the business press was trumpeting the end of brands. Everything was becoming a commodity, we were told; brand loyalty was dead. Today we know that brand identity is a company's most powerful and unique asset—one of the few things that cannot be easily copied. Hundreds of brand names are dominating their markets around the world, and growing wildly.

But don't be too quick to assume that brand managers know how to manage brands. Many business practitioners have missed the same boat as the business writers—and are diminishing their brands in the very act of marketing them. The truth is, what makes a brand powerful is the emotional involvement of customers. The ongoing customer relationships that define every great brand are possible only because customers value such relationships. They invest themselves in the goods and services they buy and have a personal stake in their success. In short, people who buy a brand have made a choice, and choice confers power on the chosen. Organizations that use that power wisely will prosper in the years ahead.

Of course, not every product enjoys such stature. Customers are motivated by many things: loyalty, comfort, amusement, style, or image. Many buyers are indifferent to the allure of a brand name, and indifference means you still have a product; you just are not yet a brand. Whether a consumer goods maker, a financial service provider, or a charity, you cannot become a brand until your customers share a history, attitude, or emotion with you. The challenge for leaders, then, is twofold: to provide long-term brand stewardship and to build a genuine organizational vision that inspires employees as well as customers.

Traditional research techniques that drive most marketing and advertising campaigns overlook the emotional richness of customer relationships and therefore tell you little about how to gain lasting competitive advantage. By relying too much on hard data and current market trends (which are seldom current by the time they are identified), decision makers miss what's most important. Remember, all products are becoming better all the time—but not necessarily better than one another. Is Toyota better than Honda? Hard to say. Both companies build a good, reliable car, but neither conveys a keen understanding of how its product fits the customer's life or lifestyle. What you offer—features, benefits, value—is one thing; how your users feel about it is another, far bigger, question.

Too often companies undermine the emotional relationship they have with customers. They introduce line extensions that trade on a great name, but that may also dilute its power, blur its image, or worst of all, erode customers' trust. They make important strategic decisions—entering a new market, repositioning themselves, redesigning a product—with little regard for customer perceptions or the iconic power of their brand. Remember New Improved Coke?

Measuring Emotional Content

By conducting a brand audit, you can uncover such intangibles as, What things—images, songs, emotions—trigger thoughts of your brand? How do you feel when you use the brand? and What stories or memories do you associate with this brand?

These questions are ultimately meant for consumers, but you first want to know how the CEO and senior management team answer them—because that's how they are going to make decisions about the brand. You then conduct a reliable sample of one-on-one customer interviews. You listen with an ear toward the intangible. You record verbatim comments, not multiple-choice checkoffs, and those comments must be read by the people who are actually interpreting the data. Despite the inevitable regional or demographic differences you find in people's responses, you also find common themes. Feelings and beliefs cross borders more readily than preferences for flavor or color. If you talk to enough people, you get rich and statistically valid data, and out of that data you make an intuitive leap. That is where the creative process starts.

You can then reposition a product or launch a new offering with a fully developed personality that is capable of building a relationship. For instance, to launch a new car in Europe called Ka, Ford developed an attitude about it and gave it a place in the world. They put the car in fashion shows. They created a philanthropic fund, the Ka Fund, for young artists. The car was young, spirited. It had an air of confidence. The product itself was innovative in many ways, but products can be quickly copied. The totality of what that product represents to people cannot, and that is what builds a brand franchise.

Building a Vision

To win the devotion of customers, leaders must build an organization worthy of that devotion. You cannot win the hearts of customers unless you have a heart yourself. Yet far too many organizations lack that essential zest. They suffer what I call heart failure. The disease has many symptoms:

- Key managers have different versions of the company's strategy, mission, or strength.

- Employees don't know what the company stands for.

- Recognition, promotions, and everyday actions show a bias against mavericks and risk takers.

- Communications within and outside the organization are marked by dry, dull, and sober language.

- Political infighting and fiefdoms prevail.

- Customer and employee feedback reveals a gap between the company's intentions and constituents' perceptions.

Organizations with heart are clear about their vision. They know how to articulate it, how to use their vision to lift spirits, build inspiration, and make tough decisions. They deliver on their promises. They never claim that employees are their greatest asset unless that claim is obvious to anyone who walks through the door. They project a strong sense of who they are as an organization. Their corporate or image advertising reflects the fullness of the company's identity and yet makes a provocative statement. It not only defines the brand for customers but also lifts the spirits of employees. That is rare in companies, which is why corporate advertising is so often bland and generic.

It is the leader's job to define what you do, why you exist, and how you judge success. The leader and the senior team have to articulate the spiritual side of their vision as well as the material side. They understand people's innate desire to have an affiliation, an emotional connection, and they make that connection with employees as well as customers. Any CEO who cannot clearly articulate the intangible assets of his brand and understand its connection to customers is in trouble. When Ray Kroc reinvented McDonald's, for instance, he had a bone-deep understanding of his company's persona, down to the stripes on the straw. It's a rare quality. You see it in the bold strokes, the single-mindedness of leaders who want to change the world. Bill Gates's goal of "a computer on every desk," for instance, is pure inspiration, and is still a powerful driver of his company, Microsoft.

When an organization matures and loses the zeal of its founders, it usually needs new leadership to rekindle that spark. Discovering the heart of an established organization is a learned art, not a mystical insight.

If you're a change agent, you have to be a missionary for that idea, every day of your life. Not everyone will agree with your analysis or decisions—which is why you need the conviction, passion, and vision to drive your message home to colleagues and customers.

Customers as Allies

If you have both a strong brand and an organizational heart, customers will let you fix almost any problems that arise. That reservoir of goodwill, inside and outside the company, is a leader's greatest ally. Even when the company stumbles, if you've built a relationship with customers, they will give you time to get on track. When American Express, for example, was losing market share to Visa and MasterCard and the other major credit cards a few years ago, the company discovered that its customers' sense of history and membership in the company provided a touchstone for renewing the relationship. In surveys customers fondly described getting their first American Express card, or using its services while traveling overseas. By drawing on that reserve of loyalty and goodwill, American Express bought time to sharpen its focus, reinvigorate its products, and reconnect with customers. Today the company is again growing market share and profitability.

Maintaining a brand identity requires a special vocabulary—fresh, honest, and unique language—in annual reports, company meetings, and messages to customers and the community. The dead language, jargon, and double-talk characteristic of so much business communication is a symptom of heart failure. It betrays a habitual concern with the internal workings of the enterprise rather than with the needs and wants of the customer. Despite all the marketing talk about "owning" customers, for instance, most of the attempts to do that are mechanistic and impersonal—sending customers a letter every six months or enrolling them in a frequent buyers' program. What you need to do is not just own customers but understand them, even love them and learn from them. Only if you really know the people who use your products can you win a place, respectfully and affectionately, in their lives. It takes good research, constant dialogue, careful listening, and passionate devotion to a cause.

Organizations that earn a place in the hearts of customers don't rest on their laurels, or on tradition. Neither should you as a leader. In setting strategy, for example, you value provocative disruption more than superficial harmony. You never take "that's not the way we do things" as an answer. You look for ways to be faster, smarter, and more agile, and you establish the new "way we do things." You have fewer hushed meetings in the hallway and more open, honest dialogue. In a state of change, you do not wait for consensus; you get a core group of supporters and you move. You make tough decisions, take your case to your customers or constituents, and generate enthusiasm for your ideas. By taking initiative and showing results, you win over the fence sitters—or at some point you suggest that they may be happier elsewhere. You understand that consensus is no substitute for leadership.

If you really understand the dynamic between the product and the user, your chances of misreading your place in the market are very low. You may learn, for instance, that you have no reputation or loyalty or friendship with the customer, in which case you move on to the next product, or you begin the long and expensive process of building that relationship. You may not have the resources to nurture customers; you may not have time or the will. Your products may still have a viable future, but they're not going to be a long-lived brand. Every generic product will eventually become vulnerable if any competitor wants a piece of the market.

The irony is that the death knell of brands was sounded largely by marketers themselves, who resorted to sales promotion and volume discounts instead of brand-building tactics. Little of it has worked. As markets become more crowded, price is the least effective way to distinguish yourself for the long term. But if you take the time to understand, respect, and cater to your customers, you're going to stand out from the crowd, become a part of people's lives, and maybe even do some good.

26 NOEL TICHY

THE MARK OF A WINNER

Noel Tichy is professor of organizational behavior and human resource management at the University of Michigan, and director of the Global Leadership Program, an executive-development consortium of thirty-six companies. He consults to corporations around the world and is author of numerous articles and books, including The Leadership Engine, *written with Eli Cohen.*

What separates winning organizations from the also-rans? I have spent twenty-five years studying both winners and losers from the inside out for an answer. Not surprisingly, winning organizations share certain financial attributes. Companies consistently ranked in the top quartile of the Standard & Poor's 500 maintain annual revenue growth of 12 percent and a 16 percent operating return on assets, according to Columbia University Business School professor Larry Selden. In contrast, gains achieved by simply slashing payroll and expense are seldom sustained in the long run. Likewise, erstwhile winners who fail to keep pace with change and thereby destroy billions of dollars in shareholder value are severely punished (witness John Akers of IBM, Bob Stempel of GM, James

Robinson of American Express, and Kay Whitmore of Kodak). The early 1990s were a watershed time in business when these and other corporate leaders were sent home for poor leadership.

At the same time, several companies have been setting new records for financial performance, enriching shareholders, building communities, and providing greater opportunities for employees. Companies such as General Electric, AlliedSignal, PepsiCo, Intel, and others are led by men and women who personally and methodically nurture the development of other leaders, at all levels of the organization. Even if you, as a leader, are smart enough to anticipate and prepare for massive economic and social shifts, you cannot respond to the ground-level demands of the moment without the energy, commitment, and ability of people throughout the organization. Effective leaders recognize that the ultimate test of leadership is *sustained* success, which demands the constant cultivation of future leaders.

This has important implications for the work you do every day. For one thing, all the money your organization invests in "leadership development"—usually the province of outside trainers and consultants—means little without an equal investment of your own time and effort. Yet the benefits of investing your time will accrue to you as well as to your organization.

If long-term success requires having more leaders at more levels than your competitors have, then teaching, coaching, and cultivating others becomes a strategic imperative for senior executives. For example, during the first eighteen months of his tenure as CEO of AlliedSignal, Larry Bossidy put all 86,000 employees through a development program he helped design. He spoke to 15,000 people the first year—presenting his vision, explaining markets and strategies, engaging in debate—in short, teaching. In the process he helped increase the market value of his company 400 percent in six years. Likewise Andy Grove at Intel, Jack Welch at GE, Gary Wendt at GE Capital, Roger Enrico at PepsiCo, Lew Platt at Hewlett Packard, Bill Pollard at ServiceMaster, and hundreds of other business, community, military, and religious leaders understand that their success depends on others, and that leading and teaching are inextricable. They spend hundreds of hours a year working with their colleagues—sometimes just five or ten at time—to share ideas, identify needs, and develop hands-on business expertise.

Three Keys for Leading

The ability to develop the leadership of others requires three things: a teachable point of view, a story for your organization, and a well-defined methodology for teaching and coaching.

Teachable Point of View

To succeed as a leader you must be able to articulate a defining position for your organization. You must be able to talk clearly and convincingly about who you are, why you exist, and how you operate. This means you need to have ideas on products, services, distribution channels, customers, and growth. These ideas need to be supported by a value system that you articulate, exemplify, and enforce.

But you also need something I call *e-cubed:* emotional energy and edge. Winning leaders seem naturally to generate positive emotional energy in others. They also have the edge to face reality and make tough yes or no decisions. That is their unique burden—not to call in consultants or convene a task force, but at crucial moments, when forced to act quickly, to make the difficult choices only they can make. It often makes them the most unpopular people in their organizations, which is why those who need to be liked are seldom effective leaders—at least not during times of crisis. But leadership is the ability to see things as they really are *and* to mobilize an appropriate response. You can make those decisions and engender that response only if you have clear ideas and values. All three components of leadership—good ideas, appropriate values, and positive energy and edge—are part of the package you present to those you hope to develop. How you apply these essential elements of leadership has changed in important ways in recent years (see Table 26.1).

Living Stories

The basic cognitive form in which people organize their thinking is the narrative story. Individuals, families, organizations, communities, and nations all have tales that help make sense of themselves and the world. There are three kinds of stories that leaders can tell. There's the "who I am" story in which leaders describe themselves. The late Roberto Goizueta, as chairman and CEO of the Coca-Cola Company, often talked about his early experiences: being forced to leave Castro's Cuba and start over in a new country with $40 in cash and a hundred shares of Coca-Cola stock. He told stories of how as a young boy he would spend days reading and talking with his grandfather, Marcelo, who had founded a sugar and real estate empire. Marcelo's lessons on the importance of cash and simplicity, among other virtues, still guided Goizueta decades later. "I am a great believer in cash flow," he said. "Earnings is a man-made convention, but cash is cash. The larger the company is, the less it understands cash flow."

There's the "who we are" story, in which you articulate for your constituents what their identity is. Chairman and CEO Phil Knight's stories at Nike are all about winning. He named the company after the Greek goddess of victory. He uses his stories of competing as a runner to explain the thrill of competition and winning. Nike is not a company to him. It is a vehicle for furthering the aspirations of customers, both famous and unknown. His message—that every employee helps customers to be winners—helps to create an organization in which everyone knows what they are aiming for and what the company represents.

But the most important leadership tale is the "where we are going" story. Martin Luther King's "I Have a Dream" speech mobilized energy around powerful images of social equality—black and white children holding hands in a transformed world.

Winning business leaders use the power of storytelling as effectively as our most gifted public leaders. Goizueta increased the market value of his company thirtyfold in fifteen years; no business

Table 26.1. The New Way of Leadership.

Leaders of winning organizations use ideas, values, emotional energy, and edge to develop future leaders throughout the enterprise. Winning leaders combine a teachable point of view with a special focus on and personal role in the development of others. Here is how the new dimensions of leadership differ from the old.

	Old Way	New Way
Ideas	Coaching is on day-to-day problems rather than on larger business issues. Development programs are theoretical, based on cases taught by professors.	Coaching is based on the leader's own ideas, challenging people to create their own points of view. Development programs are practical, based on real business issues.
Values	Leaders proclaim organizational values, which are often superficial messages for the masses.	Leaders help people integrate their personal values with the values of the workplace—and explain the paradoxes when values collide.
Energy	Programs deliver a sugar high—by the time people return to work, it's gone.	"Programs" are ongoing—leaders teaching underlying frameworks for motivation.
Edge	Professional trainers focus on time management and priority setting, not on tough decision making.	Leaders themselves help people tackle such dilemmas as what to do with people who do not meet performance or values standards.
Leadership Focus	Leadership focuses on a collection of technical skills in strategy, finance, and so on.	Leadership focuses on hard and soft issues and on personal leadership stories.
Senior Executive Role	Senior executives sponsor development programs, parading in and out of them periodically.	Senior executives are active participants, leading all or substantial portions of leadership development programs.

leader in history has done a better job of growing shareholder value. Goizueta did this by hiring managers who are entrepreneurs and risk takers—and by finding a way to energize people about the story of the company. He reminded people that the human body requires sixty-four ounces of liquid each day and that on average Coke provides just two of those ounces. His message to the troops was clear: let's get going. Further, Goizueta put individual managers at the center of his stories. The best managers are those who walk into a building and see not where Coke is but where it isn't. It is this ability to find opportunity, he told his listeners, that will make the company a winner in the future.

Dramatic storytelling is the way people learn from, and connect with, one another. That is why CEOs—Bill Gates, Andy Grove, Bill Pollard—write books. It is more for the benefit of their constituents than for the general public.

Teaching Methodology

To be a great teacher you have to be a great learner. Most effective teachers—and leaders—will tell you that they grow as much as those they teach and lead. The process of teaching can be quite simple; it starts with having a conscious system for interacting with people. Jack Welch, for instance, spends a half-day every couple of weeks teaching, wrestling with issues, and challenging his people at Crotonville, GE's leadership development center. Rear Admiral Ray Smith visits graduating classes of the Navy SEAL underwater demolition programs, and participates in the same physical training as SEAL candidates half his age. Larry Bossidy writes two- or three-page letters to the heads of all AlliedSignal's businesses after every strategy session, operating review, and people review.

You must be methodical but not mechanical in your approach to teaching. To make a difference, you must have the self-confidence to be vulnerable to others; you need to share your mistakes and doubts as well as your accomplishments. When Roger Enrico, for instance, goes off-site with ten of his senior executives for five days, he's not afraid to reveal himself. He cannot hide behind his position. It's one thing for a CEO to come in, deliver a canned speech to a training class, and escape. You can't live with your troops off-site for five days, sixteen hours a day, and be anything but genuine. Phonies and martinets will be found out by the end of day one.

Learning to Teach

Articulating your ideas and values, developing a teachable point of view, and developing stories that bring your views to life are all learnable skills. For instance, in helping people I work with develop stories about their experiences, I often ask them to "think about a time in your life when you made something happen through other people that wouldn't have happened without you. Run the video of your life and pick the proudest moment you've had as a leader." It could be a church, community, athletic, or work activity, but I have yet to find somebody who doesn't have a proud moment. If you ask people to pair up and tell their story to someone else, and then talk about why it was an example of good leadership, they all uncover some basic tenets of leadership: "I had a vision. I persisted. I embodied in my own actions the message I was trying to create. I was able to enroll people. I fought through resistance." Implicitly we know what good leadership is, and people in all walks of life can become more motivated to work on leadership by remembering when they felt proud, when they'd been in a tough situation where they could lead.

If you ask me, however, as a coach, simply to repeat this exercise throughout your organization in lieu of you, the leader, sharing your own values, ideas, and stories with people, you are probably wasting their time and your money. Outside consultants—and I am one—are the last people who can develop the long-term leadership talent in your organization. That is the job of recognized leaders, with a proven record of success, who work with their colleagues every day.

The current conventional wisdom in leadership development programs is to develop a set of competencies for what a good leader is and then figure out a way to develop people around those competencies. At the end of the day the competencies that get developed in these programs look pretty similar—having integrity, building trust, demonstrating towering competence, knowing how to overcome resistance.... What's missing is the leaders themselves teaching colleagues, not leaving the teaching to others or talking about somebody else's values. People want their leader to look them in the eye and say, "Here is where our company is going and here is what we need from leaders in order to get there."

Practice What You Teach

The military has understood this for years. After the end of the Cold War, General Wayne Downing transformed the mission, training, and appraisal of the elite Special Operations Forces (SOF). He could change the mind-set of his troops from Rambo-like warrior to "quiet professional" because he had credibility. The credibility came from living his personal ideas and values (which he developed as an SOF officer in Vietnam) and bringing to life the story of where SOF was heading. Admiral Smith, in his mid-fifties, is out there the last week of SEAL training doing the physical training and explaining to recruits the importance of what they're doing. Religious institutions have been clear on this approach to pastoral training. Medical educators know that you cannot put a professor in the operating room to demonstrate surgical techniques. You need someone who has hands-on expertise, credibility, and a teachable point of view about how to develop others' capabilities. That doesn't mean there is no role for professors and consultants, but it does mean there is not a leading role for them.

When Andy Grove shares with new hires his ideas about where the industry is going, he is learning and teaching. The young engineers know far more then he does about some of the current technology. They have ideas that he has not even considered. By being in class with those new hires, he bypasses layers of hierarchy; the closer the hierarchy gets to him, the more it thinks like him. So Grove has developed his own pipeline to get new ideas. At the same time, Grove is teaching the engineers based on his experience of decades at Intel—both his successes and his failures. He is teaching the engineers about Intel and its industry so that they can channel their ideas. To spread learning throughout the organization, Grove asks other experienced managers to teach—and bases part of their bonus on whether or not they do.

Leaders of traditional, hierarchical organizations don't get these kind of opportunities. In short, to compete in the twenty-first century, leaders need to build not just a learning organization but a *teaching* organization—one with the capacity to build leaders. They need to create an environment where leaders are teaching leaders.

Making Training Pay

Most leadership training springs from the question, Are leaders born or made? and is designed to prove that the latter is the correct answer. It's an age-old and essentially pointless debate. It's like asking whether athletes are made or born. The answer is, obviously, both. With coaching, commitment, and hard work, there isn't any group of people who couldn't improve their ability to play tennis, golf, or basketball. There aren't many, however, who are going to be world-class performers. The same with leadership. Any organization that takes the time to get more leadership out of people is going to be far ahead of its competitors. Are all managers candidates for the top job? Of course not. But can they be a lot better than they are now? Absolutely. We can all hone our ideas and better articulate our values and improve our capacity for making yes-no decisions. So it's worth the effort to develop everybody.

Losing organizations make the mistake of handicapping their field of potential leaders and investing their training and development resources only in those they think will go furthest. Inevitably they pass over a lot of talent. Winning organizations often bet their hunches, too, but they typically wait longer to do it. They look at broad leadership skills, not just at success with particular projects. And most important, they continue to invest in the development of everyone else, including those they don't expect to rise to the top. Winning companies' more inclusive approach helps get the best out of everyone—and keeps late bloomers and mavericks contributing long after others might have written them off.

Leaders who invest themselves personally in the process of developing future leaders are also building the most precious of organizational assets. The long-term success of leaders cannot be measured by whether they win today or tomorrow. The measure of their success will be whether or not their company is still winning fifteen years from now, when a new generation of leaders has taken over.

27 BOB NELSON

CREATING AN ENERGIZED WORKPLACE

Bob Nelson is author of 1001 Ways to Energize Employees *and the best-selling* 1001 Ways to Reward Employees, *among other books and numerous articles. He is founder of Nelson Motivation Inc. in San Diego and speaks often on employee involvement and motivation.*

American management is discovering that the traditional methods of motivating employees—either with carrots (bonuses, raises, stock options) or with sticks (coercion, fear, firing)—no longer work. As Peter Drucker has observed, "Economic incentives are becoming rights rather than rewards. Merit raises are always introduced as rewards for exceptional performance. In no time at all they become a right.... The increasing demand for material rewards is rapidly destroying their usefulness as incentives and managerial tools." Negative management techniques are likewise becoming a less useful option. In our legalistic culture, firing an employee—or even giving an unflattering reference—is often an invitation to a lawsuit.

On the plus side, employee motivation may represent one of the last frontiers for organizational leverage. This is true for several reasons. The business environment has fundamentally changed. Years ago, disparities in technology, market access, and production capability separated businesses from one another. As we near the end of the millennium, however, the gaps that have separated companies—and countries—are shrinking dramatically. Today, most companies have access to the same technology, markets, methods of production, and channels of distribution. The result is that traditional measures of business performance such as return on investment (ROI) and return on assets (ROA) have less significance today than does return on people (ROP). When leaders look beyond purely financial yardsticks and measure their organization's productivity, responsiveness, innovation, and knowledge base, they are measuring their ROP. Increasingly, it's the ROP that provides the most significant competitive advantage.

With the shifting business environment, we are also seeing massive change in the global workforce—both in composition and attitude. Skilled, knowledgeable employees are becoming more difficult to find, manage, and motivate. The changing demographics of an aging, more diverse, and more demanding workforce are challenging the traditional notions of management and work itself. As a result of these changes, managers have essentially two approaches to increasing their ROP. They can try to squeeze more and more output from a less and less tractable workforce, or they can energize employees, encouraging them to better direct their own efforts. Given the realities of today's workplace, leaders have little choice.

The Limits of Management

Traditional management practices produce diminishing returns due to seven business trends:

- *The need for greater employee initiative.* Employees are increasingly being asked to be self-directed, autonomous, and responsible for their own work, acting in the best interests of their customers and employers.

- *The changing role of managers.* Managers have fewer ways to shape employee behavior—coercive and authoritarian behavior is no longer an option. To be effective, today's managers must create supportive work environments that can influence, but not ordain, desired behaviors and outcomes.
- *The impact of workplace technology.* Many workers now interact more closely with their computers than with their managers and colleagues. As author John Naisbitt observed, the more high-tech we become, the more "high-touch" we need to be in our professional relationships.
- *The increasing speed of business.* As the pace of business quickens, managers need consciously to make time to focus on people. Finding "quality time" is as great a challenge at work as it is at home.
- *The need to build trust after layoffs and downsizing.* Employees need to reconnect after layoffs or reorganizations to regain a sense of security, perspective, and grounding—and they need to reconnect mostly with their managers.
- *The growing need to have meaning in work.* Workers today struggle to achieve more balance between their jobs and family life, and they are demanding work environments that they find personally rewarding.
- *The need for low-cost options for motivating employees.* CEOs aside, most employees are not collecting huge bonuses or raises, even in good years. Fortunately, simple forms of recognition and praise have proven to be effective, low-cost means for influencing performance.

The New Work Environment

As old management styles focusing on tasks and procedures become less effective, leaders are learning to get results through people. Bill Hewlett, cofounder of Hewlett Packard, has observed, "Men and women want to do a good job, a creative job, and if they are provided the proper environment, they will do so." How does one create an energized organization? The experiences of hundreds of high-performing enterprises suggest that leaders must focus on five strategies:

1. Make Communication a Priority

Employees have a deep-rooted need to be informed about what's happening at all levels of their organization. Especially during times of turbulence—which today is almost a constant—employees need to know what changes are taking place, how the changes affect them, and the benefits of the changes to them and the organization. Not all employees will agree with every change, but they will feel more secure understanding them. You can no longer rely on the chain of command or a companywide memo to do the job for you. Instead, you must find new ways to connect with employees personally.

For example, Scott Mitchell, president of Mackay Envelope in Minneapolis, has a one-to-one, twenty-minute discussion with every employee about ideas, improvements, or whatever is on the employee's mind. Mitchell devotes more than 170 hours to this every year, which he says is time well spent.

Palmer Reynolds, CEO of Phoenix Textile Corporation, an institutional linens distributor in St. Louis, invites employees from each of the company's five departments to join her for breakfast every month. By getting to know her and one another, employees are often better able to work out problems. At one such breakfast, the sales department learned that the production department also had quotas to meet, ending a long-standing tug-of-war and helping the company grow revenues from $1.4 million to $24 million in just six years.

2. Develop a Sense of Ownership

To act like owners, employees need to be treated as owners. That is mostly a function of your attitude toward employees. People want a voice in the decisions that affect them and their jobs, and the means to act in the organization's best interest, on a daily basis.

Hundreds of companies also take employee ownership literally, through employee stock programs, with impressive results. Starbucks Coffee, for instance, offers full benefits and stock options to both full- and part-time employees. Senior managers conduct quarterly open forums where they discuss expansion plans and financial results and invite feedback. As a result, employee turnover at Starbucks is about one-quarter the industry average.

Other elements that create a sense of ownership include:

- Having an opportunity to develop an idea from concept to reality, as is a common practice at 3M Company

- Knowing how one's job relates to the products and services delivered to customers, and to the viability of the organization

- Understanding and identifying with the organization's mission and values

3. Establish an Improvement Orientation

Despite the lip service given to employee involvement, too many managers resist suggestions from the front line, perhaps because they feel threatened by workers entering what was once their domain. By contrast, Boardroom, Inc., publisher of Boardroom Reports and other business publications, encourages everyone to think about the way they work and how to do better. Founder and CEO Martin Edelston asks employees to contribute two ideas every week (versus the national average of one suggestion per seven employees per year). Simple suggestion forms are available at every meeting and at key spots throughout the office. Once a week the ideas are collected and assigned to a senior manager to review. Nominal cash rewards ($2 or $5) are distributed on the spot to idea contributors, and a monthly report on suggestions and their implementation is distributed to the entire staff. In one case, a shipping clerk noticed that trimming one-sixteenth of an inch from the pages of Boardroom's books would lower its postage costs—by $500,000 in the first year alone. That's return on people.

The point is not to look for home runs every time out but to build a culture of improvement. For Boardroom, paying minimal rewards is a way to focus employees on all opportunities for improvement, big or small, and to build cooperation by eliminating the fear of having one's idea stolen by a coworker.

For suggestion systems to be successful, leaders have to set the tone personally and hold their managers accountable for soliciting and implementing suggestions. Ron Kiripolsky, former president of a five-hundred-person division of PSA Airlines (now part of USAirways), used to empty the suggestion box every day, read each suggestion, and meet with the employees and their supervisors that same day to discuss the suggestions and work out implementation. (In PSA's case, the program may have worked too well; its efficient service and loyal customer base made it an attractive target for acquisition.)

4. Encourage Flexibility

Whereas yesterday's organizations typically were rigid, bureaucratic, and rule bound, today's successful competitors are flexible, fast, and dependent on their frontline employees to act independently in the best interests of the organization. Instead of depending on policies and procedures to force employees to do the right thing, smart organizations depend on them to do the right thing on their own.

When a subsidiary of candy maker Mars, Inc., headquartered in McLean, Virginia, replaced its inch-thick set of policies with a new five-page version, employee grievances plunged from average for the industry to just a trickle. At Sprint Corporation headquarters in Westwood, Kansas, employee teams visiting a nearby utility company to study its practices were shocked by its informal culture. When the Sprint teams asked about attendance policies and dress code, their host responded that its policies were "come to work," and "wear clothes." According to Sprint benchmarking manager

Jeff Amen, "We got the biggest whack on the side of our head by the answers to those two questions. We were surprised to discover their attendance policy was not twenty-eight pages like ours. We obviously had a long way to go to make it three words."

5. Make Recognition a Way of Life

Research tells us that you get what you reward. Although employee recognition is a commonsense notion, it is far from common practice. As Tom Peters has observed, "Our problem in the U.S. isn't overemphasis on incentives; it's that so few companies offer them at all."

Ironically, the most powerful forms of positive incentives are also the easiest and least expensive to do. In one recent study of more than fifteen hundred employees in a variety of work settings, Gerald Graham, professor of management at Wichita State University, found that the most powerful motivator was personal, instant recognition from managers. According to Graham, "Managers have found that simply asking for employee involvement is motivational in itself." In one of his studies, Graham determined that the most effective ways to motivate others include:

- Congratulating employees who do a good job
- Writing personal notes about good performance
- Publicly recognizing employees for good performance
- Celebrating group successes

Despite this fact, 58 percent of employees in the study report that they seldom if ever have been personally thanked by their managers for a job well done, and about 75 percent seldom if ever have received a positive note, a public acknowledgment, or group recognition from their managers. Is it any surprise that many employees today lack the motivation to be full contributors to their organizations?

No-Cost Ways to Energize Employees

Some of the most effective things you can do to develop and sustain motivated and energized employees cost nothing. They are a function of the daily interactions that you have with employees at work. Consider the power of "the five I's":

Interesting Work. Everyone should have at least a part of their job be of high interest to them. As management theorist Frederick Herzberg put it, "If you want someone to do a good job, give them a good job to do." Find out what tasks your employees most enjoy and use that information in future work assignments.

Information. More than ever, employees want to know how they are doing in their jobs and how the company is doing in its business. Open channels of communication to allow employees to be informed, ask questions, and share information.

Involvement. Involving employees in decision making, especially when the decisions affect them directly, is both respectful and practical. Those closest to the problem typically have the best insight as to what to do about it. As you involve others, you increase their commitment and ease in implementing new ideas or change.

Independence. Most employees appreciate having the flexibility to do their jobs as they see fit. Giving people latitude increases the chance that they will also perform as you desire—and bring additional initiative, ideas, and energy to their jobs.

Increased Visibility. Everyone appreciates getting credit when it is due. Occasions to share the successes of employees with others are almost limitless. Giving your employees new opportunities to perform, learn, and grow as a form of recognition and thanks is highly motivating for most people.

The Role of Leaders

Does your organization systematically "catch people doing something right"? Or are managers' interactions with employees mainly about mistakes, problems, and criticisms? If so, instead of nurturing employee initiative and inspiring people to be their best, you will only convince people to do what they're told—and no more.

Remember, too, that money is not the number one motivator. In dozens of studies, employees rarely rank money among the top five incentives. As Rosabeth Moss Kanter has noted, "Compensation is a right; recognition is a gift." CEOs sometimes describe the impact of small, public recognition on frontline employees. These stories—which usually involve an employee waiting years to be acknowledged—are meant to be heartwarming, but they are more often sad. That T-shirts and trinkets can mean so much reminds us how little it takes to honor hard work, and how rarely it is done.

These five energizing strategies are not in themselves a sure recipe for success; they embody a necessary attitude. You can dramatically improve your return on people by clearing the obstacles standing between employees and the organization's goals. To produce more results with fewer resources—as every enterprise must—effective competitors reward their people in creative and visible ways. For example:

- At American Express Travel Related Services, former president Lou Gerstner established a Great Performers program, which featured posters picturing employees, describing their accomplishments, and seeking award nominations from their peers. The nominated employees' initiatives led to new markets, products, and services that helped increase net income 500 percent in eleven years.

- An Amoco refinery in Texas City has saved $19 million in two years by publicly awarding idea suggesters with gift certificates during lunch breaks, thanking them on the plant's internal TV system and in local newspapers, and entering them monthly in an annual employee contest.

- American Airlines supports a seventy-person staff for its employee-suggestion program, which it considers as important as any program or service the company offers. It shares 10 percent of the first-year savings with the idea contributor. A few years ago, its "Help Us Buy an Airplane" campaign yielded one-year savings worth $50 million—enough, indeed, to buy a Boeing 757.

Now it's your turn. The old ways of motivating employees no longer work. Creating energized employees demands a new set of leadership priorities. By sharing information, control, and glory, you'll create an environment that allows employees to do their best work, and to achieve the best results for you—and them—in the process.

28 JEFFREY PFEFFER

THE REAL KEYS TO HIGH PERFORMANCE

Jeffrey Pfeffer is the Thomas D. Dee Professor of Organizational Behavior at Stanford University's Graduate School of Business. He has led executive education seminars around the world and is a best-selling author of more than ninety articles and four books, including The Human Equation: Building Profits by Putting People First.

It appears that the old aphorism "People are our most important asset" is *actually true*. Compelling evidence suggests that organizational success comes more from managing people effectively than from attaining large size, operating in a high-growth industry, or becoming lean and mean through downsizing—which, after all, puts many of your most important assets on the street for the competition to employ. But although many leaders believe that putting people first makes strategic sense, all too few of their organizations do it.

What can you actually do to implement high-performance management practices and enjoy the benefits that will almost certainly accrue? Unfortunately there are no easy answers—if there were, this strategy would not be such an important foundation for sustainable competitive success. But there are things that high-performing organizations do that can spur new thinking about this question.

Achieving profits through people requires consistent leadership attention—and that is the biggest barrier to success. The scarcest resource in most organizations is time and attention—what leader has enough? Time spent focusing on one thing cannot be spent focusing on others, and too often quarterly financial results crowd out the long-term management of people. Leaders of truly successful organizations—such as Whole Foods Markets, Southwest Airlines, the Men's Wearhouse, and AES Corporation—see their role as systems architects, engaged in the critical task of building values, cultures, and a set of management practices that enable the recruitment, retention, development, and motivation of outstanding people. They also engage in the important work of building work practices that ensure that the ideas of all people become known and used.

Whole Foods, which has grown in the 1990s from $100 million to $1 billion in sales—in the grocery business, no less—is famous for its use of self-managed teams. The company shares detailed performance and financial information with all its people—so much information that, because many people own stock in the company, *all* employees are considered insiders for purposes of Securities and Exchange Commission regulations. The company even makes data about individual salaries available to all its employees. It also shares productivity gains with its people through team-based incentive compensation, in the process of fostering decentralized decision making.

The Men's Wearhouse has succeeded in the retailing industry—an industry notorious for its use of part-time, low-paid, undertrained, and poorly treated help—by doing exactly the opposite: investing heavily in training, using few part-time staff, paying above-industry-average wages, and encouraging employee stock ownership. The company recognizes that what is important is not what people *cost* but what they *do*. AES, a global developer and operator of electric power plants, has succeeded by fostering radical decentralization, sharing financial and performance information (all of its people are also insiders), recruiting on the basis of cultural fit, and eschewing bureaucracy. How many companies with several thousand employees do you know that have no human resources staff and that make business development and strategic planning part of everyone's job, not just the province of a centralized staff?

The Real Source of Success

It may seem obvious that building organizational capability and ensuring the implementation of high-commitment management practices is a key managerial responsibility. But this prescription is frequently honored in the breach. Conventional wisdom argues that senior leaders should focus on making strategy, seeking some technological edge, and worrying about financial engineering, mergers and acquisitions, and restructuring.

But the data on the sources of sustained success are clear. Is being in a high-technology industry an essential source of competitive success? It can be, but it is not necessarily. When the *Wall Street Journal* ranked industries by their five-year returns to shareholders, in 1997 only three out of the top fifteen industries were in high technology. In the paper's 1996 list, restaurants (ranked twenty-sixth) provided a higher five-year return to shareholders than did medical devices (twenty-eighth), and footwear (ranked thirtieth) outperformed pharmaceuticals (ranked forty-seventh). The computer industry ranked only seventy-eighth, behind industries such as automobile parts (thirty-fourth), heavy machinery (twenty-ninth), and even railroads (thirty-third). *Inc.* magazine's list of the fastest-growing companies in 1996 was headed by a toothbrush manufacturer, a consumer products distributor, and a human resources service company.

Does being in a rapidly growing industry matter? A study by consultants at Booz, Allen and Hamilton of more than eighteen hundred companies with a market capitalization of more than $500 million in 1994 found that industry growth rates were completely unrelated to the growth rates of individual companies, as measured by the ten-year return on shareholder equity. Another study of growing companies found a similar disconnection between company growth rates and the growth rates of their industries. The Men's Wearhouse, for instance, has enjoyed compound growth of more than 30 percent annually in both sales and profits over the past half-decade. In the relatively stagnant market of men's tailored clothing, the firm grows by taking business from the competition.

Does size matter, and in particular, does the wave of mergers and consolidations undertaken presumably to achieve economies of scale make sense? My analysis of eighty nonfinancial industries shows that in 44 percent of the industries the correlation between sales volume and return on capital is actually negative. Chrysler has been more profitable than General Motors, as has Ford. Southwest is the most profitable and efficient airline, although it is far from the largest. Even in financial services, the banks with the highest return on assets, an important measure of profitability, include virtually none of the largest. Across industries, the average correlation between size and two measures of profitability, return on assets and return on shareholders' equity, was only 0.1. This means that size is almost completely unrelated to firm profitability.

Should leaders worry about having the right strategy? Sure, but implementation is a lot more important. As a senior officer at one of the leading strategy consulting firms admitted to me, "*finding* the answer is relatively easy; *doing* the answer is frequently impossible." Richard Kovacevich, CEO of Norwest, the enormously successful financial services company, recently told the *Wall Street Journal*, "I could leave our strategic plan on a plane . . . and it wouldn't make any difference. No one could execute it." As Tom Farmer, the CEO of Kwik-Fit, the largest supplier of automotive repair services in the United Kingdom, says, "In a service business [and in today's world, all businesses are service businesses], there is only one successful strategy—providing your customers outstanding value and service—customer delight."

The evidence is also clear on the effects of downsizing and restructuring—these actions will not increase stock price (over an eighteen-month or two-year period), nor will they increase productivity or efficiency. Rather, downsizing will do only one thing: make the organization smaller. So leaders would do well to spend less time worrying about finding the right competitive niche, searching for technological silver bullets, and massaging financial statements, and spend more time developing their people to provide the competitive edge. Numerous studies indicate that managing people using high-performance or high-commitment practices can produce enormous economic returns (see box). Moreover, really making people your most important asset turns out to be difficult to copy.

Three Guiding Principles

I have observed three basic principles that leaders use to transform their organizations into a high-commitment model of management: build trust, encourage change, and use appropriate measures of performance. Each of these principles makes as much sense as the idea of building organizations that develop and apply employees' knowledge and competence. But again, experience reveals that common sense is not common in managerial practice.

Building Trust

At the most basic level, one builds trust by treating all members of the organization as though they can be trusted. This means, among other things, sharing information with everyone. When John Mackey, CEO of Whole Foods, was asked why the firm shared all of its performance information with everyone, and even made it possible for each team member to know the salary of everyone else in the company by name, he replied that to keep secrets implied that the organization didn't trust those from whom information was withheld. Knowledge is power, and sharing information entails sharing power. But not sharing information suggests that there are some in the organization who can be trusted with its secrets and others who can't. This is the wrong message to send if you want to harness the efforts and energy of everyone.

You cannot build trust without treating people with respect and dignity. It is now all too common to have layoffs in which those let go are immediately escorted off the premises. This process deprives them and those left behind of the opportunity to say good-bye and, more fundamentally, signals distrust and disrespect. Consider instead the New Zealand Post, which, since becoming a state-owned enterprise in 1987 was expected to operate like a private company, has

---

Five Cases for High-Performance Management

Studies in a wide range of manufacturing and service industries show that management systems that encourage personal commitment and competence achieve greater productivity, quality, and cost-efficiency than systems that impose direct control. Highlights of five studies suggest just how much people can deliver when supported by effective management.

Among 702 large firms in many different industries, being one standard deviation better on an index of high-commitment human resource practices resulted in an increase in shareholder wealth of $41,000 per employee, according to a study by Mark Huselid of Rutgers University and Brian Becker of the State University of New York at Buffalo.

Motor vehicle manufacturing firms implementing flexible production processes and associated practices for managing people enjoyed 47 percent better quality and 43 percent better productivity than firms relying on traditional mass-production approaches, according to a worldwide study by Wharton School's John Paul MacDuffie.

The five-year survival rates of initial public offerings showed that firms whose human resource practices scored in the top one-sixth of

accomplished amazing things (for instance, actually *reducing* the cost of a stamp). People laid off were offered generous severance, given parties on their leaving, and recognized for their contributions to the company. Indeed, the Post even let the staff help decide who would go and who would stay—for it turned out that some people the organization intended to keep wanted to leave or retire and others wanted to stay.

Building trust also means taking the organization's values seriously. At AES, the annual report discusses how well the organization is doing in living up to its four core values of fun, fairness, integrity, and

---

IPO firms had a 33 percent higher probability of surviving than those in the lowest one-sixth. Firms in the upper one-sixth in providing financial rewards to all employees, not just managers, had almost twice as much chance of surviving for five years, according to research by Theresa Welbourne of Cornell and Alice Andrews of Vanderbilt.

Steel minimills using a high-commitment approach to management required 34 percent fewer labor hours to make a ton of steel and had a 64 percent better scrap rate than minimills using a command-and-control approach, according to Jeffrey Arthur of Purdue.

Apparel manufacturing firms that had changed to modular production, relying on teams of multiskilled people paid more on a group (rather than individual piecework) basis, had 65 percent better operating profit as a percentage of sales, 22 percent higher gross margins, and 49 percent more growth in sales from 1988 to 1992 compared to firms that relied on traditional bundle manufacturing and paid single-skilled operators on the basis of individual piecework. So found John Dunlop of Harvard and David Weil of Boston University.

social responsibility. Whole Foods Market's annual report prominently presents the results of its employee satisfaction survey. These organizations signal that they take seriously their commitments to both their values and their people by publicly discussing where they are succeeding and where they are falling short—and what they are going to do about it.

Encouraging Change

Leaders can encourage change in many ways. One way is by exposing themselves and their colleagues to alternative models of management. It is useful to read about Southwest Airlines or AES or the Men's Wearhouse, but it is much more compelling to visit these companies, talk to their people, and experience firsthand what a different way of treating people feels like. When Citibank recently became interested in using quality as a way of organizing and motivating change, it invited people from Motorola to visit. The reverse of that process—having Citibankers spend time actually experiencing Motorola—might have been even more powerful.

Another way that organizations can encourage change is by doing things that break old ways of organizing. The New Zealand Post did two such things. First, it reorganized frequently. Putting people in new roles in a new organizational structure almost automatically ensured that they would have to do things differently and not be bound by old habits and assumptions. In addition, the company physically reconfigured the workplace to promote new ways of working and thinking about customer service processes. At the Dallas plant of AT&T in the late 1980s, the new plant manager, Ken Weatherford, encouraged change by making visible changes to the plant's operations—changing the dress code so that ties were no longer worn, moving the engineers out to the production area, reorganizing the plant into four focused factories by moving equipment and rearranging production processes. In a world in which new initiatives are greeted with skepticism, the easiest way to convince people that this time it's for real is to begin doing things that demonstrably signal that change is occurring and that put people in new places with new work roles that require them to work in new ways.

Measuring What Matters

Finally, leaders who have successfully built high-performing workplaces make sure to measure the practices that constitute high-commitment management. They also measure related management processes that determine how the organization is functioning. The problem is simple: most financial reporting systems provide tremendous detail about what *has* happened, but much less information about the organization's present condition or the reasons for its performance. It is, as the saying goes, like trying to drive by looking in your rear-view mirror. A positive response to this problem is Robert Kaplan and David Norton's balanced scorecard approach, in which financial measures are weighed against measures of customer satisfaction and retention, employee attitudes and retention, new product and new business development, or readiness for change. Some of these indicators are more difficult to measure than past financial performance, but sophisticated leaders recognize that measurement systems focus organizational attention, and that the adage "what gets measured gets done" is accurate.

Every business has a few key drivers of success. It is the job of management to lead a process in which these key success factors are understood, measurements for them are developed, and attention is then focused on those measures. If people are an important source of competitive advantage, then the attraction, retention, development, and spirit of an organization's people requires as much attention as the financial statement. At the SAS Institute, a $650 million, privately held developer of statistical software for business applications, employee recruitment and retention are key measures of performance. A visitor hears much more discussion about the number of people applying for jobs and the company's turnover rate than about sales or finances. The CEO, James Goodnight, recognizes that in a knowledge-intensive business, if you can hire and retain the best people, the other results will follow.

Measuring what really matters, not what the current information system happens to track routinely, is critical. It is no accident that great companies develop unique standards of performance—and that these often involve people. For example:

- Hewlett Packard evaluates managers on their subordinates' assessment of managerial behavior and adherence to HP values.

- Motorola has had a goal of giving each employee at least forty hours of training per year, and measures managers by the proportion of their people who get the requisite amount of training.

- Singapore Airlines spends *15 percent* of its payroll costs on training—no wonder the firm is a model of service. What is most important, however, is that the firm takes its commitment to training seriously enough to track it.

- The SAS Institute measures employee turnover; managers know their numbers and talk about them.

- Southwest Airlines tracks the number of job applicants (currently more than 120,000 a year). Some would see processing so many applicants as a waste of resources, but Southwest views this activity as critical to ensuring access to the best possible workforce.

It is also possible for organizations to assess the proportion of the workforce working in teams, the number of people who know the organization's strategy and its performance measures, the number of layers in the hierarchy (a reasonable indicator of decentralization), and similar factors related to a firm's people management practices.

Wise leaders use measures not only to focus attention but also to drive change and continuous improvement. Comparisons across teams at Whole Foods Market stimulate everyone to do better in an atmosphere of friendly competition. At the Men's Wearhouse, sales per square foot, sales per employee, and the size of the average sale are all tracked and reported internally. This measurement and comparison process stimulates internal benchmarking and the sharing of sales and merchandising ideas among people and across stores, providing a standard for continuous improvement.

A New Role for Leaders

In today's world, knowledge and capability have become keys to success because everything else—product offerings, marketing strategy, sourcing schemes—is easily acquired or imitated. Putting people first, or at least taking people issues seriously, is more important than ever. But implementing high-commitment practices requires a different view of management and competitive advantage. From this perspective, leaders build systems—systems that build distinctive competence and capability and that, because of their internal coherence, are robust even as the competitive landscape and the macroeconomic environment change. These leaders don't necessarily make a lot of business decisions, even decisions about strategy, or worry a lot about financial engineering and restructuring. They make more important decisions about systems for recruiting, motivating, and developing people that, if successful, will ensure that the organization has the talent necessary both to develop an effective strategy and to execute it. It may seem strange to see the leader's role as being the chief people (or culture) officer, but that is exactly what you will find in organizations that have really achieved profits through people.

In hindsight, it is relatively straightforward to assess whether or not this effort at systems architecture has been successful. Some years ago, three colleagues completed a study of productivity in the worldwide automobile industry over a forty-year period. Using sophisticated statistical methods, they were able to estimate not only overall productivity growth but also, more specifically, growth in labor and capital productivity and the effects of various CEOs' tenures on all this. With one exception, every automobile manufacturer showed the results of a particular CEO's strengths or weaknesses. For instance, Donald Petersen at Ford was associated with continual increases in productivity. In other companies, some CEOs had positive effects, others negative. The one company in which there was no CEO effect was—could you guess?—Toyota. That makes perfect sense. Toyota, after all, is famous for its Toyota Production *System*. Although that system has been refined over time, the point is that it is, in fact, a system—a set of interrelated elements that has provided the company with competitive advantage during dramatic changes in the value of the yen, in the location of manufacturing facilities, and in product mix and consumer tastes. I can think of no better example of the power of systems architecture.

An organization need not be born doing the right thing with respect to people. The New Zealand Post wasn't, nor was Ford Motor Company. As long as leaders recognize the importance of building business success around their people and learn to manage with trust, encourage change, and make sure that their measurement systems contribute rather than cause problems, organizations of all sizes and in all sectors can accomplish great things. It just requires leaders to focus on what is, after all, their most important asset.

29 LINDA A. HILL

DEVELOPING THE STAR PERFORMER

Linda A. Hill is the Wallace Brett Donham Professor of Business Administration at the Harvard Business School and is course head for the required M.B.A. Leadership program. She is author of Becoming a Manager: Mastery of a New Identity *and has written or contributed to the multimedia CD-ROM programs* High-Performance Management *and* Coaching. *Her consulting work has included change management, career development, and personal leadership.*

Management phobia is running rampant in corporate America, according to a recent *Wall Street Journal* article. In contrast to previous decades, many employees now have no interest in becoming managers. Managers in the 1990s tend to occupy demanding and insecure positions that offer significantly fewer perks than ever before. Not surprisingly, senior executives are finding that recruiting people capable of leading their enterprises into the next century is a long, difficult, and frustrating process. However, with a global trend toward organizational restructuring and streamlining, executives need to develop managers who can cope with the ever-changing marketplace and increasing responsibilities. Without capable managers, the flatter, leaner organizations cannot sustain quality, service, and financial performance. Developing new managers is therefore a critical strategic challenge for organizations that hope to prosper in the years ahead.

As you might expect, the competition for top management talent is fierce. The pool of talent already within an organization is an invaluable resource for the future—if the organization knows how to develop it. So how does an organization develop and retain the talent it needs to support a growing business in a competitive world? How does it create an environment in which star individual contributors can be nurtured and prepared to play critical managerial and leadership roles in the organization?

It has become a business imperative for senior executives to devote more time and attention to these issues. More and more organizations, especially professional service firms, have come to believe that the strategic management of talent will be their competitive advantage. As a consequence, organizations are beginning to look more closely at what it takes to be an effective manager, and at how people actually learn to manage and lead. One of the best ways to understand these issues is to consider the experiences of individuals as they first move into managerial assignments. Evidence suggests that the first managerial assignment is a pivotal development experience for future executives. It is a time that profoundly shapes their basic leadership style and philosophy. Furthermore, it is generally during transitions between roles that individuals are most receptive to learning new skills and behaviors. To take advantage of this unique opportunity, organizations must help people make sense of and master these earliest managerial experiences.

Becoming a Manager

For star performers who have been handsomely rewarded for their individual contributions and who have come to expect wide latitude in how they work, *manager* is often a dirty word. Helping them grow into that role can be at once a difficult, exhilarating, and unsettling process. Some career transitions involve changes akin to the minor adjustments a pilot makes to a flight plan to keep the plane on course; other transitions require charting an entirely new destination. The transition from performer to manager is such a change. It is a turning point in one's career.

Many new managers have to unlearn the deeply held attitudes and habits they developed when they were responsible for only their own performance. Instead, they must see themselves as responsible for setting and implementing an agenda for a whole group. To set the agenda for a group and to motivate and inspire others to accomplish that agenda is much more complicated than most people anticipate, particularly in flat, fast-moving organizations.

As one new manager in a software company remarked, seeing himself as a network builder and a leader was a fundamentally different way of looking at who he was and what he was supposed to do. It meant learning to frame problems in ways that were much broader, more holistic, more long term. It meant learning to cope with the stresses associated with his new "schizophrenic" condition (producing actual work while managing a team of other people) as well as discovering new ways to derive satisfaction from work.

In interviewing and observing hundreds of first-time managers, I have seen that mastering the managerial role requires what educator Douglas Hall terms two kinds of learning: *task learning*—the technical, organizational, or conceptual competencies necessary to be an effective manager—and *personal learning*—the attitudes, mind-set, and values consistent with the work of management. The personal learning is usually far more difficult than anticipated, and far less likely to be addressed in management development efforts. New managers grapple with four complex transformational tasks:

- Learning what it means to be a manager
- Developing interpersonal judgment
- Coping with emotions and stress
- Gaining self-knowledge

Organizations can help new managers master these tasks by appreciating what they are going through. And new managers can help themselves by preparing for what lies ahead.

What It Means to Manage

Becoming a manager means coming to terms with the difference between the myth of management and the reality. As one rising star at a chemical company found out, management meant much more than just doing what she had been doing all along, "only with more power and control." She had been an accomplished performer and had received better-than-average management training. She stepped into a product development management position with impeccable credentials, high hopes, and a deep appreciation for the company's values. Three weeks later her comments were startling: "Becoming a manager is not about becoming a boss. It's about becoming a hostage. There are many terrorists in this organization who want to kidnap me. It is awful. I used to love my job. People listened to me. People liked me. I'm the same person now, but no one listens and no one cares."

Unfortunately, many new managers report similar experiences. When individuals have been star performers, they often experience average or even solid performers as incompetent, unmotivated, or antagonistic. When most people first become managers, they focus on their formal authority—the rights and privileges associated with getting a promotion. They expect to have more authority and freedom. They soon discover, however, that what they have actually gained are new duties, obligations, and interdependencies. Instead of feeling free, most feel incredibly constrained—especially if they were accustomed to the relative freedom of being a star.

New managers soon learn that formal authority is a very limited source of power. One can ask people to do something, but they often don't respond; they do their own thing. (Some new managers recognized the irony of their situation, admitting that they didn't always listen to their bosses either. But things look different when you're supposed to be in charge.)

The fact is, most of the people who can make a manager's life miserable are people over whom one has no formal authority—that is, bosses and peers. Management has just as much, if not more, to do with negotiating interdependencies as it does with exercising formal authority (see Table 29.1).

New managers therefore have to learn two sets of responsibilities. One is to manage their team. The other is to manage the context within which their team resides. That means managing the boundaries—the relationships of their team with other groups both inside and outside the organization. New managers often narrow their horizons too much; they mistakenly focus only on their own team of direct reports. But in fact, unless they look up and around, their teams are going to have inappropriate expectations placed on them and they will lack the resources necessary to do their jobs. Thus, managing the context means identifying and building effective relationships with the key people and groups on which their teams depend.

As solo performers, these individuals had the luxury of worrying about only their own interests. As managers, by definition, they must balance competing interests in complex situations. They have to learn to be supportive, yet tough-minded. They must accommodate

Table 29.1. What It Means to Manage and Lead.

	Myth	Reality
Operative Principles:	Authority	Interdependency
Source of Power:	Formal authority	"Everything but"
Key Players:	Subordinates	Includes those outside your formal authority
Desired Outcomes:	Control, compliance	Commitment, empowerment
Key Competencies:	Technical	Technical, human, conceptual

individual needs while accomplishing group goals, and they must use their clout to defend their group's interests without undermining the performance of their organization. Every day they have to make decisions that have no right answer. "Nothing is black and white," one new manager observed. "It is all gray. My job is to manage trade-offs and dilemmas."

Developing Interpersonal Judgment

New managers have to learn to manage people, not just tasks, and they must develop interpersonal judgment in three critical areas: establishing credibility rather than relying on formal authority, building subordinate commitment rather than seeking subordinate control, and leading the team rather than managing individuals.

One rising star at a theatrical rigging company learned a quick and painful lesson about the nature of management, the exercise of authority, and the power of group dynamics. During his first week as a manager, a subordinate with long tenure in the company asked if he could have the one parking spot that had just become available. Wanting to get off to a good start and be viewed as a "good guy" the manager concluded, "Why not?" Within the hour one of his most experienced people, a big moneymaker, stormed into his office threatening to quit. It seems that the winner of the parking place was widely viewed as incompetent, and the manager's decision was unfathomable to the star. (Understand that this was in Texas and the parking spot was in the shade; it was a valuable commodity and of pragmatic and symbolic importance to the office.)

The manager told me, "They didn't teach this in the management development program. This is not the kind of thing that I'm supposed to be worrying about." He eventually smoothed the ruffled feathers as he began to recognize that every decision about particular individuals also affected the collective. This manager had made a typical mistake of new managers: he had equated supervising each individual with leading the team. He had assumed that if he could establish rapport and a good relationship with each person who reported to him, his whole team would click. Of course that is often not the case.

Team leadership means having responsibility for the whole. It means understanding the dynamics that can make the whole far more (or much less) than the sum of its parts. The real trick is providing the leadership necessary to establish a high-performance, high-commitment team culture. Grasping this notion can be especially elusive for up-and-comers who have been able to accomplish so much on their own. Effective managers realize that every group has its informal leaders, who often have greater standing with the group than the boss. The Texan manager eventually learned to listen to these leaders always, to defer to them often, and to let them announce a tough decision occasionally. And he came to see that by sharing power in this way, he was actually gaining power.

This became clear when his subordinates began asking his advice. They began to trust that he would look out for their interests and keep them informed. The more trust people had in his ability to make good decisions, the less often they required him to have proof of delivery on a promise. Trust is a function of how an individual perceives a manager in three areas: competence (Does he know the right thing to do?), character (Does he want to do the right thing?), and influence (Can he get it done?). Building trust is critical to leadership, and a delicate part of any manager's job.

Learning to assess trustworthiness in others is also key. To delegate effectively, a fundamental managerial skill, new managers need to be able to make judgment calls about whom they can trust. Managers also have to decide how much leeway to give subordinates—too little and they feel overcontrolled, too much and they feel unsupported and neglected—based on trustworthiness. To further complicate matters, managers must learn that, ironically, to treat people fairly is to treat them differently. The right amount of delegation for one employee may be wrong for another. Thus, to manage people is to manage paradox.

Managers must:

- Embrace individual differences and collective identity and goals
- Focus on performance and on learning and development
- Balance managerial authority and team member discretion and autonomy

Gaining Self-Knowledge

Stress is inherent in organizational life these days. Managers, even the most experienced, often report feelings of overload, conflict, ambiguity, and isolation. New managers are surprised by the "burdens of leadership"—having to make decisions that affect people's lives in profound ways, particularly when they are unsure about what the right answer is in a given situation. They often find themselves playing psychotherapist, listening to the personal problems of a recalcitrant direct report. As one manager put it, "I never knew a promotion could be so painful." New managers have to learn how to manage themselves and their emotions. Otherwise the inevitable feelings of stress and anxiety can profoundly affect their daily functioning. Many rookie managers will find themselves all too willing to revert to the familiar, individual "doer" role when faced with these messy managerial responsibilities. That is seldom a productive response.

Learning to manage is a task of the head and the heart. To be effective in handling the stresses of leading others, people have to learn a great deal about themselves—their personal values, styles, strengths, and weaknesses. They often discover new sides of themselves as new competencies are called upon. Time and again they find themselves revisiting the questions: Why did I become a manager? Do I have what it takes? And who am I becoming? It is no accident that most effective leaders are self-aware. As role models for their teams, new managers begin to understand that they must view themselves as instruments who can have a profound effect on the culture and outcomes of their teams. Only through reflective introspection can they fully appreciate who they are and their impact on others.

Learning to Lead

To be successful, new managers have to become self-directed learners. Ultimately, no one can teach them how to manage and lead; they have to teach themselves. Learning to manage is largely the result of learning from experience—from doing and interacting with others. Managers must be willing and able to reflect periodically on their experiences, to collect feedback, analyze it, and alter their behavior when necessary.

The myriad challenges encountered when one becomes a manager are difficult to shoulder alone. Unfortunately, new managers can be reluctant to ask for help; it doesn't fit their conception of the boss as expert. One manager explained that she avoided participating in the company training program offered to new managers. "If they realize how little I know," she said, "they will think I am a promotion mistake."

By refusing to share her struggle with others, however, this manager (and many like her) made her job more difficult. Often those managers who have a more extensive and varied network and who are willing to ask for help find it easier to adapt to their new role. Relationships with peers, both past and current, can be invaluable. Because such discussions tend to be relatively informal and nonthreatening, managers can feel free to disclose problems and engage in joint problem solving on how to address them.

Developmental Strategies for Leaders

The first step in developing the managerial talent an organization needs is understanding *what* people have to learn—the transformational tasks of management—and *how* they learn them—through experience and their interactions with others.

Among the most powerful learning experiences are stretch assignments—giving people goals that are a little beyond what they're capable of doing. It is not about throwing talented people into the pool and letting them sink or swim; even a star athlete, asked to climb a ladder that is missing most of its rungs, will probably fall. Instead it is about matching an individual's developmental needs and capacities to a well-sequenced set of specific, meaningful opportunities. These opportunities should allow performers to acquire expertise while also establishing relationships with people who can help them make the most of those experiences. Given the appropriate opportunity, they can then produce results, establish a track record, build credibility, and be prepared to pursue bigger stretch assignments.

Individuals should be encouraged to pursue assignments in which their strengths are really needed, their weaknesses are not a serious drawback, and their core values are consistent with the job at hand; the stretch should not be too big or the risk too great. Risk should be commensurate with the individual's ability to cope with and responsibly manage that risk (for the sake of both the organization and the individual). In general, the risk is probably too great if someone is likely to need more than six months of learning to produce meaningful results. Well-selected stretch assignments have three qualities. They offer:

- *Autonomy.* The chance to develop and display leadership.

- *Relevance.* Work that is of strategic importance to the organization.

- *Visibility.* A way to become known—and held accountable—for personal efforts.

As career theorist David Thomas has shown, people who do not have access to stretch assignments, or who do not establish developmental relationships, will actually lose skills over time.

It is thus important to think about developing management talent over the long term. Think strategically about how you will give star performers the right portfolio of experiences to prepare them for management (for instance, heading a global task force on a key strategic issue, or introducing a new product, or assisting an executive who is turning around a division). Senior management needs to send strong signals that they expect a balance to be maintained between current performance and the learning and development of future managerial talent. This can be a difficult balance to maintain, given today's competitive pressures and the focus on customer satisfaction. However, business and human resource strategies must be more fully integrated. As a firm identifies new business opportunities, it must simultaneously begin to think through the kind of talent it will need and the kind of experiences that will help junior people develop those talents.

Management Development Versus Management Selection

It is important to remember that once individuals move into managerial assignments, the organization's job is not over. Given the complexities of their new responsibilities and all that they have to learn, new managers, no matter how gifted, still need coaching. And the immediate superior of a new manager plays a critical role in that manager's development. All too often new managers report that their immediate superiors are a threat rather than an ally in their development. Work-producing managers, in sales and professional service firms especially, voice these concerns; their bosses give lip service to the notion that the new producing manager is to take his or her managerial responsibilities seriously, but in reality they only reward them for short-term outcomes such as generating revenue.

Mistakes by subordinates can be costly to new managers' immediate superiors, despite the nod their organizations might give to learning and development. It is not surprising, therefore, that many new managers report they have very few safe places to go for help; many sheepishly describe actively avoiding their superiors (star performers in particular often prefer to work things out on their own). The more pressure there is in an organization for current performance, the more reluctant people are to seek assistance proactively. Consequently, most organizations miss the unique opportunity to influence positively the leadership philosophies and styles of their new managers.

There are some notable exceptions, however. The most effective bosses of new managers provide supportive autonomy; they hold the new manager accountable to high standards but adopt a joint problem-solving approach when the inevitable missteps occur. These bosses recognize the trouble spots for new managers—for example, in neglecting key peer relationships, delegating, and leading the team. They seek out the new managers, recognizing their insecurities. They tend to adopt a Socratic method, encouraging the new managers to reflect on and consolidate the lessons of their experiences.

In the end, they hold the new managers responsible for their own development and work to provide them with some of the tools they will need to take advantage of their on-the-job experiences. They encourage new managers to think strategically about their careers—the experiences they should seek and the relationships they should try to build. One of the most important ways to help people grow is to help them learn to be good protégés.

Too often aspiring managers have wrongheaded ideas about developmental relationships; they suffer from the myth of the "perfect mentor." They see their task as finding a mentor who will guide them over the course of their careers. Implicit in their approach is the myth of a benevolent, experienced counselor who will be willing and able to help a younger colleague navigate through the world of work. Such perfect mentors are rarely found; mentors are neither omnipresent nor omnipotent. Indeed, mentor-protégé relationships demand considerable investment and risk on the part of both partners.

Rather than seeking perfect mentors, new managers should learn to become "perfect protégés," so that people will want to mentor them. The perfect protégé is smart enough to know what she doesn't know, is willing to disclose information that will allow others to help her, and is open to receiving feedback. She not only looks to a single mentor for guidance but also has a diverse personal board of directors to help her learn. She accepts that successful mentoring relationships are always two-way streets. The mentor offers advice and opportunity; the protégé delivers results—and can provide a ground-level view of the organization's workings.

Transforming star performers into effective managers has always been a difficult process, but in today's economy it is even more challenging. There are few shortcuts and no magic formulas. Only by adopting a strategic mind-set about talent development can organizations continually renew the intellectual and financial capital they need to compete. That is arguably senior management's most important job.

30 LEONARD BERRY

LEADING FOR THE LONG TERM

Leonard Berry holds the JCPenney Chair of Retailing Studies and is professor of marketing and director of the Center for Retailing Studies at the Lowry Mays College and Graduate School of Business, Texas A&M University. The most prolific writer on services marketing in the United States, he is author of numerous articles and books on service excellence, including On Great Service.

As any leader knows, past glory does not guarantee future success. Organizations prosper only as long as they provide value to those they serve. And providing long-term value for customers is especially difficult for enterprises that deliver services. Services are performances, which means they are usually labor intensive. Service providers are the product, and sustaining their energy, commitment, and focus is never easy. Leaders who sustain success do so by managing three equally important but sometimes conflicting pressures: operating effectively when growing rapidly, operating effectively when managing costs, and remaining entrepreneurial.

Operations Versus Growth

For many people, growth is synonymous with success. But balancing growth with the need for consistent delivery is one of the biggest challenges. Ironically, the greater the involvement of people in the process of serving customers, the more difficult the challenge. The organization must protect its principles while selecting, orienting, and educating new managers and employees. Effective internal communications, vibrant vision and culture, and excellent service quality—essential success factors—are all tested by expansion. The process requires greater leadership and discipline than exist in many companies.

Service companies like ValuJet and CompUSA stumbled by placing growth ahead of execution. Even while receiving accolades for its rapid growth—well before the tragic crash that led to an FAA shutdown—ValuJet was a deeply troubled company with lax controls. In the early 1990s, computer retailer CompUSA was the fastest-growing retail company in America. However, by early 1994 the company's survival was threatened as a result of weak financial controls, undisciplined merchandising practices, and poor in-store operations. Rapid growth had outstripped the small-company systems in place at the time. New management halted the expansion, centralized merchandising, revamped store operating practices, strengthened the balance sheet, and then cautiously ramped up new store expansion. The company reported record sales and profits in 1996, but the lesson of out-of-control growth still reverberates in the CompUSA boardroom.

Execution Versus Price

Although the fit and feel of a suit or the styling of an automobile can give customers reasons to choose a more expensive product, most service offerings are harder to differentiate. It usually comes down to questions of execution and price. (Think about what went into your choice of long-distance provider, insurance agent, or cleaning service.) Although higher service quality is what sustains customer relationships, most providers opt to compete on price. It is an appealing strategy because it can be implemented quickly and marketed easily. Unfortunately, it can also undermine service.

Consider one of the most volatile service industries: telecommunications. Preparing for deregulation and expected price competition, local telephone service providers have eliminated thousands of workers from their payrolls in recent years—just as demand for services has skyrocketed. More demand combined with less capacity has hurt service delivery, resulting in rising consumer complaints and regulator activism. In 1996, New York's Public Service Commission ordered Nynex to credit $50 million to five million consumers because of slow repair and installation services. Also in 1996, Wisconsin's Public Service Commission sued Ameritech for slow, unreliable service. In California, customers' local telephone service complaints more than doubled between 1990 and 1995.

These companies, and thousands of others, have mistakenly assumed that value and price mean the same thing to customers. They do not. Customers understand that value represents the benefits received for the burdens endured. Burdens have both a financial and a nonfinancial component (for example, uninformed service staff, slow delivery times, and voice mail systems from hell).

The benefits/burdens equation is why retailers at both the high end and low end of the market can prosper. To deliver value to their customers, both Neiman Marcus and Wal-Mart must do the same thing: maximize the most important benefits to targeted customers and minimize the most critical burdens. Successful service providers understand that price is simply price; *value* is the customer's total experience.

Entrepreneurship Versus Maturity

Maintaining an entrepreneurial culture that celebrates continuous improvement and discovery is another ingredient of success. Innovative entrepreneurship springs from conditions more typical of newer, smaller organizations than of mature, larger organizations: the dream of building a great business and the fear of failure. But as long-term performers have learned, it is possible to encourage entrepreneurship consciously, even in large organizations.

Entrepreneurship is personal. It requires inspiration, which is jeopardized as the business grows and institutes more formal policies and systems. Memos and supervisory layers replace impromptu visits from the owner. The power of the dream, the sense of mission, can easily fade as the company becomes not only more successful but also bigger, more complex, and more bureaucratic.

Service staff closest to the customer need inspiration to invest the energy and undertake the risks of innovation. They need inspiration to develop better ways to perform their service and to speak up when they see their company going in a wrong direction.

Most service positions involve discretionary effort, which is the difference between the maximum energy an individual can bring to a job and the minimum necessary to avoid penalty. Personal entrepreneurship is an optional activity. Managers cannot *command* people to be entrepreneurial; they can only hope to inspire them to try something new or go the extra mile for a customer. That is why Peter Drucker urges managers to consider employees to be "volunteer workers."

Companies such as Eastern Airlines (now defunct), Kentucky Fried Chicken, and Holiday Inn were great entrepreneurial service companies in their youth. But the entrepreneurial spirit of these firms declined as they grew, aged, changed leadership, and shifted ownership. The founders' dreams, embraced in young, feisty organizations, faded away. The emotionally rich journeys taken by early employees were transformed into mere jobs as the years passed.

Sustaining Success

Although many initially successful service companies have been unable to sustain their success, other enterprises such as Charles Schwab and United Services Automobile Association (USAA) have not only sustained their early success but accelerated it. Assets under custody at Charles Schwab grew from $20 billion in 1989 to $253 billion in 1996; earnings increased by 36 percent in each of the last five years. USAA, expanding from its base in auto insurance to a full range of financial services, achieves record revenues and net income year after year. Serving a military clientele, customer retention is remarkably high (98 percent) and employee turnover is remarkably low (7 percent).

Service companies that have achieved ongoing success do a number of things right, but these four characteristics are common to all:

Customer-Centered Values

The organization's core values, strategies, and everyday practices revolve around creating superior value for customers. The primacy of the customer's experience with the company, continually communicated and reinforced within the organization, drives decision making. Recognizing that every employee makes decisions that directly or indirectly affect customers, managers use customer-centered values to guide these decisions. The focus on customers helps organizations to overcome the hazards of growth and competition.

Many companies profess to be customer-focused, but relatively few organize their operations almost completely around the quality of the customer experience. Gallery Furniture in Houston, Texas, is one such company. Gallery Furniture is the most successful single-store furniture retailer in the United States, with 1996 sales in excess of $90 million. Gallery delivers furniture to customers on the same day it sells it to them, possibly the only furniture store in the world that offers guaranteed same-day delivery. This practice requires a warehouse facility that operates twenty-four hours a day, seven days a week—but it delights customers who usually have to wait days, weeks, or even months for their furniture. Gallery's credo: "Find a way—or make a way—to take care of the customer."

Preaching this message each day is Gallery's founder and owner, Jim "Mattress Mac" McIngvale. McIngvale's office is open and in the middle of the sales floor. He can usually be found greeting customers at the front door, solving problems on the sales floor, personally delivering furniture so the store can keep its same-day delivery promise, or appearing in one of the store's daily television commercials, talking up Gallery's "reason for being" and reaching employees as well as customers in the process.

Gallery currently turns over its inventory 30 times a year, with a goal of 50 times a year. The retail furniture store average is 2.5 turns. Jim McIngvale comments: "The customer is the business and the business is the customer. Most retailers are hung up on how well they are doing today or this month versus last year. We are hung up on how we can improve our service to the customer."

Amid rapid market change and growing organizational complexity, customer-centered values provide a beacon. As Charles Schwab CEO David Pottruck writes in a 1997 essay, "Faced with the reality of constant change, even a highly successful retailer can become confused about its identity, lose its way. A radiantly clear vision to guide you is imperative." Southwest Airlines chairman Herb Kelleher (see Chapter Six) makes the same point: "I have seen brilliant entrepreneurial strategies falter as an organization grows and matures. Obviously you manage a $25 billion company differently than you do a $25 million company. But you change your *practices*, not your principles."

Listening-Based Innovation

Continuing success comes from value-creating innovation stimulated by disciplined listening. Occasional surveys are insufficient. Organizations need to build listening systems that capture, summarize, and disseminate the unmet dreams and unfulfilled wants of multiple customer groups, including existing, prospective, and internal customers (employees).

Listening systems uncover fresh marketplace intelligence, help guide decision making, and nurture creative thinking. Effective listening systems involve both formal and informal methods, conversations with customers, the use of trend data to reveal changing patterns, the distribution of relevant information to all employees, and active discussion and application of findings in work groups.

Listening leads to learning, which sets the stage for innovation. Innovation is more likely when employees are well informed about the customer, unafraid to try something new, and committed to the organization's success. Charles Schwab uses multiple methods to listen for customers' dreams that often start with the phrase, "I know it's not possible, but I wish. . . ." Schwab's top management travels extensively to interact with customers in informal settings. Branches host monthly customer receptions, and at least once a week in different cities Schwab holds town hall meetings to hear employees' ideas, suggestions, and concerns.

Schwab's mutual fund business took off after the company launched OneSource, a service that enables customers to buy hundreds of no-load mutual funds through Schwab with no transaction fee. Previously, mutual fund customers had the option of buying no-load funds from separate sources or buying a variety of funds from Schwab and paying a commission. Inspired by customers' wishes, Schwab persuaded mutual fund companies to provide the revenue and created OneSource, today a $50 billion business.

Charles Schwab actively nurtures innovation by encouraging managers to listen intently to customers and by defining acceptable failure:

- It can't put the company at risk.

- Reasonable precautions against failure should be taken.

- Failure must produce learning.

Failures that meet these tests—and Schwab admits to many—are considered a necessary part of building a strong business.

Gary Hoover, who has created three innovative businesses (Bookstop, *Hoover's Handbooks*, and TravelFest), claims that the customers always get what they want. It is just a matter of who gives it to them and when. Companies that sustain success continually search for new ways to create value for customers. They choose to lead rather than follow, to act rather than wait, to heed the customer instead of the competitor.

Acting Small

Organizational smallness has its virtues. Quick responses to changing market conditions are easier. Internal communications are more direct. Employees' sense of contribution to the organization's success is more pronounced. Promises to customers to deliver personalized service are more credible. Yet scale also has its virtues, such as more complete service lines, broader geographic coverage, and bigger promotion budgets. An important success sustainer is finding ways to reap the benefits of smallness in a large organization.

Innovative organizational structures can enable large organizations to act small, and these structures are often built on an engaging metaphor or model. Rosenbluth International, one of America's largest travel management companies, with 1996 sales of more than $2.5 billion, is made up of more than one hundred units—which CEO Hal Rosenbluth calls "family farms"—serving clients in specific regions. Corporate headquarters functions as the "farm town" in which "stores" (for example, the accounting store) provide necessary resources to the farms. Although the company uses e-mail, company conferences, and other communications vehicles to share ideas, decision making and learning about customers are localized at the farm level.

Lakeland Regional Medical Center in Lakeland, Florida, an 851-bed hospital, teams a registered nurse and one or more licensed health-care providers to perform up to 90 percent of the hospital's services for assigned patients. Five of these small teams form a "care team" that delivers twenty-four-hour, seven-day service to four to eight patients. Care teams provide such services as preadmission testing, charting, X-rays, respiratory therapy, physical therapy, EKG exams, and in-hospital transportation. The care team not only serves the same patients throughout their stay but also serves the same doctor. Pharmacists, social workers, dietitians, physical therapists, and other specialists are part of the extended care team.

Continuity of care has helped to boost patient satisfaction dramatically. Patients are served by far fewer personnel in the restructured organization than in the traditional hospital. Although large, Lakeland functions more like a small hospital, for the benefit of both patients and caregivers.

Innovative applications of information technology can also enable big organizations to act small. USAA illustrates as well as any large organization how high technology, properly deployed, can support high touch. Although USAA's military "members" reside throughout the world and change locations frequently, serving their needs over the telephone and through the mails is usually seamless. Each member's complete service file is accessible on-line to service representatives. Customer correspondence and other additions to an account are electronically imaged and immediately appended to the file. Preparation of new policies, changes to existing policies, claims, and billing, among other processes, are also automated. Although it is a $7 billion business, USAA serves its clientele quickly and personally.

Service companies need not sacrifice the benefits of smallness—nimbleness, responsiveness, teamwork, personalization—when they grow. Large organizations can act small, but they must be prepared to combat formally, continuously, and creatively the creeping bureaucracy sown by scale.

An Ownership Attitude

Employees who feel like part owners of a company are more likely to do what is necessary to sustain the firm's success. That McDonald's franchised stores are significantly more successful than its company-owned stores is unsurprising. Franchisees own their businesses;

managers of company-owned stores do not. Cultivating an ownership attitude in an organization intensifies personal commitment to its success. Owners not only gain more if a company succeeds, they lose more if it fails.

Ownership is a sense of commitment and responsibility stemming from both financial sources (for example, employee stock ownership) and emotional sources (for example, feeling trusted by management). Combining financial and emotional ownership is ideal. Every service company should seriously consider programs that encourage employee stock ownership. As AlliedSignal CEO Larry Bossidy states in *Fortune*: "We've got to have everyone in the company own our stock so that if the company prospers, they can prosper too." Starbucks Coffee Company's stock option plan, called Bean Stock, is available to all employees, including part-timers. The plan is structured on a five-year vesting period. It begins one year after the option is granted, then vests at 20 percent each year. Employees also receive a new stock-option grant each year, initiating a new vesting period. The grant's percentage is related to the company's profitability.

LensCrafters, the world's largest optical retailer, nurtures an ownership attitude by linking part of employees' compensation to the customer satisfaction ratings of their store or region. Non–customer contact employees are also included in the system. Linking customer satisfaction to pay reminds people of what's most important to the company's success—finding new ways to satisfy the customer.

Tattered Cover Book Store in Denver nurtures an ownership attitude by giving new employees a key to the store on their first day of employment. New employees spend the first day of a week-long orientation course (called Boot Camp) learning about the company's value system from chief executive Joyce Meskis. New associates at Rosenbluth International spend their first two days at company headquarters attending mandatory orientation. Regardless of their location or job title, *every* new Rosenbluth associate visits the corporate farm town—Philadelphia—to learn the company's philosophy. During the orientation, senior management serves the new recruits tea, an especially symbolic experience. Rosenbluth periodically hosts a companywide event called "Live the Spirit," to which all associates are invited to meet other associates, learn new skills, and be part of the family. All associates can communicate directly with Hal Rosenbluth by phoning "Hal's Hotline."

Employees with an ownership attitude manage themselves to a significant degree in creating value for their internal or external customers. They are more likely to work hard, account for their own performance and the company's, and take prudent risks in pursuit of innovation. An organization has created an ownership attitude when its success is also the employees' success.

The greater the involvement of people in the value-creation process, the more difficult it is for organizations to sustain performance and growth. Long-term success demands customer-centered core values, listening-inspired innovation, organizational agility, and a genuine sense of employee ownership. An organization's future success is never assured. The actions, creativity, and commitment of individual employees, multiplied thousands of times over many years, determine an organization's long-term success. That is the ultimate test of excellence, and of leadership.

Part VI

BUILDING GREAT TEAMS

31 WARREN BENNIS

THE SECRETS OF GREAT GROUPS

Warren Bennis is distinguished professor and founding chairman of the Leadership Institute at the University of Southern California. He has advised four U.S. presidents and numerous CEOs and is author or editor of more than twenty books on leadership, change, and management, including Organizing Genius.

Personal leadership is one of the most studied topics in American life. Indeed, I have devoted a big chunk of my professional life to better understanding its workings. Far less studied—and perhaps more important—is *group* leadership. The disparity of interest in those two realms of leadership is logical, given the strong individualist bent of American culture. But the more I look at the history of business, government, the arts, and the sciences, the clearer it is that few great accomplishments are ever the work of a single individual.

Our mythology refuses to catch up with our reality. So we cling to the myth of the Lone Ranger, the romantic idea that great things are usually accomplished by a larger-than-life individual working

---

Note: See also *Organizing Genius*, Addison-Wesley, 1997.

alone. Despite the evidence to the contrary—including the fact that Michelangelo worked with a group of sixteen to paint the ceiling of the Sistine Chapel—we still tend to think of achievement in terms of the Great Man or the Great Woman, instead of the Great Group.

As they say, "None of us is as smart as all of us." That's good, because the problems we face are too complex to be solved by any one person or any one discipline. Our only chance is to bring people together from a variety of backgrounds and disciplines who can refract a problem through the prism of complementary minds allied in common purpose. I call such collections of talent *Great Groups*. The genius of Great Groups is that they get remarkable people—strong individual achievers—to work together to get results. But these groups serve a second and equally important function: they provide psychic support and personal fellowship. They help generate courage. Without a sounding board for outrageous ideas, without personal encouragement and perspective when we hit a roadblock, we'd all lose our way.

The Myths of Leadership

Great Groups teach us something about effective leadership, meaningful missions, and inspired recruiting. They challenge not only the myth of the Great Man but also the 1950s myth of the Organization Man—the sallow figure in the gray flannel suit, giving his life to the job and conforming to its mindless dictates.

Neither myth is a productive model for behavior, and neither holds up to current reality. In fact, I believe that behind every Great Man is a Great Group, an effective partnership. And making up every Great Group is a unique construct of strong, often eccentric individuals. So the question for organizations is, How do you get talented, self-absorbed, often arrogant, incredibly bright people to work together?

The impetus for my current work in groups was a meeting more than forty years ago with anthropologist Margaret Mead. I had heard her speak at Harvard, and afterward I asked her whether anyone had ever studied groups whose ideas were powerful enough to change the world. She looked at me and said, "Young man, you should write a book on that topic and call it Sapiential Circles." I gasped, and she went on to explain that *sapiential circles* meant knowledge-generating groups. Like a lot of good ideas, it took a while to gestate, but over the years the power of groups became a recurrent theme for me. Recently, work by leading thinkers such as Michael Shrage in the nature of technology and collaboration, Hal Leavitt and Jean Lipman-Blumen in *Hot Groups*, and Richard Hackman in his writing on the remarkable Orpheus Chamber Orchestra highlights the significance of this inquiry.

To see what makes Great Groups tick, I studied some of the most noteworthy groups of our time, including the Manhattan Project, the paradigmatic Great Group that invented the atomic bomb; the computer revolutionaries at Xerox's Palo Alto Research Center (PARC) and at Apple Computer, whose work led to the Macintosh and other technical breakthroughs; the Lockheed Skunk Works, which pioneered the fast, efficient development of top-secret aircraft; and the Walt Disney Studio animators. Every Great Group is extraordinary in its own way, but my study suggests ten principles common to all—and that apply as well to their larger organizations.

- *At the heart of every Great Group is a shared dream.* All Great Groups believe that they are on a mission from God, that they could change the world, make a dent in the universe. They are obsessed with their work. It becomes not a job but a fervent quest. That belief is what brings the necessary cohesion and energy to their work.
- *They manage conflict by abandoning individual egos to the pursuit of the dream.* At a critical point in the Manhattan Project, George Kistiakowsky, a great chemist who later served as Dwight Eisenhower's chief scientific advisor, threatened to quit because he couldn't get

along with a colleague. Project leader Robert Oppenheimer simply said, "George, how can you leave this project? The free world hangs in the balance." So conflict, even with these diverse people, is resolved by reminding people of the mission.

- *They are protected from the "suits."* All Great Groups seem to have disdain for their corporate overseers and all are protected from them by a leader—not necessarily the leader who defines the dream. In the Manhattan Project, for instance, General Leslie Grove kept the Pentagon brass happy and away, while Oppenheimer kept the group focused on its mission. At Xerox PARC, Bob Taylor kept the honchos in Connecticut (referred to by the group as "toner heads") at bay *and* kept the group focused. Kelly Johnson got himself appointed to the board of Lockheed to help protect his Skunk Works. In all cases, physical distance from headquarters helped.

- *They have a real or invented enemy.* Even the most noble mission can be helped by an onerous opponent. That was literally true with the Manhattan Project, which had real enemies—the Japanese and the Nazis. Yet most organizations have an implicit mission to destroy an adversary, and that is often more motivating than their explicit mission. During their greatest years, for instance, Apple Computer's implicit mission was, Bury IBM. (The famous 1984 Macintosh TV commercial included the line, "Don't buy a computer you can't lift.") The decline of Apple follows the subsequent softening of their mission.

- *They view themselves as winning underdogs.* World-changing groups are usually populated by mavericks, people at the periphery of their disciplines. These groups do not regard the mainstream as the sacred Ganges. The sense of operating on the fringes gives them a don't-count-me-out scrappiness that feeds their obsession.

- *Members pay a personal price.* Membership in a Great Group isn't a day job; it is a night and day job. Divorces, affairs, and other severe emotional fallout are typical, especially when a project ends. At the Skunk Works, for example, people couldn't even tell their families what they were working on. They were located in a cheerless, rundown building in Burbank, of all places, far from Lockheed's corporate headquarters and main plants. So groups strike a Faustian bargain for the intensity and energy that they generate.

- *Great Groups make strong leaders.* On the one hand, they're all nonhierarchical, open, and very egalitarian. Yet on the other hand, they all have strong leaders. That's the paradox of group leadership. You cannot have a great leader without a Great Group—and vice versa. In an important way, these groups made the leaders great. The leaders I studied were seldom the brightest or best in the group, but neither were they passive players. They were connoisseurs of talent, more like curators than creators.

- *Great Groups are the product of meticulous recruiting.* It took Oppenheimer to get a Kistiakowsky and a Niels Bohr to come to his godforsaken outpost in the desert. Cherry-picking the right talent for a group means knowing what you need and being able to spot it in others. It also means understanding the chemistry of a group. Candidates are often grilled, almost hazed, by other members of the group and its leader. You see the same thing in great coaches. They can place the right people in the right role—and get the right constellations and configurations within the group.

- *Great Groups are usually young.* The average age of the physicists at Los Alamos was about twenty-five. Oppenheimer—"the old man"—was in his thirties. Youth provides the physical stamina demanded by these groups. But Great Groups are also young in their spirit, ethos, and culture. Most important, because they're young and naive, group members don't know what's supposed to be impossible, which gives them the ability to do the impossible. As Berlioz said about Saint-Saens, "He knows everything; all he lacks is inexperience." Great Groups don't lack the experience of possibilities.

- *Real artists ship.* Steve Jobs constantly reminded his band of Apple renegades that their work meant nothing unless they brought a great product to market. In the end, Great Groups have to produce a tangible outcome external to themselves. Most dissolve after the product is delivered; but without something to show for their efforts, the most talented assemblage becomes little more than a social club or a therapy group.

New Rules for Leaders

These principles not only define the nature of Great Groups, they also redefine the roles and responsibilities of leaders. Group leaders vary widely in style and personality. Some are facilitators, some are doers, some are contrarians. Leadership is inevitably dispersed, however, sometimes in formal rotation, more often with people playing ad hoc leadership roles at different points.

Furthermore, the formal leaders, even when delegating authority, are catalytic *completers*; they take on roles that nobody else plays—cajoler, taskmaster, protector, or doer—and that are needed for the group to achieve its goal. They intuitively understand the chemistry of the group and the dynamics of the work process. They encourage dissent and diversity in the pursuit of a shared vision, and they understand the difference between healthy, creative dissent and self-serving obstructionism. They are able to discern what different people need at different times.

In short, despite their differences in style, the leaders of Great Groups share four behavioral traits. Without exception, the leaders of Great Groups

- *Provide direction and meaning.* They remind people of what's important and why their work makes a difference.

- *Generate and sustain trust.* The group's trust in itself—and its leadership—allows members to accept dissent and ride through the turbulence of the group process.

- *Display a bias toward action, risk taking, and curiosity.* A sense of urgency—and a willingness to risk failure to achieve results—is at the heart of every Great Group.

- *Are purveyors of hope*. Effective team leaders find both tangible and symbolic ways to demonstrate that the group can overcome the odds.

There's no simple recipe for developing these skills; group leadership is far more an art than a science. But we can start by rethinking our notion of what collaboration means and how it is achieved. Our management training and educational institutions need to focus on group development as well as individual development. Universities, for instance, rarely allow group Ph.D. theses or rewards for joint authorship. Corporations usually reward individual rather than group achievement, even as leaders call for greater teamwork and partnership.

Power of the Mission

It's no accident that topping both lists—the principles of Great Groups and the traits of group leaders—is the power of the mission. All great teams—and all great organizations—are built around a shared dream or motivating purpose. Yet organizations' mission statements often lack real meaning and resonance. Realistically, your team need not believe that it is literally saving the world, as the Manhattan Project did; it is enough to feel that it is helping people in need or battling a tough competitor. Simply punching a time clock doesn't do it.

Articulating a meaningful mission is the job of leaders at every level—and it's not an easy task. In Shakespeare's *Henry IV, Part 1*, Glendower, the Welsh seer, boasts to Hotspur that he can "call spirits from the vasty deep," and Hotspur retorts, so can I, so can anybody—"but will they come when you do call for them?" That is the test of inspiring leadership.

I learned firsthand how critical a sense of mission—or its absence—can be to an employer. Several years ago, I had an assistant who handled the arrangements for my speeches and travel; at night she did volunteer work for a nonprofit, self-help organization. Her work for me was acceptable but perfunctory. It was clear that she was much more involved and committed to her unpaid work. Frankly, I was jealous. I came to resent the fact that I was not getting her best efforts; after all, I was paying her and they weren't. We talked about it, and she was very honest about the fact that it was her volunteer work that had real meaning for her; there she felt she was making a difference. So you can't expect every employee to be zealously committed to your cause. But you can accept the fact that part of the responsibility for uninspired work lies with the leader.

Great Groups remind us how much we can really accomplish by working toward a shared purpose. To be sure, Great Groups rely on many long-established practices of good management—effective communication, exceptional recruitment, genuine empowerment, personal commitment. But they also remind us of author Luciano de Crescanzo's observation that "we are all angels with only one wing; we can only fly while embracing one another." In the end, these groups cannot be managed; they can only be led in flight.

32 JON R. KATZENBACH

MAKING TEAMS WORK AT THE TOP

Jon R. Katzenbach is a director of McKinsey & Company in Dallas, specializing in strategy, organization performance, leadership, and change for business and nonprofit institutions. He is author of Teams at the Top *and coauthor of the best-seller* The Wisdom of Teams.

Most top executives pay lip service to their "team at the top" but achieve only a small portion of the actual team performance potential of the senior leadership group. Others, who champion a team approach at all levels, become frustrated that they cannot run the company more as a team. Both extremes are missing the point: real team efforts at the top of large organizations have performance value only when applied to legitimate team opportunities.

In other words, the senior leadership group (that is, all the CEO's direct reports) need not try to become a real team. As obvious as this may seem, few senior leadership groups are disciplined about when and how they pursue team opportunities. As a result, they struggle for team performance when it makes no sense, and miss opportunities for team performance when it offers high potential.

This happens even in companies that have mastered the use of teams in other parts of the organization.

The reasons are simple to describe but difficult to overcome. Shortfalls in team potential occur when leadership groups

- Do not appreciate the discipline of teams and the performance potential that teams can offer—even at the top

- Do not differentiate between—nor make an explicit distinction in how they pursue—team and nonteam opportunities

- Depend on crisis-type events to trigger team behavior

- Rely exclusively on the familiar discipline of executive leadership, which conflicts with—and typically overpowers—the discipline required for team performance

- Regularly overlook new options for team composition, modes of behavior, and leadership roles they can play to build real teams in the right places

The Prevailing Mind-Set

When we think of a team at the top composed only of the CEO's direct reports, we presume that all companies have one, for better or for worse. We also presume that this senior executive group can function together in only one of two ways: as a hierarchical group or as a collaborative team. If these are the primary options, then most top teams certainly are not "real teams," because the CEO calls the shots. Moreover, it is virtually impossible to change that reality without changing the style of the CEO, which rarely happens. Hence we observe very little team performance in the executive suite of most organizations. This mind-set further leads to two different sets of myths about so-called teams at the top: the strong leader myths and the real team myths. Both result in a loss of performance potential within senior leadership groups.

Myths of the Strong Leader

The underlying assumption of those who favor strong executive leadership is simply that strong leaders cannot—and probably need not—function as part of a real team; that sort of behavior makes more sense down the line or in the workplace. This premise leads in turn to five fallacies surrounding senior leadership behavior.

1. *The CEO determines whether a company wins or loses.* What board of directors does not believe that if you pick the right CEO your problems are solved? The view is not restricted to corporate boards, however; analysts, consultants, and journalists as well as most executives appear to share this belief. In fact, it is close to heresy to suggest otherwise.

The reality is that the leadership requirements of winning companies (particularly those that stand the test of time) go well beyond the CEO. It is not that the CEO role is somehow less important, or that the leader's personal attributes have little influence on corporate performance; obviously, they do. Rather, it is that the broad leadership and organizational system is more important over time. As James Collins and Jerry Porras argue in *Built to Last*, "the success of visionary companies—at least in part—[comes] from underlying processes and fundamental dynamics embedded in the organization and not primarily [from] a single great idea or some great, all-knowing, godlike visionary who made great decisions, and had great charisma, and led with great authority."

2. *The CEO has to make all the key decisions.* No self-respecting boss admits to backing off when a tough decision is needed. This is particularly true in turnaround situations. This view causes most of us to believe that a real team (wherein the leadership and decision-making role shifts among the members) is really impossible at the

top, because real teams do not have a single leader or decision maker.

In reality, however, the CEOs of large companies cannot make all the key decisions, nor do they try. Instead, a strong cadre of leaders down the line is constantly making important decisions that never reach the attention of the CEO. More and more companies are disaggregating their businesses to create even more decision makers closer to both the marketplace and the workplace. Many of these decision makers avail themselves of real team decisions. Furthermore, real teams can and do function within a construct that permits the senior leader (or CEO) to decide key issues. This need not prevent a shifting of leadership roles within teams when opportunities require it.

3. *It is a team because we say so!* CEOs, managers, analysts, consultants, academics, and writers freely label the senior leadership groups of large and small companies "the executive team" or "top team." Everyone knows who they mean, despite the nonteam behavior that generally characterizes these groups.

The reality—which everyone knows as well—is that these groups seldom if ever function as real teams if one is rigorous about defining the term, applying the discipline it implies, and measuring the kinds of results it should produce. Labeling the leadership group a team does not make it so.

4. *The right person in the right job leads to the right team.* The very best companies devote major portions of their human resource system to getting right person–right job matches. At some companies it becomes a slogan, if not a reality. At the top, the primary focus of new leaders is how to structure and fill the top jobs in the company—particularly those that comprise the CEO's direct reports. The understandable presumption is that the right person will somehow figure out how to shape his own team—and will instinctively team up with other executives as need be to get the job done.

The fact is, real teams at the top happen naturally only when a major, unexpected event forces the issue—and only when the instincts of the senior leader permit the discipline of team performance to be applied. Unfortunately, that means a lot of valid team opportunities are overlooked.

5. *The top team's purpose is executing the company mission.* While senior executives are, in fact, responsible for carrying out the organization's mission and strategy, that is far from the whole story. To produce the kind of shared sense of commitment necessary to execute strategy, they must also focus on collective work products or joint leadership.

The achievement of mission depends on much more than the decisions of senior executives, some of which may warrant joint decisions. Good decision making alone, however, will seldom provide the focus, commitment, and mutual accountability that a real team effort must have. While it is possible for senior leadership groups to shape effective team behavior around key decisions, they seldom do.

As pervasive as these myths are, the result of embracing any or all of them is virtually to preclude real team performance at the top—except when a crisis breaks the strong executive leadership behaviors that prevail in most organizations.

Myths of the Real Team

Equally constraining is a set of strongly held beliefs about the importance of real team performance within a senior leadership group. These beliefs are increasingly evident among top executives, and have been at the heart of much of the research that has been published about executive team behaviors. Unfortunately, they are as counterproductive as the myths of the strong leader. Five beliefs in particular hamper the very team performance they are designed to stimulate:

1. *Teamwork at the top will lead to team performance.* This myth argues for more attention to the "four C's" of effective teamwork—communication, cooperation, collaboration, and compromise. It also recognizes that many senior leadership groups need to practice

more supportive behaviors or teamwork. In fact, most of us assume that teamwork is probably the only kind of team effort that senior groups can be expected to pursue.

The reality is that teamwork is not the same thing as team performance. Teamwork is broad-based cooperation and supportive behavior; a team is a tightly focused performance unit. Hence, by focusing on teamwork as a generic virtue, the senior group is less likely to discern when and where they need to apply the discipline required to achieve real team performance. They may improve their ability to communicate and support one another, but they will not obtain team performance without applying team discipline to a specific task.

2. *Top teams need to spend more time together building consensus.* We often assume that consensus-based decisions are somehow better than individual decisions, particularly with respect to critical corporate actions. Unfortunately, we also assume that building consensus is synonymous with reducing conflict, and that less conflict leads to more teamlike behavior.

The reality is that most executives have little time to spare as it is, and the idea of consuming more of that scarce resource struggling to build consensus makes little or no sense to them. In fact, many decisions—such as whether to appoint an individual to a new job or how to choose between two equally attractive strategies—are better made individually than collectively. Moreover, spending time together seeking consensus is not the same thing as actually working together, as a real team, to yield a higher performance result. The further reality is that in a real team the right person or persons make the decisions; group consensus is not required. Most important, real team efforts do not avoid conflict; they thrive on it. Conflict is virtually unavoidable among top decision makers, who must deal with ambiguity, high stakes, and frank debate as a matter of course.

3. *CEOs need to change their style to obtain team performance.* Those who see the strong, decisive style of the CEO and others as the major obstacle to team performance would admonish top executives to stop making all key decisions, and to learn to be more col-

laborative. Some even advocate personal counseling and leadership training to that end.

Most senior executives cannot fundamentally change their style. However, rather than trying to be someone they are not, if they simply learn to play a different role, they can often stimulate real team efforts, if not function as members and leaders of such efforts. Their underlying beliefs and everyday activities turn out to be much more important than their personal leadership styles. For instance, Andrew Sigler, the former CEO of Champion International, would probably not be anyone's first choice as the ideal team leader. He was a strong, individual leader with a single-minded focus on the best way to lead his company forward. Nonetheless, he understood the value of teams and, through word and deed, genuinely supported their growth throughout the organization. His successor, Richard Olson, has a very different leadership style, much of it developed while working under Sigler's strong executive style. Olson is a natural team leader who is able to lead Champion's senior group—both as a team and as a single-leader unit. Both Sigler and Olson achieved remarkable team results throughout the company, although Olson gets more team performance at the top. The key is in learning to differentiate between team and nonteam situations within the senior group, and to ensure that the appropriate discipline is applied—even if it means that someone else should lead the group's team efforts.

4. *The senior group should function as a team whenever it is together.* This myth presumes that every task for the senior leadership group could qualify as a team opportunity, regardless of how that task is best carried out within the group. But that view leads to team-building sessions that can drive tough, skeptical executives up the wall. As a result, a lot of time can be wasted attempting to achieve team behaviors in situations that warrant more efficient, leader-driven approaches.

In reality many senior leadership interactions are simply not real team opportunities and do not warrant the application of team disciplines. Team efforts at the top make sense only part of the time—when they address specific issues that require senior executives to do real work together. If, by contrast, the task is simply a matter of reviewing and approving the work of others, or communicating syndicated decisions—as much senior executive activity has become—it is seldom best accomplished by a team. Individual efforts can often be faster and more effective, particularly when the potential value of the collective work products is low or unclear.

5. *Teams at the top need to "set the example."* To suggest that teams down the line cannot perform as real teams unless the top leaders act as role models presumes too much about the power of senior managers—and too little about the abilities of others. Nevertheless, believers in this view argue for "daily examples" of team behavior among the leadership group.

The reality is that daily contact is seldom even possible among the members of the management group. Fortunately, most real team efforts down the line are unaffected by how the senior leadership group behaves, as long as the top leaders believe in the value of team performance down the line and are supportive of such team efforts. The support matters far more than the example. Many of the team efforts at the top, however, are of necessity carried out behind closed doors because of the confidential nature of the crisis events that produce true team action.

The myths that grow out of the real team premise can be as constraining on senior leadership performance as those growing out of the strong leader premise. For that reason, it makes sense to consider seriously a different mind-set that seeks to integrate these two extreme points of view. Simply stated, a team at the top should be able to vary its composition, behavior, and leadership roles to optimize—and better integrate—individual, team, and nonteam performance. Obviously, this is an argument for a balanced leadership approach.

Achieving Balance at the Top

Expanding and tapping into the leadership capacity throughout the organization is important for virtually any enterprise that anticipates growth and change, be it Mobil Oil, Hewlett Packard, Champion International, or Ben & Jerry's. It doesn't seem to matter whether the company is large or small, industrial or financial, global or regional—leadership capacity is in short supply at all levels.

This has always been true, and will probably always be true—dynamic organizations can never have enough leadership capacity. On the other hand, just because the aspiration is elusive does not mean that we can afford to ignore the need. In leading a complex enterprise to an increasingly high set of balanced aspirations, team performance is but one of several approaches that leaders must consider. At the same time, I believe that team performance is the approach with the most potential for immediate results—and the one that is most neglected within top leadership groups.

The forces at work in any large organization can easily undermine senior executives' interest in learning how to increase their team performance. Paradoxically, these very same leaders are often in serious pursuit of greater leadership capacity. Yet they continue to overlook the value of the team approach in enhancing the potential of any small group. Real teams learn how to shape working approaches that exploit the leadership capabilities of all their members. They also learn how to develop those individual and collective capabilities to the fullest. The full potential, however, of a team at the top cannot be realized unless and until the leadership group is able to

- Sharpen its ability to recognize high-potential team opportunities and differentiate them from equally important nonteam situations

- Learn to shift its mode and composition to fit differing opportunities and apply the appropriate discipline

- Become comfortable in shifting the leadership role among its members without eroding the ultimate authority of the CEO

What worries me most when able leaders are first exposed to the notion of fluid team dynamics is their tendency to conclude "we already do that." Discussions of shifting roles and responsibilities among senior leadership groups invariably produce a great deal of head nodding, knowing glances, and side comments of support—followed by the sighs of relief that "we don't really have to worry about being a team after all—we just have to keep delegating work to subgroups."

This is an understandable reaction, because much of what effective leaders do instinctively is what works best for teams at the top. In moments of crisis—a plant disaster, a takeover threat, any unexpected and serious disruption of service—people break the hierarchical norms of the organization and work together to accomplish whatever needs to be done. Most leaders are also relieved to learn that their personal styles do not usually need to change, that they need not feel guilty about functioning as single-leader working groups, and that strong individual leadership still counts for a lot. Indeed, subordinate groups working without the executive's direct participation are often the best way to obtain team performance, and as we have seen, unexpected events will probably trigger true team behavior anyway. No wonder "we already do it that way" is a common reaction among senior executives.

So why not just keep doing it in the way you are most comfortable? The answer, of course, is that instinctive adherence to executive leadership disciplines will snuff out team discipline. Any senior leadership group may get team performance in crucial situations, but will not obtain it in many other important opportunities. Teams excel when

- The task requires a truly collaborative work product
- Real value accrues from rotating leadership roles among team members
- Members hold themselves mutually accountable

But understanding the difference between team and nonteam situations is not enough. Learning how to recognize those differences, consciously making the trade-offs between the speed of individual action and the performance potential of team action, integrating the two disciplines, and applying the right discipline at the right time are acquired skills for most leaders who run things at any level. To that end, the following six specific suggestions can help any senior group that aspires to more team performance at the top:

1. *Determine the group's level of common commitment to real team efforts.* Openly discuss each member's beliefs as to the potential value of more team performance within the group. Unless and until group members truly believe in the extra value of team performance, executive leadership discipline will prevail.

2. *Do not try to be a real team all the time.* Learn the difference between a real team effort and a single-leader working group; recognize that both have value within the construct of the senior leadership group.

3. *Be disciplined, but be selective.* Learn to apply the six elements of team discipline—small size, complementary skills, common purpose, clear performance goals, explicit working approach, and mutual accountability. Real team performance demands that members of the group understand and apply this simple discipline, as well as deal with the inevitable conflicts that team basics create for advocates of executive discipline. Until the group recognizes the value of both disciplines and is selective about when to apply each, valuable leadership capacity will be lost.

4. *Go beyond your "personal favorite" leadership approach.* Learn to shift in and out of a real team mode of behavior and vary the roles played by each member without eroding the senior leader's ultimate authority. This suggests an open discussion of the relative areas of individual experience and know-how, as well as the design of a working approach for the group that permits role shifts among the members as different kinds of performance issues arise.

5. *Obtain the right skill mix.* Vary the membership of each team situation to fit its purpose and goals; do not presume that all "direct reports" should be involved in all team issues at the top. Seek out the appropriate skill mix for each situation, even if it requires skills from outside the senior group.

6. *Concentrate team efforts where they count the most.* Periodically (say, every six months) explicitly identify the half-dozen or so team opportunities that deserve priority attention of the senior leadership group. Ensure that the six elements of team discipline are being applied to each of these situations.

The good news is that team performance at the top is much more doable than commonly assumed. The bad news is that most small groups that run things can obtain team performance only by changing their approach, learning new skills, applying multiple disciplines—and doing more real work together. The potential benefits of doing so are too great to ignore.

33 J. RICHARD HACKMAN

WHY TEAMS DON'T WORK

J. Richard Hackman is Calmers-Rabb Professor of Social and Organizational Psychology at Harvard University. He conducts research on the performance of work teams, social influences on individual behavior, and the design and leadership of self-managing units. He has consulted with a number of organizations on issues of work design, leadership, and team performance, and is author or editor of seven books, including Groups That Work.

A few years ago, Paul Osterman, an economist at MIT, did a careful national survey of innovative work practices in U.S. manufacturing firms. He found that more than half the companies surveyed were using teams—and that some 40 percent of these companies had more than half of their employees in teams. How well do all of these teams perform? To judge from management

---

Source: Adapted from J. Richard Hackman, "Why Teams Don't Work," in R. S. Tindale, J. Edwards, and E. J. Posavac (eds.), *Applications of Theory and Research on Groups to Social Issues*. New York: Plenum. Copyright © J. Richard Hackman.

books and articles, the answer is clear: teams markedly outperform individuals, and self-managing teams do best of all.

Here are some reports from the field, cited by Jack Orsburn and his colleagues in their 1990 book *Self-Directed Work Teams: The New American Challenge*. At Xerox, the authors report, "plants using work teams are 30 percent more productive than conventionally organized plants. Procter & Gamble gets 30 to 40 percent higher productivity at its 18 team-based plants. . . . Tektronix Inc. reports that one self-directed work team now turns out as many products in 3 days as it once took an entire assembly line to produce in 14 days. . . . Federal Express cut service glitches such as incorrect bills and lost packages by 13 percent. . . . Shenandoah Life processes 50 percent more applications and customer service requests using work teams, with 10 percent fewer people."

It makes sense. Teams bring more resources—and more diverse resources—to bear on a task than could any single performer. Moreover, teams offer flexibility in the use of those resources—the capability to redeploy member talents and energies quickly and to keep the work going even when some members are unavailable. Teams composed of people from different units can transcend traditional functional and organizational barriers and get members pulling together toward collective objectives. And of course teams offer the potential for synergy, that wonderful state when a group clicks and members achieve more than any of them could have accomplished alone. These are major benefits, worthy of the attention of the leaders of any enterprise. No wonder Osterman found teams to be so popular.

But there is a puzzle here. Research evidence about team performance shows that teams usually do less well—not better—than the sum of their members' individual contributions. When interacting teams are compared to nominal groups (that is, groups that never meet, whose output is constructed by combining the separate contributions of those who would have been members), nominal groups usually win.

This fact was driven home for me a few years ago after some colleagues and I had completed an intensive study of thirty-three different work groups of all different kinds—athletic teams, industrial production workers, top management teams, prison guards, airline crews, economic analysts, and more. We pulled our findings together in a book I wanted to call *Groups That Work*, a catchy phrase with what I thought to be a clever pun. Our editor told us that he'd be happy to publish the book, but not with that title: there were just too many groups in our study that barely worked at all. He was right. Probably four of our thirty-three groups were actually effective teams. The rest had problems so severe that our analysis was mainly about what had gone wrong with them. So the book was published with a parenthetical phrase after my clever title: *Groups That Work (and Those That Don't)*. Anyone who actually reads through it will discover, as our editor did, that most of our groups lie within the parentheses.

What, then, are we to make of all the team successes reported in the managerial literature? It is possible, of course, that the published claims are exaggerated, as writers have sought to catch the wave of enthusiasm about teams—to sell books, to build consulting practices, to market training programs, to become team gurus. That is not a sufficient explanation. Indeed, I trust the accuracy of the numbers about productivity and service gains that are reported in the popular books about teams. My concern, instead, is whether those numbers really mean what they seem to mean.

The implementation of any new management program, be it self-managing teams or anything else, invariably involves intense scrutiny of the unit where the changes will occur. Taking a close look at any work unit that has been operating for a while almost always surfaces some inefficiencies and poor work procedures. These incidental problems are corrected as part of the change process—it would be foolish not to correct them. But in making these corrections, an interpretive ambiguity is introduced. Was it the team design that resulted in the improvements found, or was it that a shoddy work system was shaped up? Virtually any intervention that is not itself destructive has a better-than-even chance of generating short-term improvements, simply because of the value of intently inspecting a work system. The question, then, is whether short-term improvements associated with the introduction of teams are sustained over time as inefficiencies begin to creep back into the system. It is not possible to know for sure—at least not without an appropriate longitudinal research design.

My own observations suggest that work teams tend to clump at both ends of the effectiveness continuum. Those that go sour often do so in multiple ways—clients are dissatisfied with a team's work, members become frustrated and disillusioned, and the team becomes ever weaker as a performing unit. Such teams are easily outperformed by smoothly functioning traditional units. On the other hand, teams that function well can indeed achieve a level of synergy and agility that never could be preprogrammed by organization planners or enforced by external managers. Members of such teams respond to their clients and to each other quickly and creatively, generating both superb performance and ever-increasing personal and collective capability. Teams, then, are somewhat akin to audio amplifiers: whatever passes through the device—be it signal or noise—comes out louder.

What differentiates those teams that go into orbit and achieve real synergy from those that crash and burn? The answer has much more to do with how teams are structured and supported than with any inherent virtues or liabilities they may have as performing units.

Mistakes Managers Make

In the course of several research projects, my colleagues and I have identified a number of mistakes that managers make in setting up and leading work teams, mistakes that invariably cap a team's performance potential.

- Mistake 1. *Use a team for work that is better done by individuals.* There are some tasks that only a team can do, such as performing a string quartet or carrying out a multiparty negotiation. There are other tasks, however, that are inimical to team work. One such task is creative writing. Not many great novels, symphonic scores, or epic poems have been written by teams. Such tasks involve bringing to the surface, organizing, and expressing thoughts and ideas that are but partially formed in one's mind (or in some cases, that lie deep in one's unconscious), and they are inherently better suited to individual than to collective performance. Even committee reports—mundane products compared to novels, poems, and musical scores—invariably turn out better when written by one talented individual on behalf of a group than by the group as a whole working in lockstep.

The same is true for executive leadership. For all the attention given to top management teams these days, my reading of the management literature is that successful organizations almost always are led by a single talented and courageous human being. Among the many executive functions that are better accomplished by an exceptional individual than by an interacting team is the articulation of a challenging and inspiring collective direction. Here, for example, is a mission statement posted in a company cafeteria: "Our mission is to provide quality products and services that meet the needs of individuals and businesses, allowing us to prosper and provide a fair return to our stockholders." I don't know how that particular statement was prepared, but I'd wager that it was hammered out by a committee over many long meetings. The most engaging and powerful statements of corporate vision, by contrast, invariably are the product of a single intelligence, set forth by a leader willing to take the risk of establishing collective purposes that lie just beyond what others believe to be the limits of the organization's capability.

There are many other kinds of tasks that are better done by individual human beings than by teams. It is a mistake—a common one and often a fatal one—to use a team for work that requires the exercise of powers that reside within and are best expressed by individuals.

• Mistake 2. *Call the performing unit a team but really manage members as individuals.* To reap the benefits of teamwork, one must actually build a team. According to organizational scholar Clayton Alderfer, real teams are bounded social systems whose members are interdependent for a shared purpose, and who interact as a unit with other individuals and groups in achieving that purpose. They can be small or large, face-to-face or electronically connected, and temporary or permanent. Only if a group is so large, loosely connected, or short-lived that members cannot operate as an intact social system does it have no chance to become a team.

Managers sometimes attempt to capture the benefits of teamwork by simply declaring that some set of people (often everyone who reports to the same supervisor) is now a team and that members should henceforth behave accordingly. Real teams cannot be created that way. Instead, explicit action must be taken to establish and affirm the team's boundaries, to define the task for which members are collectively responsible, and to give the team the autonomy that members need to manage both their own team processes and their relations with external entities such as clients and coworkers. If the performing unit is to be a team, then it should be a real team—and it should be managed as such.

Creating and launching real teams is not something that can be accomplished casually, as is illustrated by research on airline cockpit crews. It is team functioning, rather than mechanical problems or the technical proficiency of individual pilots, that is at the root of most airline accidents. Crews are especially vulnerable when they are just starting out; the National Transportation Safety Board reported in 1994 that 73 percent of the accidents it investigated occurred on the crew's first day of flying together—and 44 percent of those accidents happened on the crew's very first flight.

This research has clear policy implications. Crews should be kept intact over time, preflight briefings should be standard practice, and captains should be trained in the skills needed to conduct briefings that get crews off to a good start. Yet in most airlines, crew composition is constantly changing because of the long-standing practice, enforced by labor contracts, of assigning pilots to trips, positions, and aircraft as individuals—usually on the basis of a seniority bidding system. Creating and launching real teams is a significant challenge in organizations such as airlines that have deeply rooted policies and practices that are oriented primarily toward individuals rather than teams.

- Mistake 3. *Fall off the authority balance beam.* When a manager sets the direction for a team, anxieties inevitably rise—especially when the manager must balance between assigning a team authority for some parts of the work and withholding it for other parts. Because both managers and team members tend to be uncomfortable in such situations, they may implicitly collude to "clarify" who is really in charge of the work. Sometimes the result is the assignment of virtually all authority to the team—which can result in anarchy or in a team heading off in an inappropriate direction. Other times, managers retain all authority for themselves, dictating work procedures in such detail that many of the advantages that can accrue from teamwork are lost.

To maintain an appropriate balance of authority between managers and teams requires that anxieties be managed rather than minimized. Moreover, it is insufficient merely to decide how much authority a team should have. Equally important are the domains of authority that are assigned to teams and retained by managers. Our research suggests that team effectiveness is enhanced when managers are unapologetic and insistent about exercising their own legitimate authority about direction, the end states the team is to pursue. Authority about the means by which those ends are accomplished, however, should rest squarely with the team itself.

Contrary to traditional wisdom about participative management, to set authoritatively a clear, engaging direction for a team is to empower, not disempower, it. Having a clear direction helps align team efforts with the objectives of the parent organization, provides members with a criterion to use in choosing among various means for pursuing those objectives, and fosters members' motivational engagement. When direction is absent or unclear, members may wallow in uncertainty about what they should be doing and may even have difficulty generating the motivation to do much of anything.

- Mistake 4. *Dismantle existing organizational structures so that teams will be fully empowered to accomplish the work.* Traditionally designed organizations often are plagued by constraining structures that have been built up over the years to monitor and control employee behavior. When teams are used to perform work, such structures tend to be viewed as unnecessary bureaucratic impediments to group functioning. Thus, just as some managers mistakenly attempt to empower groups by relinquishing all authority to them, so do some attempt to cut through bureaucratic obstacles to team functioning by dismantling all the structures that they can. The assumption, apparently, is that removing structures will release the pent-up power of groups and allow members to work together creatively and effectively.

If anything, the opposite is true: groups with appropriate structures tend to develop healthy internal processes, whereas those with insufficient or inappropriate structures tend to be plagued with process problems. It is nearly impossible for members to learn how to interact well within a flawed or underspecified team structure.

Our research suggests that an enabling structure for a work team has three components. The first component is a well-designed team task, one that engages and sustains member motivation. Such tasks are whole and meaningful pieces of work that stretch members' skills, that provide ample autonomy for doing what needs to be done to accomplish the work, and that generate direct and trustworthy feedback about results. Second is a well-composed group. Such groups are as small as possible, have clear boundaries, include members with adequate task and interpersonal skills, and have a good mix of members—people who are neither so similar to one another that they are like peas in a pod nor so different that they are unable to work together. Third is clear and explicit specification of the basic norms of conduct for team behavior, the handful of "must do" and "must never do" behaviors that allow members to pursue their objectives without having to discuss continuously what kinds of behaviors are and are not acceptable.

The key question about structure, then, is not how much of it a team has. Rather, it is about the kind of structure that is provided: Does it enable and support collective work, or does it make teamwork more difficult and frustrating than it needs to be?

- Mistake 5. *Specify challenging team objectives, but skimp on organizational supports.* Even if a work team has clear, engaging direction and an enabling structure, its performance can falter if it has insufficient organizational support. Such teams often start out with great enthusiasm but then become frustrated in trying to obtain the organizational supports they need to accomplish the work.

If the full potential of work teams is to be realized, organizational structures and systems must actively support competent teamwork. Key supports include (1) a reward system that recognizes and reinforces excellent team performance (not just individual contributions); (2) an educational system that provides teams, at their initiative, any training or technical consultation they may need to supplement members' own knowledge and expertise; (3) an information system that provides teams with the data and forecasts that members need to proactively manage their work; and (4) the mundane material resources—equipment, tools, space, money, staff, or whatever—that the work requires.

It is no small undertaking to provide these supports to teams, especially for managers whose experience has mainly involved supporting and controlling work performed by individuals, in organizations that are fine-tuned to support individual work.

- Mistake 6. *Assume that members already have all the skills they need to work well as a team.* Once a team has been formed and given its task, managers sometimes assume that their work is done. A strict hands-off stance, however, can limit a team's effectiveness when members are not already skilled and experienced in teamwork—a not uncommon state of affairs in cultures where individualism is a dominant value.

It can be helpful, therefore, for leaders and managers to provide some coaching to individuals in honing their team skills and to the team as a whole in developing good group performance practices. There is no one best way to provide such help, nor is there any one best coaching style. Like teaching a class, coaching a group is done best when the leader exploits his or her own personality and style to get the lesson across.

There are, however, certain times in the life of a team when members are likely to be especially open to coaching: the beginning, when a group is just starting its work; the midpoint, when half the work has been done or half the allotted time has passed; and the end, when a piece of work has been finished.

Although I am uneasy about applying sports metaphors to business, the behavior of good athletic coaches does illustrate the different coaching functions that can be performed at different times in the life of a work group. Just before the game, coaches tend to focus on matters of *motivation*, establishing that the contest about to begin will be quite challenging but that the team has a real chance to win if members play hard and well. Halftime, back in the locker room, is a time for *consultation*, revising the game strategy for the second half of play based on how things have gone thus far. The next day, when the team has gathered to review the game films, is when coaches focus on *education*, helping to build individual and team proficiency in preparation for the team's next contest. Although good coaches can do many other things to foster team effectiveness, these three times in the life of a group offer openings for coaching that may be especially welcomed by and helpful to team members.

No matter how good coaching interventions are, they do not help much if a team's overall performance situation—that is, its direction, structure, and context—is poor. When these elements are present, on the other hand, the team reaps a double benefit: it is likely to have less need for coaching interventions (because it encounters fewer problems that require outside help), and the coaching that it does receive is likely to be more helpful (because members are not preoccupied with more basic, structurally rooted difficulties). Such teams have the potential of entering into a self-fueling spiral of ever-increasing team capability and performance effectiveness—just the kind of pattern that is described in all the popular books that tout the benefits of organizational work teams.

What It Takes

The conditions that foster team effectiveness are simple and seemingly straightforward to put in place: a real team with work that lends itself to teamwork; a clear and engaging direction; a group structure—task, composition, and norms—that promotes competent teamwork; team-friendly reward, educational, and information systems; and some coaching to help team members take advantage of their favorable performance circumstances. All the evidence suggests that teams for which these simple conditions are in place are likely to perform very well indeed. Yet one or more of these conditions is absent in the great majority of the teams studied.

Why should this be so? The conditions themselves are not subtle, complex, or difficult to understand. Indeed, they are just the kinds of things that an alert manager surely could learn from experience. The problem is this: to put these simple conditions in place is also to change the answers to four fundamental questions about how an enterprise operates:

- *Who decides?* Who has the right to make decisions about how the work will be carried out, and to determine how problems that develop will be resolved?

- *Who is responsible?* Where do responsibility and accountability for performance outcomes ultimately reside?

- *Who gains?* How are monetary rewards allocated among the individuals and groups that helped generate them?

- *Who learns?* How are opportunities for learning, growth, and career advancement distributed among organization members?

The answers to these four questions express some of the core values of any enterprise, and it can be maddeningly hard to change them. Indeed, it may be that such changes can be implemented in an established organization only when it has become destabilized for some other reason—for example, the departure of a senior manager, the rapid growth or dissolution of an organizational unit, the approach of financial disaster, or the introduction of a new technology that requires abandonment of standard ways of operating. Fundamental change cannot be accomplished either as an add-on (as managers in some corporations appear to wish) or as a one-step transition to utopia (as members of some ideologically driven cooperative enterprises appear to wish).

Creating organizational conditions that actively support work teams, therefore, is in many organizations more a revolutionary than an evolutionary undertaking, one that requires a different way of thinking about teams and the factors that affect their performance. As a metaphor, consider constant tinkering with a nation's interest rates, money supply, and tax policies versus getting fundamentally sound economic conditions in place and letting the economy run itself; or micromanaging the development of a child versus creating a good family context that promotes healthy autonomous development by the family's youngest members; or managing a physical injury such as a moderately serious burn with surgery and multiple drugs versus fostering the general health of the patient and letting the body heal itself.

In all of these instances the better strategy is to devote the first and greater portion of one's energies to establishing conditions that lead naturally to the desired outcomes and the lesser portion to on-line process management. The same considerations apply to the design and management of social systems, including work teams in organizations.

The implications for leaders and members of work teams are clear. Their first priority should be to get in place the basic conditions that foster team effectiveness—a far-from-routine undertaking in many organizations. In fact, establishing the preconditions for evolutionary, adaptive change is often a revolutionary act requiring new models of leadership and organization. Once the basic conditions are in place, however, leaders and members can "manage at the margins," making small adjustments and corrections as needed to smooth a group's progress toward its objectives. As organizational psychologist Ruth Wageman has pointed out, dealing with emergent team problems and opportunities is many times easier—and far more likely to be successful—if conditions favorable to team performance are already in place. Until we begin to accept the risks of revolution and break out of our traditional ways of construing and leading social systems, I fear that articles such as this one will continue to be about why teams don't work rather than about why they do.

34 MARSHALL GOLDSMITH

COACHING FOR BETTER TEAMWORK

Marshall Goldsmith is founding director of Keilty, Goldsmith and Company, based in San Diego, which consults to leading U.S. corporations. He was rated by the Wall Street Journal *as one of the top ten executive development consultants in the country.*

As leaders we always preach teamwork, but we often excuse ourselves from its practice—and even more often fail to hold people in our organizations accountable for living this value. This inconsistency invites corporate cynicism, undermines credibility, and can sap organizations of their vitality. The failure to uphold espoused values in general—and teamwork in particular—is one of the biggest frustrations in the workplace. In our research, involving thousands of participants at more than thirty large companies, employees rated their manager's ability to "effectively deal with individuals whose behavior undermines teamwork" dead last among ninety-two elements of effective leadership.

If everyone, including senior executives, acknowledges this challenge, why is it so difficult for leaders to promote change among those whose behavior they can most readily influence—their direct reports?

One reason is that leaders, like most people, want to be liked. Leaders are often afraid that confronting people about poor teamwork or other behavioral shortcomings (as opposed to performance problems) will cause them to be disliked. The paradox is, leaders would be more respected, not less, if they delivered the bad news. Outside consultants often provide behavioral coaching to leaders, and leaders usually appreciate the help. Surveys show that people highly value honest feedback—whether or not the feedback itself is positive.

The nature of the performance-review process itself accounts for much of the problem. Historically, when assessing others, most managers were forced to play the role of judge—and, potentially, executioner. The consultant, by contrast, is usually seen as an objective third party who is providing analysis, suggestions, and feedback gathered from multiple sources. A person receiving bad news from a consultant is more likely to separate the message from the messenger than a person hearing the same news from the manager.

Fortunately, leaders have at their disposal a valuable aid already in place at many leading companies—360-degree feedback. Carefully designed processes that include 360-degree feedback can allow a leader to practice consultative coaching, as opposed to merely exercising personal judgment. The results can be profound—and not just for department heads evaluating their frontline employees. The executive coaching process can help any manager whose work involves personal interaction. In fact, senior management teams at some of the world's leading companies—American Express, Avon, GE, Netscape, Nortel, Texaco—use 360-degree feedback as part of an overall process to help align corporate values and individual behavior.

Before You Begin

Although this process can improve behavior, it will definitely not solve all performance problems. Before you get started, ask yourself if any of the following conditions prevail. If so, behavioral coaching may be a waste of time.

- *The person you're coaching is not willing to make a sincere effort to change.* Behavioral coaching will work only if the manager you are coaching is willing to make the needed commitment.

- *The person has been written off by the company.* Sometimes organizations are really just documenting a case to get rid of someone. If that's the case, don't bother going through this process.

- *The person lacks the intelligence or functional skills to do the job.* If a manager does not have the capacity or experience required, don't expect behavioral coaching to help.

- *The organization has the wrong mission.* Coaching is a "how to get there" process, not a "where to go" process. If the organization is headed in the wrong direction, behavioral coaching will not make it change course.

Getting Started

On the other hand, if you're dealing with people who have the will and capacity to change their behavior, who are operating in an environment that gives them a chance to change, and who work for an organization that is headed in the right direction, this process will work; the nature of the process itself ensures its success. The approach I recommend involves eight steps:

1. *Identify desired attributes for the manager you are coaching.* You shouldn't have to start from scratch. I generally work with my clients to develop custom leadership profiles, but there are many useful inventories on the market (from Jim Kouzes and Barry Posner, the Center for Creative Leadership, and others) that can be a big help. Once you've determined the behavioral characteristics of a successful manager in a given position—such things as accessibility to colleagues, recognition of others, and listening—ask that

manager if he or she agrees that these are the right kind of behaviors. Securing agreement will boost commitment to the process.

2. *Determine who can provide meaningful feedback.* Key stakeholders may include direct reports, peers, customers, suppliers, or members of the management team. Strive for a balanced mix that does not stack the deck for or against the manager, and gain agreement that these are the appropriate reviewers.

3. *Collect feedback.* Assessment is often best handled in a written, anonymous survey, compiled by an outside party into a summary report and given directly to the manager being coached.

4. *Analyze results.* Talk with the manager about the results of his or her peers' feedback. The manager may choose not to disclose individual stakeholders' comments, or even numerical scores. The point is simply to discuss the manager's key strengths and areas for improvement.

5. *Develop an action plan.* The most helpful—and appreciated—outcome of any assessment is specific advice. Developing "alternatives to consider" (rather than mandates) shouldn't be difficult. If, for example, you asked the manager to suggest four things you could do to be a better listener, you'd probably get a pretty good list—things like don't interrupt people, paraphrase what they say, make eye contact, and pause five seconds before responding to their remarks. The problem isn't figuring out what to do; the problem is doing it. Focus on one or two key behaviors and develop a few action steps to improve each.

6. *Have the manager respond to stakeholders.* The manager being reviewed should talk with each member of the review team and collect additional suggestions on how to improve on the key areas targeted for improvement.

7. *Develop an ongoing follow-up process.* Within three or four months conduct a two-to-six-item minisurvey with the original review team. They should be asked whether the manager has become more or less effective in the areas targeted for improvement.

8. *Review results and start again.* If the manager has taken the process seriously, stakeholders almost invariably report improvement. Build on that success by repeating the process quarterly for the next twelve to eighteen months. This type of follow-up will ensure continued progress on initial goals and uncover additional areas for improvement. Stakeholders will appreciate the follow-up—no one minds filling out a focused, two-to-six-item questionnaire if they see positive results. And the manager will benefit from ongoing, targeted steps to improve performance.

Moving Beyond the Basics

You may want some coaching yourself from a trusted colleague, friend, or family member on how to approach the task, but this is not a mysterious process. It requires more discipline than talent, more integrity and commitment than behavioral science expertise. Simply by sitting down with the manager and analyzing the perceptions of his or her colleagues, you will be able to change your relationship with that person. And the person will change, too. Managers who want to improve, who talk to people about ways to improve, solicit feedback, and develop a rigorous follow-up plan, will almost always improve. (Certainly they won't get worse.) And when people improve, their self-confidence goes up. They keep doing what works, and they keep getting better.

By becoming an effective coach, you can become a more credible leader and an active agent of change. You can help people develop an essential habit for personal or organizational success—follow-through. By delivering what you promise—that is, measuring others on the behaviors and attributes you say you value—you cement the bonds of leadership with your constituents. And by having others follow through on their own progress toward agreed-upon goals, you can help create a more responsive, positive, and cohesive organization.

It may be difficult for leaders to give and receive honest feedback—and to make the time for genuine dialogue. Executive coaching is simple, but not easy. It is just one tool in a total strategy of performance appraisal, compensation, and promotion that can reinforce positive behavioral change. But if you're serious about your espoused values, shouldn't you ensure that the managers in your organization demonstrate the values you promote?

Part VII

LEADERSHIP ACROSS THE SECTORS

35 JOHN W. GARDNER

LEADERSHIP IN THE CITIES

> *John W. Gardner served as Secretary of Health, Education and Welfare from 1965 to 1968. He chaired the National Urban Coalition and founded the citizen's lobby Common Cause and the nonprofit alliance* INDEPENDENT SECTOR. *He currently teaches at Stanford University. He is author of seven books, including* On Leadership.

In the large, complex systems through which the contemporary world gets its work done, dispersion of initiative and responsibility downward and outward through the system is essential. The larger and more diverse the system, the less likely it is that a centrally designed, one-size-fits-all solution will work. There must be individuals in every segment and at every level authorized to take leaderlike action to solve problems in their part of the system. Centrally designed programs must leave ample room for ground-level creativity. Corporations have been learning that lesson in the course of twenty hard years of restructuring. The federal government is just beginning to learn it.

The lesson portends a substantially more significant governance role for the cities and their metropolitan areas in the years ahead.

Observers of the political scene should not be confused by congressional voices that are promoting devolution of power for their own short-term political, budgetary, or ideological purposes. For example, some are using devolution as a smoke screen to camouflage political agendas that weaken or destroy programs essential to American cities. In challenging such contrivances, however, we should recognize that a measure of devolution is necessary, indeed inevitable.

Whatever policies emerge from Washington, it is clear that local government cannot begin to accomplish the task alone. It must forge new partnerships with the private sector and with for-profit and nonprofit organizations. Collaboration will be the rule.

Leaders from all sectors can play an essential role in building bridges. Their skills, experience, and commitment can make a visible difference in the lives of people within and outside their organizations. Less visible, but just as powerful, is their influence on colleagues unaccustomed to crossing boundaries and building alliances. Both tasks—sharing resources to foster change and inducing others to participate—can help renew the cities.

Obstacles to Progress

The nature and patterns of leadership due to emerge will present us with a much bigger puzzle than we have yet admitted. Here are five considerations that complicate the task of leadership in our cities.

1. *Fragmentation is the rule in the city.* Affluent sections are not in touch with impoverished sections. The city is separated from its suburbs. Municipal agencies often communicate poorly with one another. Government generally has uneven relations with the business community. The mayor and city manager are often out of touch with neighborhood leaders. And nonprofit groups that could play a significant knitting-together role are too often rivalrous and territorial. Whipsawed by the elements of this fragmented scene, the city flounders. Most students of urban problems now recognize that

the only answer is to help new patterns of collaboration evolve among all the fragments.

2. *Collaboration requires leaders with special gifts.* Effective leaders are skilled in boundary crossing, in consensus seeking, in coalition building, in mediation and conflict resolution. And because many of the new players will be citizen-leaders from the professions, corporations, neighborhoods, churches, and the like, they may have a lot to learn.

3. *Citizens have lost a sense of ownership.* If we are to repair the individual's disastrous loss of civic faith, citizen involvement is essential. Everyday people must feel that they are listened to, that they are respected, that they can make a difference. Again, this places special requirements on leadership.

4. *Leaders are needed to represent all the various levels and diverse segments of city life.* That means recruiting business leaders, neighborhood leaders, city council members, and leaders in the schools and in religious congregations—leaders who will move beyond their special segment and take sustained interest in the whole community. There are never enough. Not that there isn't an ample supply of individuals capable of leadership. Most cities have enough leadership talent among their citizens to run a medium-sized nation. But it isn't available because of our patterns of selecting and using talent. Many potential community leaders have been siphoned off into highly remunerative professional or executive roles. Others simply feel no responsibility for the city in which they live—none whatever. Some have a fleeting sense of responsibility but are deeply bored by the whole subject of local government. Most of the literature on leadership deals with the tasks, attributes, strategies, and training of leaders; very little attention has been paid to the vexing question of how we persuade qualified but indifferent citizens to step forward and play their part.

5. *New kinds of leadership require new organizational structures.* Leaders generally function in some kind of structure or institutional setting. The military may offer the clearest example. It is one of the

most dramatic examples of leadership in that its leaders must send their people out to face willingly—even aggressively—the possibility of being killed. Perhaps because of the gravity of the assignment, the military provides its leaders with elaborate supportive arrangements: suitable equipment, logistical support, extensive training, a strong tradition, and a thoroughly developed structure of rules to guide conduct.

The chief executive officer of a corporation is supported by comparable, if less precisely defined, arrangements. The executive has a well-understood role, explicit authority, staff support, and much more. The same may be said for the head of a government agency.

In other words, leaders generally provide leadership in a well-developed context of supportive arrangements. So when we ask, in any given situation, "Where are the leaders?" we must ask the related question, "Are there leadership structures, established roles, and support for any leaders who do arise?"

It is a critical question in the cities today. Leaders are going to have to emerge from quite diverse segments of the community and work together to forge new kinds of partnerships among officials of local, state, and federal government; among neighborhood leaders; among business leaders; and among leaders from the many agencies and institutions of the nonprofit world. But in most cities we lack any of the appropriate supports for such citizen leaders—no designated jobs or titles; no clear, credible sponsorship or authority; no tradition; no rules or guidelines; and no staff support.

New Organizational Forms

I have no doubt that in twenty years such arrangements, structures, and traditions will exist in most cities. It would be foolhardy to try to predict exactly what they will look like, or what the new duties and the new leadership might consist of. Probably innovation will take many forms.

Some groups will consider the entire city their concern. For example, the Atlanta Project, launched by Jimmy Carter and supported by Ronald Reagan, George Bush, and Bill Clinton, has cut red tape and brought together business, government, nonprofits, and private citizens in a five-year campaign against poverty.

Some will focus on one or more neighborhoods. The Sandtown/Winchester Project used the construction of new public housing in West Baltimore as an opportunity to transform the entire community of ten thousand people.

Some will cover a whole state. The Oregon Progress Board tracks trends and helps government agencies, businesses, and nonprofits achieve 259 benchmarks for workforce development, quality-of-life improvement, and economic growth.

Some groups, such as California's Healthy Start (which marshals diverse resources in local communities on behalf of children), will be led by government; some will be led by the nonprofit sector (for instance, Success by Six, a twenty-year United Way plan for preparing youngsters for school).

A university or foundation could make a groundbreaking contribution by examining the various structures now in place across the nation, looking for ones that might be forerunners of things to come. Which of them seem most adequate to the tasks ahead? Which most effectively bridge the government–private sector gap? Which best meet the requirements for diversity and citizen participation?

Some groups will be deliberative bodies in which people from very different backgrounds learn to communicate with one another and reason together. Others will have a research function. Even if they do not have legislative or executive powers, they can be empowered to place proposals before government and to require action within a specified time. Some will be conventional nonprofit organizations. Some will be chartered by government. Their tasks will be to foster partnerships, bring about collaboration, build community, engage in conflict resolution through mediation and arbitration, envision the future, evaluate the past and present—and much more. The rules and guidelines will have to be developed by each city or state and will vary from one place to the next.

One hazard of such community bodies—as of all human organizations—is a gradual hardening of the arteries, a process in which flexibility, creativity, and problem solving disappear over the years, causing the group, ultimately, to engage in irrelevant routine exercises. Perhaps a complete renewal every fifteen years should be built into the arrangements for such bodies. One of the simplest solutions to this problem, pioneered by nonprofit organizations, is to impose term limits on the members of boards.

Selection, Training, and Tasks of Leaders

The leaders of these new entities would have to be selected for their capacity to work across boundaries with diverse segments of the population. Some may be facilitators, some mediators, some motivators. Some may be indistinguishable in style and temperament from the most able of today's legislators (even if they don't legislate).

Various sorts of formal training can be imagined and will no doubt be developed, but a process of self-selection will lead many individuals who think they are fitted for particular tasks to test themselves in volunteer roles for limited periods of service.

There should be ample provision for turnover. Burnout and stale-out are problems for both volunteers and staff working in the tumultuous world of citizen politics. Any civic group tends to become something of a hobby, a social club, and a source of ego satisfaction for a small group of citizens who embed themselves in the inner circle and hang on for dear life. Again, specified terms of service linked with systematic recruitment of younger leaders can keep these groups fresh.

It will be the task of the citizen leader to draw all segments of the community into a continuous conversation. Segments that have felt excluded or discriminated against must come to believe that they will be respected, given their chance to speak, and listened to. Government officials must be spared knee-jerk government bashing but must do their part by softening the attitude of professional elitism that implies they are the only ones who know how to run the city. University people—who have much to contribute, particularly in terms of research—must come to understand that they will not be putting their academic souls in peril by plunging into the roiling waters of citizen politics. The social agencies must learn to work together. The corporations must learn that they have a healthy and natural position of influence—good for them and good for the city—if they can resist throwing their weight around for the sake of short-term self-interest. (And incidentally, all corporations must have a line on their executive evaluation sheets that addresses the executive's contribution to local community life.)

Years of economic and social turmoil have convinced us of the need to lead and act in new ways. But we must also learn to think in new ways. The first step is to understand that most good work is accomplished with the help of allies. Our cities can be wellsprings of the innovation and human capital essential to every enterprise—if we learn to find common ground with people outside our own organizations.

It is fruitless to call for leadership in our cities without understanding the obstacles to progress, the institutional contexts in which we operate, and the need for collaboration. From one city to the next, the solutions will vary. But we can begin discussing the shape of the future now. The sooner we get on with it, the better.

36 REGINA HERZLINGER

FULL DISCLOSURE

A Strategy for Performance

Regina Herzlinger is the Nancy R. McPherson Professor of Business Administration at the Harvard Business School. She is an authority on the health care industry, nonprofit management, and financial management control. She is the author of numerous articles and books, including Market-Driven Health Care.

Americans expect results from their business, government, and nonprofit organizations. We also expect information about the performance of those institutions: Who's in charge? How is money spent? And what have they accomplished? In the business world, the demands imposed by lenders and investors—and of course by the Securities and Exchange Commission (SEC)—force companies to disclose precise details of their operations—earnings, expenses, performance, and levels of executive compensation relative to peer groups.

Despite the grumbling of some managers, organizations are helped by such scrutiny. Many companies, for example, measure the performance of different divisions, rank them, and share the results among all divisions. They do so because it serves to boost performance. And public disclosure has brought extraordinary accountability and credibility to business—and to the capital markets that ensure corporate growth. It is doubtful that millions of middle-class Americans would have invested billions of dollars in the stock market without access to basic information that allows them to make informed judgments.

Yet when it comes to 39 percent of the national economy—the nearly $3 trillion consumed by government and social sector organizations—Americans have few instruments for collecting information and comparing results. For all the talk of reinventing government and strengthening the social sector, there is still no way to gather and disclose information about their performance systematically.

Our public and voluntary institutions are literally the public's business. They are entrusted with taxpayer and donor dollars to educate our children, preserve and enrich our culture, and ensure the health and security of all citizens. They are too important to be excused from the obligations of performance and accountability. They cannot afford the erosion of public confidence that has followed recent scandals at some of our best-known nonprofits and that has dogged government for decades.

Most of these organizations perform remarkably well under difficult circumstances. But because they are run by humans, they sometimes let us down. Problems can range from inefficiency—for instance, arcane procurement practices that result in the military's legendary $600 hammers—to malfeasance, as in the recent fundraising scandal at the Foundation for New Era Philanthropy or the 1995 fraud conviction of the former president of United Way. Institutions can also fall victim to the private inurement of insiders and the unchecked financial risk of asset investments.

To alert responsible leaders to such potential problems—and more important, to restore public confidence in our most crucial institutions—we need strong medicine. Local, state, and federal agencies should implement the same kind of financial reporting as publicly traded companies, and should share that information with their constituents. And state and federal government—that is, we the voting public—should require our large nonprofit organizations to do the same.

Public and nonprofit organizations may lack the clear financial measures that drive business, but they can develop useful measures of performance by asking themselves four questions:

- *Are the organization's goals consistent with its financial resources?* An organization's leaders may aim too high relative to the available resources—or too low. For example, the Robert Wood Johnson Foundation had assets of $2.6 billion in 1990 but spent only $66 million in actual grants.

- *Is the organization practicing intergenerational equity?* Agencies must balance the needs of present and future beneficiaries by neither hoarding assets for a distant future nor consuming them all today.

- *Are the sources and uses of funds appropriately matched?* Fixed expenses such as salaries and mandated benefits should not be funded by variable revenues such as research grants or interest income.

- *Is the organization sustainable?* Even if the answers to the first three questions are positive, the organization might find itself overly dependent on a single individual, project, or funding source. Today's blue skies can turn stormy with little warning.

The answers to these questions will yield a revealing snapshot of your organization's financial and nonfinancial performance. For instance, to determine whether your organization's goals are consistent with its financial resources, you need to ask whether the organization achieved its stated goals, how much money it used to achieve them, and how significant its outcomes were relative to the money spent. It forces you to ask questions like, How healthy are our patients relative to a control group? How are our students doing relative to a comparable group? How are we faring with the homeless compared to other cities? But ultimately, performance outcomes must be measured relative to cost. If you're feeding twice the people as a neighboring charity but are spending ten times the money, how well are you really doing?

Every organization must determine for itself how effectively and efficiently it is achieving its mission. But the foundation on which to make that assessment should be established jointly by a cross section of interested parties. In the private sector, for instance, accounting standards for public documents are determined not by the SEC (though that agency has the power to do so) but by the Financial Accounting Standards Board—an independent agency representing businesses, investors, and citizens. Oversight must be rigorous but mutable—new bodies for setting accounting standards have been established as the concerns of the public and of business have changed over recent time. What's important is that we must have a mutually accepted process that is responsive to changing values in the community.

Radical changes in government and nonprofit management are inevitable. The push will come from the public, and eventually from the organizations themselves, who will benefit from greater credibility. As more and more money goes to state and local governments, we will see more questions about financial management and service delivery. Likewise, as nonprofits step up to the enormous social task being handed them, we're going to see more questions about their performance.

The evidence that we are already demanding more vigilance of our public and nonprofit institutions is growing. In the health care arena, for example, many organizations are more closely examining their own performance—and sharing that information with payers and consumers of their services. Yet those are only first steps, and mostly taken under duress. The health care report cards provided by many hospitals and HMOs are a step in the right direction, but they have focused on *process* measures—rates of immunizations, mammography, glaucoma testing. What's really important are the *outcomes* of such processes and the satisfaction of patients with the service they receive. Health care, after all, is a trillion-dollar industry, consuming 15 percent of our gross national product. That we don't have better measures of its performance is outrageous.

In other cases, public watchdogs are doing the job for us. For example, John Palmer Smith, executive director of the Mandel Center for Nonprofit Organizations at Case Western Reserve University, has developed his own report card to track the performance of the City of New York. He tracks crime statistics, health statistics, graduation rates, educational performance scores, the time cops spend out in the street as opposed to doing paperwork, and their overtime. Such doggedness helps keep city government accountable for its performance. But the average citizen does not have the means to gather such data; the city does, and it should share them with the public. Ironically, Smith has found that in recent years most measures of city performance have improved, so politically it could be a plus for officials to disclose such data.

I propose a four-part process that will largely remedy the woeful gaps in our understanding of public and voluntary sector performance. I call it *DADS,* for disclosure, analysis, dissemination, and sanctions. I spoke recently with four organizations, each of which has taken seriously its duty to account for its performance. Independently, each has developed a strategy that illustrates a different aspect of DADS.

- *Disclosure.* The United Way of America is an example of an organization that's reaching for more disclosure, partly in response to the damaging actions of its past president. United Way has pioneered a serious effort to measure not only the outcomes of programs but also their impact on the community. But even at United Way, which is far ahead of most nonprofits, evaluation processes are uneven. Ninety-eight percent of its participating organizations measure the volume of services delivered, but only 17 percent measure participant satisfaction. And 18 percent are attempting to assess the results of their programs in the form of measurable changes in the community. If those numbers sound low, it is because the concept is so new. Unlike the business world, for public and nonprofit agencies the notion of tracking constituent satisfaction is revolutionary.

- *Analysis.* Stephen Goldsmith, mayor of Indianapolis, exemplifies how analysis can improve government performance. He invited a national accounting firm to introduce activity-based costing and performance measures into local government. That information enabled city employees to compete against private sector vendors to provide municipal services. The results have been dramatic. Competition has generated more than $240 million in savings and has allowed the city to reduce its nonpublic safety workforce by 44 percent since 1992.

When the city's fleet services were opened to competition, the union beat out three national firms by increasing productivity and service quality. Subsequent savings to the city totaled $8 million. Likewise the street repair division used activity-based costing to reveal hidden overhead, and won a competition to fill potholes. Line employees redesigned their work and in the process cut their costs by 25 percent. In every area in which competition has been introduced, costs have plummeted, services have improved, and customer satisfaction (as measured by city surveys) has increased.

- *Dissemination.* When John Moorlach, the treasurer who is guiding the financial turnaround of bankrupt Orange County, ran against the former incumbent, he told voters the prosperous county was on the brink of bankruptcy—and people thought he was nuts. Why? They never saw the financial statements. Now, every month Moorlach produces a public statement that resembles a monthly money market report. He lists the investments by type of investment, indicating inflows and outflows, rates of return, monthly balances. Anyone who wanted to spend thirty minutes reviewing such a report would know whether the county was in trouble.

Furthermore, if you're a taxpayer in Orange County and you call Moorlach with a question, he'll respond personally. You cannot legislate that kind of personal responsiveness. But if you mandate the disclosure of comprehensive information, it forces a whole agency to be more accessible.

- *Sanctions.* Donald Berwick, who directs the Institute for Healthcare Improvement, is widely known as an early advocate of the once-preposterous notion that the quality of health care can and should be measured by somebody other than physicians. As a senior executive of the Harvard Community Health Plan in the early 1980s, he won praise for putting that principle into practice. Berwick soon concluded that the problem was not measurement alone but also involved changing the caregiving process. But any organization is subject to inertia and politics, and Berwick discovered that even if you measure a process, parts of your organization will resist doing anything with the results. So we need to educate and, failing that, apply sanctions to those who do not measure up. In health care, that could mean loss of accreditation or disqualification for providers of employer-paid health benefits.

A meaningful national sanctioning system is important because our past enforcement practices have been insufficient. If a nonprofit organization misbehaves, it is subject to revocation of its tax-exempt status by the Internal Revenue Service. But that is, in effect, a death sentence for the organization, and therefore rarely applied. All-or-nothing alternatives are seldom the best choices. What's most often needed—and has recently been enacted into law—is a series of incremental sanctions that give an organization an opportunity to acknowledge shortcomings and improve performance. DADS would further that process, and increase citizen participation in public institutions.

Increased disclosure appears to go against the political grain, involving as it does increased government oversight and regulation. But the process would not be as onerous as some will claim. Small local organizations should be exempt from public oversight, just as private businesses are exempt from many SEC requirements. The need is simply not as great. A day care program, for instance, might serve just twenty-five clients, all of whom are intimately involved in its activities; if the program does a lousy job, clients know it and will simply seek other services. Likewise, local religious organizations, arts programs, or activist groups have tremendous impact on the community and have such a small base of local support that if they fail in their mission, they're gone. But at some point—and that point must be determined through the political process—an organization becomes so big that the local base loses its voice.

Furthermore, the kind of oversight I propose is consistent with a powerful force in modern society—decentralization. Decentralization is impossible without good information. The best example of that is Johnson & Johnson—arguably the most decentralized corporation in the world. Johnson & Johnson comprises more than 150 companies, and the CEO of each company is captain of his or her ship. It's hard for a company as big as J&J to grow as much as it has, to keep making good products and good profits, without giving its operating divisions real autonomy.

But to think that an organization as decentralized as Johnson & Johnson has no accountability would be naive. In fact, it has more measures of performance, more oversight, and better communication between top management and unit management than do most centralized organizations. Decentralization means giving responsibility and authority to local levels, not abrogating oversight. So if Americans are serious about decentralized decision making, they had better find ways to monitor performance.

Each of the four organizations described here was forced to innovate as a result of disaster. The United Way suffered a public relations meltdown—and saw a precipitous drop in donations. Indianapolis, like most industrial cities, has struggled with a declining economic base, hard-pressed public services, and an aging infrastructure. Orange County endured the largest municipal bankruptcy on record and laid off more than a thousand workers. The Institute for Healthcare Improvement waged an uphill fight to reform a wasteful, unwieldy system that nearly everyone agrees has to change.

But the point of monitoring performance is not simply to help see organizations through times of crisis—though that is a benefit.

The point is to boost public confidence in vital institutions and thereby broaden their financial base. Just as SEC oversight has created credible, efficient financial markets and Food and Drug Administration approval has assured the safety and efficacy of medical devices and drugs, prudent regulation of the public and nonprofit sectors will pay off—literally—for the institutions who embrace DADS.

Unfortunately, even in the forward-looking efforts outlined here, improved accountability is mostly the result of extraordinary individual effort. John Moorlach, for example, intends to do his period of public service, then leave. Likewise, the approaches championed by Goldsmith and Berwick may or may not survive their tenures. Unless we institutionalize such practices, the public trust will depend on the good will, competence, and commitment of individuals. But if we want institutions that are as good as the people in them, it's up to us to take the first step.

37 JAMES E. AUSTIN

THE INVISIBLE SIDE OF LEADERSHIP

James E. Austin is John G. McLean Professor of Business Administration at Harvard University Graduate School of Business Administration. He is cochair of the school's Social Enterprise Interest Group and has served as an adviser to corporations, international agencies, and nonprofits, and as a special adviser to the White House. He has authored or edited fifteen books, including Managing in Developing Countries.

Businesspeople exercise leadership in the community as well as in the commercial world, yet we know little about the magnitude, form, and significance of their engagement in this other leadership arena. In many ways it has been the invisible side of leadership. We know that community involvement is widespread: a 1993 Conference Board survey of 454 companies revealed that more than 90 percent have formal volunteer programs for their employees and that 86 percent encourage their executives to serve on boards. But research at the Harvard Business School documents involvement that is deep, important to business leaders and their communities, and clearly beneficial to their businesses (see box).

The Other Leadership Arena

Surveys of more than 9,800 Harvard Business School graduates and 316 Fortune 500 company CEOs offer the following snapshot of community involvement:

Involvement is very high. Eighty-one percent are involved with nonprofits and 57 percent are board members.

Community service is not just a late life phenomenon; it begins early and grows. More than 60 percent of the recent graduates (twenty-five to twenty-nine age group) are involved with nonprofits. This rises to about 90 percent by age fifty-five, at which point board membership reaches about 70 percent.

CEOs are heavily involved. They generally serve on four boards, double the number for the average executive, with 30 percent sitting on five to eleven boards; most spend five to twenty hours per month, twice the average.

Involvement is broad but education dominates. Half of the board service was with educational institutions, followed by human services (28 percent), advocacy (23 percent), arts (22 percent), religious organizations (18 percent), health (14 percent), grantmaking (7 percent), and environment (6 percent).

Community service is an integral part of executives' lives and careers. Sixty-three percent considered their nonprofit involvement to be "very important" to them and another 35 percent considered it to be "moderately important."

A rigorous analysis of Standard & Poor's 500 companies by professors Sandra Waddock and Samuel Graves revealed that strong corporate social performance both benefits from and contributes to strong financial performance in a "virtuous circle." Nonprofits, too, benefit in important ways. Surprisingly, nonprofit executives cite their board members' business skills and managerial perspectives as being more significant than their personal donations or access to corporate contributions.

John Whitehead, former chairman of Goldman Sachs, believes it is myopic to view community service as simply altruistic: "Don't think that this is a charitable thing where you will get rewarded in heaven. You get rewarded right away because you'll be known as a company that is conscious of its social responsibility, you'll attract better quality employees, your stock will sell at a higher multiple." Our surveys, interviews, and company studies reveal that while executives primarily serve to "give back" to their communities, they also perceive important benefits accruing to their companies in three areas: human resource management, culture building, and business generation.

Human Resource Management

Managers cite specific benefits in recruiting, motivation, professional development, and assessment.

Recruiting

A company's capacity to create competitive advantage starts with its ability to attract talent. Increasingly, graduating MBAs are questioning firms' attitudes and activities regarding community involvement. For employers trying to differentiate themselves, this dimension of leadership may be decisive. Charles Perrin, former CEO of Duracell, explains, "The younger generation wants an involved corporation, a company that is making a contribution. A lot of them have concerns about working with a big company to begin with, so we put ourselves on a more human scale."

Community service also helps companies identify new sources of talent. For instance, Duracell provides college scholarships and internships to African Americans through the National Urban League; 80 percent of those interns end up as employees. Ninety percent of managers surveyed by the Conference Board said that volunteer programs helped them attract better employees.

Motivation

We found a widespread belief among executives that supporting employees' community service activities enhances employee commitment and retention. Financial incentives can be matched by firms trying to lure away managers, so the glue that makes an employee stay is often noneconomic. In the realm of intangible assets, value congruence looms large. A senior executive of a financial services firm says, "It's important to keep the people within my ranks involved and happy in the community to avoid being attracted to move elsewhere. If they have ties with a charity, it's going to be a lot harder for them to uproot and move elsewhere." Community engagement creates exit barriers.

Community service is a form of job enrichment. Studies confirm that volunteer programs significantly increase employee morale, loyalty, and productivity, all of which contribute to enhanced business performance.

Professional Development

Working with nonprofits, particularly as a board member, is seen as developmentally useful for both junior and senior managers in four ways.

- *Expanding practice opportunities.* Board service may enable younger managers to engage in tasks such as mission and policy formulation, strategic planning, and resource allocation that they would not yet do in their daily jobs. Many managers report that such experiences—obtained at lower risk to the company and themselves—increased their self-confidence as well as skills.

- *Enhancing core capabilities.* Helene Curtis Inc. has created the Development Through Service program to provide "an opportunity for experiential learning that can assist employees' personal and professional development." The company assesses twenty-eight business skill areas (including project management, planning, organization, team building, and presentation), identifies opportunities for employees to practice these skills through nonprofit involvement, and tracks the process to help employees meet developmental expectations. General Mills and Federal Express found that their community service programs enhanced employee skills in leadership, teamwork, organization, listening, and decision making.

- *Broadening perspectives.* For more senior managers, professional development comes from broadening exposure to people and organizations. The expanded interaction enables executives to escape their insularity. The added stimuli of interacting with more diverse colleagues enriches perspectives and enhances creativity. Breadth of view and understanding are vital capabilities for top leadership.

- *Learning collaborative leadership.* William Madar, CEO of the industrial firm Nordson Corporation, sees nonprofit involvement as a way to develop consensus-building skills: "You learn quickly that if you are in charge of a nonprofit's committee, you can't order people to cooperate. It's leadership in an environment where people don't necessarily have to follow. It's these very characteristics that we are trying to nurture within the business." A focus group of senior managers agreed that what they learned most in nonprofit settings is how to work with a diverse group of volunteers. They had to lead with their ability, passion, and conviction, not their formal authority.

Assessment

Community service can reveal an individual's capabilities, values, and attitudes and can sharpen the capacity for initiative, commitment, caring, time management, and organizing. How companies take this into account varies. Only a few of the companies studied had formally incorporated their managers' community involvement into their personnel evaluation process, but almost all the executives indicated that such participation is relevant to their judgments about people. A McKinsey partner provides the firm's perspective: "What we basically do is reward people who exercise leadership in any fashion, and we look favorably upon people who take responsibility outside of work." Another senior executive stated, "It's a way of standing out from the pack in a large organization—of getting noticed."

In contrast to such informal assessment, one professional services firm uses degree of community involvement as an explicit promotion criterion. One top executive says he prefers to hire managers involved in nonprofits because they are better team players. In some companies community involvement is seen as obligatory. For example, managers in one cable television company are disciplined if they do not serve outside the workplace, because positive community relations are seen as essential to the company's success. And nonprofits, which depend on volunteers for more than one-third of their workforce, need all the help they can get.

Culture Building

In foresighted companies, community service is not an add-on but rather a central force shaping and reinforcing values vital to the success of the business.

- *Service-oriented culture: empathy and caring.* Nordson's William Madar explains how community service helps reinforce the company's culture: "The values that are key to making an organization responsive to customers, to suppliers, and to each other are the very same values of caring that lead to concern for our neighbors and participation in the community. Community involvement is part of the whole. It is integral to the success of the business."

- *High-involvement culture: making a difference.* Boot and apparel maker Timberland Company, whose sales catapulted from $196 million in 1990 to $650 million in 1994, is led by Jeff Swartz. His strategy of "boots, brand, and beliefs" rests on a culture of service, broadly defined: "As a company we have both a responsibility and an interest in engaging in the world around us. By doing so, we offer the consumer a company to believe in and get involved with; we offer our employees a set of beliefs that transcend the workplace; we offer the community an active and supportive corporate neighbor; and we offer shareholders a company people want to both buy from and work for." The centrality of community service to the Timberland culture and its positive effects on attitudes, motivation, recruitment, and teamwork were confirmed in employee interviews.

- *Crisis glue: cohesion through core values.* A corporate culture provides an institutional anchor that stabilizes the organization during storms. In 1995, after years of explosive growth, Timberland had to weather financial difficulties. Its first-ever downsizing was traumatic, but the company's community service commitment helped deal with this, as one manager describes: "The service events last year told people that this was the same company. You have to find new opportunities for people to feel good. You can't give them money. You can't promote them. The service projects were a relatively painless way to do that."

IBM, too, has had to undergo major downsizing, with its workforce and corporate giving dramatically slashed. Chairman Lou Gerstner preserved community involvement as a key principle guiding the restructuring of IBM by focusing on K–12 education. During its downsizing, the company wished to send a signal internally and externally that community participation was still important, so it converted its annual office party into a community service day. IBM managers spoke of such involvement as a source of pride and renewal during a time when the company was widely criticized for poor performance.

- *Values compatibility check: partner assessments.* Community involvement can also play an important role in determining and reinforcing compatibility of corporate cultures in mergers. According to top management at Chase Manhattan, a shared commitment to community service contributed to the successful 1996 merger of the Chase and Chemical banks. In fact, the first public act of the merged corporation was a forum on major issues facing the nonprofit community. Likewise, EDS has used its global volunteer day to integrate employees from an acquired firm into the EDS culture by facilitating informal interaction between managers and staff.

Business Generation

Some might consider it inappropriate for individuals or businesses to realize economic dividends from a social contribution. But rather than question motives, we should ask whether such involvement adds value to the nonprofit and its social purpose. If the manager or the company gains at the expense of the community, then exploitation occurs. If both the community and the company gain, then the engagement has made a positive contribution. Private gain is not incompatible with public benefit.

- *Reputation enhancement.* Community service activities enhance a company's image and increase name recognition. A Citicorp executive describes the nature of the reputation-building process: "It's a competitive advantage. It takes a long time to build a sense of 'Let's go to Citibank instead of the other guy down the street because they are good corporate citizens.' But the feeling that you can trust the company does sway decisions people make." The direct service involvement by employees personalizes the company and creates human interactions that have deeper and more lasting reputational effects than standard public relations methods.
- *Goodwill banking.* A top executive at Duracell saw community service as protecting the business: "What you're always most fearful of is bad publicity. Community involvement builds a little

bit of a bank account. The benefit will come the day that something unforeseen happens, an environmental accident or a strike, or something that is going to thrust Duracell into the forefront, when we are going to have to start making some withdrawals from that bank of goodwill that hopefully we have built up over a period of years."

- *Network creation and relationship building.* Involvement with nonprofits expands one's circle of contacts. In many types of businesses, the more extensive one's personal and professional network, the more business that is ultimately generated. Community service creates a distinctive forum and process for developing relationships. Trust is frequently the determining factor in winning a client, and as one Citibanker comments, "Especially on hard-working boards, you develop a rapport with people rooted in respect and trust. Based on these board relationships, people feel obliged to help each other."

- *Market development.* For some types of immovable business, where the local community is their market, involvement in community activities is seen as an integral part of senior managers' jobs. This is frequently the case for manufacturing companies with plants in smaller towns or for big companies in their headquarters city. The new Chase Bank is New York's largest employer and has most of its customers in the city. An executive vice president says, "The quality of life for our people is married to the state of health of New York City. The better the city, the less likely our customers will be to move out and be gobbled up by other banks." Of course, when major companies are merged or acquired by outside interests, the level of philanthropic giving is often cut. Corporations often deal with these financial cuts, however, by increasing their direct service involvement.

Achieving Effective Community Engagement

Community service is clearly an integral part of business leaders' lives. Their engagement in the social sector is broad, deep, and personally satisfying. Their activities also yield significant dividends for their companies and therefore merit strong support. The challenge is how best to do this. Actions in five areas will enable companies to achieve more effective community engagement.

1. *Integrate community service into corporate strategy and culture.* Companies that have viewed community involvement as part of their core values have harvested greater benefits for the company, the employees, and the community. Those that treat it as a peripheral, public relations function are forgoing value-creation opportunities. The Conference Board survey revealed, for instance, that 77 percent of the companies believe that volunteer programs help them reach their strategic goals.

Many U.S. corporations have been shifting from a traditional charity perspective to "strategic philanthropy," which attempts to integrate corporate donations and community service activities with business operations and interests. But even the term *philanthropy* may be an impediment to full integration. It conjures up passive donation, with the spotlight on "How much are we giving?" The more appropriate question is, "How are we involved and what impact are we having?" Thus strategic engagement better communicates these companies' goals: proactive, deep, and multifaceted involvement that is an integral part of the company's strategy.

For example, Citicorp has made community service an integral part of its global strategy, which is to be an embedded corporation in each of the communities in which it operates, part of the institutional fabric. According to top management, this means "assessing the impact of business decisions on the community and mitigating any negative consequences, and engaging in activities—volunteer and philanthropic—that help build the community . . . all of which supports our global image as a trusted brand name." The company explicitly measures managers' performance on community betterment along with five other key areas. As one executive put it, "We are talking here about how we run our business, not just about contributions, volunteerism, and PR."

This strategy better integrates community service into the corporation's being. Some companies have separate foundations and community relations departments, but they work together, with a common corporate strategy for community engagement providing the guidance. Structure appears to be less critical than process in determining results.

Strategic engagement requires focus. Doing everything would be as nonsensical in the social arena as it is in the marketplace. Priorities should be set, resources focused, and synergies captured. A company should delineate those social needs areas that are most important to its communities and those that have the best fit with the corporation's interests and competencies.

Integrating community involvement with corporate strategy is half the task. The other half is ensuring that such involvement is central to the company's culture. It is clear that values are a powerful force in shaping corporate performance and that initiative, vision, commitment, energy, caring—the characteristics of those who volunteer in the community—are the same attributes needed to excel in the marketplace. Community service flows from and fosters the creation of a leadership organization.

2. *Make it a top-down and bottom-up process.* The CEO is the molder of the company's values. Coming from the chief belief-builder, the CEO's words and deeds are critical to the creation of a high-engagement corporation. Top management's blessings and active encouragement are essential to mobilizing widespread involvement. Those below listen acutely, and for a leader to say nothing is to say a great deal. Leaders need to be actively engaged in the community in significant and visible ways. Knowing that their CEO is volunteering time for community service increases employee loyalty to the company and its chief executive.

For community engagement to permeate the organization, the process must foster initiative from below as well. One can tap extraordinary amounts of latent energy and creativity by empowering line management and employees as architects and administrators of community service actions. Employee ownership is a prerequisite to institutionalizing such engagement into the company's culture and practices. Nordson, like many companies, created "Community Involvement Committees" in all its operating locations and then made block grants to them from the corporate foundation as a way to decentralize the decision making.

Companies that are implementing strategic engagement generally have created small corporate staff departments with responsibilities for community relations. Such entities can focus and energize widespread involvement. Challenges exist, however. Complete delegation to the community relations staff can isolate these activities from the company's core strategy formulation. Effective community relations departments see their role as facilitators, getting line managers and employees to assume primary responsibility. They also foster internal and external communications about the company's community service activities. Although there does not appear to be any inherently superior way to organize these activities, communicating, coordinating, and motivating are critical tasks.

3. *Remove barriers to involvement.* There are two main impediments to employee involvement in community service: the difficulties in locating activities and in finding the time to carry them out. Companies can facilitate employee involvement by providing a matching service (either from an outside agency or internally) that takes an inventory of employee service interests and connects them with appropriate nonprofits. There are about 450 Volunteer Centers around the country that recruit volunteers for community service, and there are seventy Corporate Volunteer Councils serving businesses. General Mills's Volunteer Connection program maintains its own database of volunteer interests and service opportunities. Both the contribution and the satisfaction will be greater if employees are engaged in an activity that they care about and that makes good use of their talents. Misplacement can be counterproductive, particularly for board service.

The biggest obstacle the managers cite in their service activities is inadequate time. If companies promote community and board service, then they should recognize that these activities are a valid use of time. Most companies provide paid release time. Some, like Timberland, give an explicit quota of annual work time (thirty-two hours) that their employees may use in service work; others organize single "days of caring." Many simply consider board-related meetings during business hours a fact of corporate life. A small number lend employees to nonprofit organizations or public service for many months. Companies are generally granting employees more time for service activities, with flexibility appearing to be more important than the absolute amount of release time.

4. *Enhance volunteer effectiveness.* Employees involved in community work are de facto "company ambassadors," so it is in the company's interest to ensure that they are well trained and supported in their service responsibilities.

Provide training. Particularly for board service, preparation is important. Training that will enable employees to perform more effectively is a form of representational insurance. Most managers' knowledge of boards and nonprofits, however, is quite limited. Local service agencies such as Cleveland's Business Volunteerism Council or Boston's United Way Board Bank sometimes provide training in board service. Publications on board responsibilities and related issues are available from many sources, including the National Center for Nonprofit Boards in Washington, D.C. Sometimes the nonprofits themselves will provide helpful orientations to the incoming board members. But too often this is not the case.

Give material support. The executive's service input on a board can be leveraged if the company supports that involvement with a contribution of funds, goods, or services to the nonprofit. Providing an employee-managed fund to cover incidental expenses related to employee group volunteer projects can also increase the quality of the volunteer experience. Providing in-kind services, such as use of copying machines or facilities for meetings, can enhance employees' efforts because they provide access to infrastructure that would not otherwise be available to the nonprofit.

Encourage peer consultation. Executives should have opportunities to share their board service experiences, concerns, and insights with one another, perhaps in special discussion lunches. There is a tendency to keep these activities off-line. Making them an integral part of corporate conversation fosters lateral learning, reinforces the legitimacy and importance of these activities, provides emotional support, and contributes to greater cohesion among employees by providing new grounds for interacting and sharing.

5. *Give recognition.* Almost all companies provide some recognition for volunteer service. This is not, however, as straightforward as recognizing outstanding job performance, because of the special nature of community service. There is a delicate divide between company life and personal life. Some individuals prefer to keep these quite separate, while others seek to integrate them. Some consider community activities as part of their constellation of personal activities and would not savor recognition. Those who do actively participate in company-sponsored or facilitated community service, however, generally enjoy and appreciate acknowledgment.

The individual, the corporation, and the nonprofit all benefit from their collaboration. But for these gains to be fully realized, corporations need to integrate community involvement into the company's strategy, culture, and operations. Leaders must set examples through their own service activities and empower employees to initiate and operate involvement programs. They can leverage their employees' impact through policies and procedures that encourage volunteerism and prepare them to perform social sector duties more effectively. As we move into the next century, businesses and business leaders will increasingly play the dual role of creators of wealth and generators of social capital. Their legacy will depend on the ability to succeed at both.

INDEX

A

Accountability: management, 19, 118; public-sector, 366–373
Accounting standards, 368
Adult education, demand for, 135–136, 137–138
AES Corporation, management practices of, 276, 281–282
Ala-Pietila, Pekka, 85, 86
Alderfer, Clayton, 339
AlliedSignal, management practices of, 256, 310
Amen, Jeff, 271
American Airlines, employee-suggestion program of, 274
American Express: customer loyalty to, 251; rewards program of, 273
Amoco, rewards program of, 273–274
Apple Computer: competitive failure of, 205, 207; teamwork at, 317, 318
Argyris, Chris, 65
Assessment: innovation and, 63–66; interpretation component of, 63–64; performance, 5–6
AT&T, bureaucracy of, 205
Atlanta Project, 361
Austin, James E., 375

B

Baldrige Award, 218, 240
Beers, Charlotte, 247
Behaviorial coaching, 350–354
Bennis, Warren, 315
Berry, Leonard, 301
Berwick, Donald, 371
Boardroom, Inc., suggestion system of, 269–270
Bossidy, Larry, 256, 260, 310
Brand identity, 247–248
Brooks, Rodney, 163
Business trends, 266–267
Business-guru system, 121–122

C

Career development, changing patterns of, 134–135
CEOs: community service involvement of, 385; public profile of, 122; role of, 212; and strong leader myth, 325–326
Change, organizational: coalition building in, 75–76; core values in, 243–244; decision-driven versus behavior-driven, 97; eight-step process of, 70–71; failures of, 95–96, 155–156; improvisation in,

389

102; leadership of, 217–220; loyalty and, 161–162; managing for, 69–79, 98–100, 155–161; mismanagement of, 70–73; ongoing, as multiphase process, 73–75; performance mapping for, 102–104; and process change, 234; principles of, 104–105; sustaining of, 130; vision and, 74, 76–78

Change, social: affiliations in, 127; career development and, 134–135, 139–140; community and, 136–138, 140–142; and institutional change, 127–128; sustaining of, 130

Character, in leaders, 220, 224–225

Charles Schwab, sustained success of, 305, 306, 307–308

Chase Bank, community service and, 382–383

Citibank, management practices of, 282

Citicorp: community service and, 382, 384; competitive strategy of, 209–210

Cities: citizen leaders of, 362–363; devolution of power in, 357–358; new organizational forms in, 360–362; performance measures for, 369; task of leadership in, 358–360

Coalition building, 75–76

Coca-Cola Company: leadership of, 258–259; mission of, 118

Collins, James, 237, 325

Commitment: in changing work environment, 161–162; to community, 223–224; in future organizations, 161–162; leaders' withdrawal from, 17; strategy and, 92

Communication: employee-management, 211, 268, 269–270; meaningful conversation in, 157

Community(ies): corporate role in building of, 13, 16, 18; diversity, as economic asset, 181–182; edge cities as, 136–138; global competitiveness strategies for, 176–179; innovation practiced in, 67; intentional, 141–142; legacy and, 16; nonprofits and, 140–141; organizational commitment to, 223–224; technological revolution and, 138

Community service, 140–141, 180–182, 375–388; benefits of, 181; business culture and, 380–382; economic dividends from, 382–383; innovation in, 53–56; strategies for involvement in, 383–388

Compensation, of leaders, 17, 19

Competition: brand identity and, 248; global, benefits of, 176; information-age technology and, 145, 147; leaders' strategies in, 49–50, 208–212; in new industrial landscape, 81–82; return on people and, 266

CompUSA, management failures of, 302

Conflict handling, 231

Convenantal relationships, 18

Corporate models, information-era challenges to, 195–196

Covey, Stephen R., 215

Cultural norms, innovation and, 62–63

Culture, corporate: emotions in, 47; empowered, 230–231; knowledge work and, 16–17; of openness and genuine inquiry, 64–65, 145; personality-based, 43–50; service-oriented, 380–382; of software industry, 186–187; technology's impact on, 143–149; of values, 217–218

Customer relations, emotional aspects of, 247–249

Customers, brand loyalty of, 247–249, 251–253

D

de Geus, Arie, 58, 60

De Pree, Max, 15, 39

Decentralization: accountability and, 372; rewards of, 133

Delegation, by leaders, 19–20
Deming, W. Edwards, 62–63
Diversity: community, as economic asset, 181–182; organizational, 13; team, 90
Downing, Wayne, 262
Downsizing and restructuring, 223, 267; financial effects on organization of, 279; service-oriented culture and, 381; trust and, 280–281
Drucker, Peter F., 53, 109, 134, 169, 265
Duracell, community service of, 382–383
Dyson, Esther, 143

E

Edelston, Martin, 269
Education system, future trends in, 129
Effectiveness, personal, seven habits of, 216
Emotions: in corporate culture, 47; and customer relations, 247–249; and new managers, 294; strategy and, 92
Employee(s): communication with, 268; development, as success factor, 277–279; front-line, communication with, 211, 269–270; globalization and, 181; opposing management views of, 57–58; partnership, 47–49; sense of ownership, 268–269, 309–311. *See also* Motivation, employee
Employee-suggestion programs, 269–270
Empowerment, defining, 230–231
Enrico, Roger, 260
Entrepreneurs, local support for, 178
Environmental scans, 209–210
Executive coaching, 350–354
Executive team. *See* Senior leadership group
Executives. *See* CEOs; Leaders
Experimentation, in strategy development, 93–94. *See also* Innovation

F

Failures, organizational: leaders' self-destructive attitudes in, 206–207; of successful companies, 201–207
Farson, R., 38–39
Federal Express, community service program of, 379
Ford Motor Company: and Japanese threat, 204; marketing strategy of, 249
Foster, Kent, 94
Framer, Tom, 278
Frank, Viktor, 221
Frost, Carl, 22
Future: challenges of, 109–120; city arrangements and structures of, 360–362; education system of, 129; executive of, 114–115; labor force of, 110–112; network economy of, 163–171; organization of, 114–115, 161–162, 195–199; society of, 119; work and social affiliations of, 127

G

Gallery Furniture, management practices of, 305–306
Gandhi, Mohandas, 223
Gardner, John, 224, 357
Garreau, Joel, 136
Gates, Bill, 207, 251
Gateway Computer, networked technology of, 196–197
General Electric: corporate culture of, 230–231; job rotation in, 227–228; managing change in, 234
General Mills: community service programs of, 379, 386
Gerstner, Lou, 273
Global economy, 175–182; competition in, 175, 194–195; corporate cost sharing in, 194–195; information technology in, 191–193; leaders' role in, 195–199; local development and, 176–179; and new enterprises, 195–199; regional economies in, 189–199; universal

consumer cultures and, 193–194; workforce needs in, 147
Goizueta, Roberto, 212, 258–260
Goldsmith, Marshall, 349
Goldsmith, Stephen, 370
Goodnight, James, 284
Goodwin, D. K., 25
Graham, Gerald, 271
Granite Rock Company, continuous improvement in, 240
Graves, Samuel, 377
Great Groups, 315–322; common principles of, 317–320; leaders' characteristics in, 320–321; mission of, 321–322
Grove, Andrew, 209, 262–263
Grove, Leslie, 318

H

Hackman, J. Richard, 335–347
Hall, Douglas, 289
Hamel, Gary, 81
Handy, Charles, 121, 139
Health care organizations, public accountability for, 368, 371
Helgesen, Sally, 133
Herman Miller: legacy of community in, 16; moral mission of, 23
Herzlinger, Regina, 365
Hesselbein, Frances, 9, 215
Hewlett, Bill, 267–268
Hewlett Packard: competitive strategy of, 210; performance standards of, 284
Hill, Linda A., 287
Hock, Dee, 61
Hoover, Gary, 308
Hope, organizational function of, 20
Hubbard, David, 22
Human resources management, 277; community involvement and, 377–380; language and, 22–23
Hunt, Michele, 23, 24

I

IBM, community service of, 381
Improvement orientation, 269–270

Industries, successful, ranking of, 277
Information-age technology: community impact of, 138; competition and, 145, 147; corporate models in, 195–196; and cultural changes, 143–149; in global economy, 191–193; global standards for, 193–194; network economics and, 163–171; nonprofits' adaptability to, 148; in service companies, 309; worker demand in, 183–184. *See also* Software industry
Innovation: abandonment and, 64; assessment of, 63–66; core practices of, 54; difficulties, 57–58; discipline of, 53–56; employee commitment in, 57–58; inquiry skills in, 65–66; listening-based, 306–308; managing for, 13; mission and vision in, 58–62. *See also* Strategy innovation
Inquiry skills, of effective leaders, 65–66
Intellectual capital, demand for, 183–184
Intellectual property, electronic distribution of, 146
Internet, business use of, 146, 149, 165. *See also* Network economy
Internet-related companies, capitalization of, 81

J

Job rotation, 227–228
Jobs, Steve, 319
Johnson, Kelly, 318
Johnson, Lyndon, 25–28, 33–34, 35–36
Johnson & Johnson, decentralized structure of, 372

K

Kanter, Rosabeth Moss, 175, 273
Kaplan, Robert, 283
Katzenbach, Jon R., 323
Kearns, David, 208
Kelleher, Herb, 43, 306
Kelly, Kevin, 163

Kennedy, John, 28–29, 34–35, 36
Kerr, Steven, 227
King, Martin Luther, Jr., 258
Kiripolsky, Ron, 270
Kistiakowsky, George, 317–318
Knight, Phil, 258
Knowledge companies: corporate culture of, 16–17; employment and work arrangements in, 146–147; market value of, 121–123; organization and management of, 112–113, 117–118
Kotter, John P., 69
Kouzes, James M., 37
Kovacevich, Richard, 278
Kroc, Ray, 251

L

Lakeland Regional Medical Center, 308–309
Language: of leaders, 10, 40–42; organizational change and, 96; of organizations, 22–23, 250
Leaders: accountability, 19, 118; brand-building tactics of, 247–249, 251–253; as change agents and managers, 12, 69–79, 95–105, 155–161, 217–220, 231–234; character and qualities of, 30, 78–79, 185, 220; as chief people officer, 285–286; as coach, 350–354; confidence of, 30; compensation of, 17, 19; credibility of, 39; entrepreneurial, management of, 184–185; and follower, responsibilities to, 20–21; of future, 114–115; in global economy, 195–199; of Great Groups, 320–321; individualism and self-interest of, 17; innovative, 53–56; mission and, 78; legacy of, 159; lessons for, 34–35; as mentors and role models, 3–7, 21–22, 298–299; as missionary, 130–131, 251; of new managers, 297–299; personal restraint and, 19; relationship-building skills of, 25–26; required reading for, 232–233; and risk taking, 21–22; senior, information technology and, 144; as servant, 44; as systems architects, 276; as talent brokers, 35; as teachers, 256–264; teams and, 100–101; trust-building practices of, 279–282; unique voice of, 39–42; winning, energy of, 257
Leadership: of cities, 357–363; core elements of, 19–20; for partnering, 12; as process, 37–42; presidential styles of, 25–36; principle-centered, 215–226; in self-organizing system, 158–160; of successful company, failures of, 201–212
Leadership development: competencies in, 261–262; leader's teaching of, 256–264; personal learning in, 289; pitfalls in, 234–235; strategies for, 227–228, 232–234, 295–297
Learning: formal, 211; personal, 289; self-directed, 295; stretch assignments for, 296; from teaching, 6
Legacy, of leaders, 15–16, 159
LensCrafters, management practices of, 310
Listening systems, 306–308
Lockheed Skunk Works, teamwork of, 317, 318–319
Loyalty, in changing organization, 161–162

M

Mackay Envelope, employee-leader communication in, 268
Mackey, John, 279
Madar, William, 379, 380
Malaysia Multimedia Super Corridor (MSC), 191–192
Malcolm Baldrige Award, 218, 240
Management: circular system of, 11; command-and-control, 151–153; diversity and, 13; for innovation, 13; mission and, 12–13; of organizational change, 69–79; practices, constants in, 118–119. *See also* Self-management

394 Index

Management, high-performance, 275–286; leaders' role in, 285–286; measurement systems in, 283–285; organization change strategies of, 282–283; principles of, 279–285; trust-building practices of, 279–282
Managers, new: authority and power issues for, 290–291; emotional aspects of leadership for, 294; immediate superior and, 297–299; interpersonal judgment of, 292–293; self-directed learning of, 295–297; transformational tasks of, 289
Manhattan Project, teamwork of, 317–318
Mars, Inc., grievance process at, 270
Matsushita, Konosuke, 73–74
McGregor, Douglas, 57
McIngvale, Jim, 306
Men's Wearhouse, management practices of, 276, 278, 285
Mentors, leaders as, 21–22
Mergers, service-oriented culture and, 382
Merlin Metalworks, global market of, 176
Meskis, Joyce, 310
Meyerson, Mort, 156
Microsoft, diversity in, 90
Mission: defining, 118; innovation and, 55, 58–62; managing for, 12–13; and mission-based organization, 59–60; morality and, 23; senior executive and, 327; statement, 339; vision and, 59, 61–62
Mistakes, learning from, 29
Mitchell, Scott, 268
Mohamad, Mahathir, 191, 192
Moorlach, John, 370, 373
Morality: mission and, 23; personal retraint and, 19
Motivation, employee: changing business environment and, 265–266; community engagement and, 378; intrinsic, as source of purpose, 62–63; low-and no-cost options for, 267, 272; material rewards as, 265; recognition as, 271; strategies for, 268–274
Motorola, performance standards of, 284

N

Nadler, David A., 201
Nadler, Mark, 201
Naisbitt, John, 267
Narratives, of leaders, 258–259
Nelson, Bob, 265
Network economy, 163–171; compound value in, 166–167; efficiency and, 168–169; electronic currency in, 165–166; fax effect in, 167
New Zealand Post, management practices of, 280–281, 282
Nike, leadership of, 258
Nokia of Finland, strategy innovations of, 83–89
Nonprofit organizations: accountability of, 366–373; information technology and, 148; as models for private sector, 170, 229–230; monitoring and oversight of, 371–373; performance analysis of, 370; performance disclosure for, 369; sustainability assessment of, 367
Nordson Corporation, community service and, 379, 386
Norton, David, 283
Norwest, strategic planning of, 278

O

O'Brien, Bill, 64
Ohmae, Kenichi, 189
Ollila, Jorma, 84, 85, 88
Olson, Richard, 329
Oracle Corporation, strategy innovation in, 91–92
Oregon Progress Board, 361
Organizations: actions aligned with values in, 237–245; as citizen company, 124–125; command-and-control, 115; consolidation and decentralization of, 148; diversity

in, 13, 90; employability and sustainability in, 161–162; exponential growth model for, 166; future of, 114–115; and law of increasing returns, 166; public disclosure and, 365–366; renewal process in, 225–226; strategies for energizing, 268–274; visionary, 237–245; winning, attributes of, 255–256
Orsburn, Jack, 336
Osterman, Paul, 335

P

Participative management, 21–22
Partnering: community building and, 13; in organization change process, 75–76
Passion: and intrinsic motivation, 62–63; of leaders, 131–132; strategy and, 92–93
Performance: misleading indicators of, 206–207; of self-managed teams, 152
Performance review: example of, 5–6; executive coaching in, 343–345
Personality, in organizational culture, 43–50
Peters, Tom, 271
Petersen, Donald, 286
Pfeffer, Jeffrey, 275
Philanthropy. *See* Community service
Phoenix Textile Corporation, employee-leader communication in, 268
Planned abandonment, 13, 64
Porras, Jerry, 325
Posner, B., 37, 39
Postindustrial economy: cities and communities in, 136–138, 141–142; social affiliations in, 138–140; training demands in, 135–136, 137–138; women's career development in, 134–135
Pottruck, David, 93, 306
Professional development: community service and, 378–379; and training, 135–136; of women, 134–135, 139–140

Profit motive, in network economy, 169–170
Profitability, and size, 278
Promotion, emphasis on, 112
PSA Airlines, suggestion system of, 270
Public sector: accountability and, 366–373; community building and, 13; monitoring and oversight of, 371–373; performance analysis of, 370; performance disclosure for, 369; sanctions for, 371; sustainability assessment of, 367
Purpose, organizational, effective leadership and, 78, 126. *See also* Mission

R

Recruitment, community involvement and, 377–378
Relaxation, practice of, 32–33
Respect, and friendship, 6
Responsibility: of leaders, 20–21, 29, 30; social, of organizations, 222–224
Retirement, early, 110–111
Retreats, off-site, 244–245, 259–261
Rewards and incentives, 228–230; effectiveness of, 271; material, demand for, 265; recognition as, 271, 273
Reynolds, Palmer, 268
Risk taking, of leaders, 21–22
Roddick, A., 40
Roosevelt, Franklin D., 30–33, 34, 35
Rosenbluth, Hal, 308, 311
Rosenbluth International, management practices of, 308, 310–311

S

SAS Institute: management practices of, 283–284; performance standards of, 284
Scholes, Jim, 81
Search for meaning, as growth industry, 125–127
Selden, Larry, 255

Self-management, 153–162; and change strategies, 155–157; leaders' role in, 154–155, 158–160; productivity and, 152
Self-organization theory, 153
Senge, Peter M., 12, 57
Senior leadership group, 323–334; consensus in, 328; fluid dynamics of, 331–332; and real team myths, 327–330; role modeling by, 330; and strong leader myths, 324–327; suggestions for, 333–334; 360-degree feedback for, 350; value and legitimacy of, 324
Service companies: customer-centered values in, 305–306; employees' ownership attitude in, 309–311; entrepreneurial, 304; execution versus price in, 302–303; information technologies in, 309; listening-based innovation in, 306–308; size and scale in, 308–309; success factors of, 301–302; sustaining success in, 305–311
ServiceMaster, outsourcing of, 114
Shareholders, roles of, 122–124
Sigler, Andrew, 329
Singapore Airlines, performance standards of, 284
Size: and profitability, 278; and scale, of service providers, 308–309
Smith, Douglas K., 95
Smith, John Palmer, 369
Smith, Ray, 260
Social responsibility, 222–224. *See also* Community service
Social sector, community building and, 13. *See also* Nonprofits
Society for Organizational Learning (SoL), 66, 68
Software industry: fluid cultures of, 186–187; managing talent in, 185; recruitment in, 183–184, 187
Southwest Airlines: leadership philosophy of, 43–50; performance standards of, 284

Spirituality, and organizational vision, 250–251
Sprint Corporation, 270–271
Starbucks Coffee Company: employee turnover at, 269; management practices of, 310
Strategy: experimentation and, 93; legacy and, 15–16; personality and, 45–46; of successful firms, 278
Strategy innovation: emotions and commitment in, 92; preconditions for, 89–94; process, 86–88
Stress management, 221, 294
Success, organizational: downsizing and, 279; employee development as source of, 277–279; findings on, 277–279; pitfalls of, 201–212; of service providers, 301–311
Sun Microsystems: charitable activities of, 181; competitive strategy of, 208, 209
Swartz, Jeff, 381

T

Tattered Cover Book Store, management practices of, 310
Taylor, Bob, 318
Teams: authority of, 341; behavioral coaching for, 351–354; benefits of, 336; complementary, 220–221; diversity in, 90; empowerment of, 341; enabling structure for, 342–434; Great Groups as, 315–322; leaders' performance on, 100–101; management mistakes in, 338–345; manager's failure to support, 349; organizational transformation and, 76; performance, compared to nominal groups, 336; self-managed, productivity of, 152; structure and support for, 343, 345–347; successful, 335–336, 337–338. *See also* Senior leadership group
Technology. *See* Information-age technology

Telecommunications industry, service delivery in, 303
Thomas, David, 296
360-degree feedback, 350
3M, core values of, 238–239, 240–241
Tichy, Noel, 255
Timberland Company, culture of service in, 381
Timing, sense of, 26
Toyota, management system of, 286
Training: and committed partnerships, 49; new market for, 135–136
Trust: building of, 279–282, 293; downsizing and, 267; and leaders' credibility, 27–28; organizational culture of, 46; in participative environment, 154–155; partnership and, 116–117

U

United Parcel Service, technology of, 197
United Services Automobile Association (USAA), 305
United Way, accountability and, 366, 369

V

Values: aligned with action, 237–245; core, 238–239, 241–244; of leaders, 18; in organizational culture, 217–218
ValuJet, management failures of, 302
Virtual businesses, 192
VISA International, innovative governance system of, 60–61
Vision: basic concept of, 237–238; building of, 249–251; of change, 76–78; defining of, 36, 61–63; mission and, 59, 61–62; and organizational change, 74; spirituality and, 250–251; statement, 339
Volunteer work. See Community service

W

Waddock, Sandra, 377
Wageman, Ruth, 347
Walt Disney Studio animators, teamwork of, 317
Wealth creation, and strategy innovation, 81–94
Weatherford, Ken, 282
Welch, Jack, 10, 75, 159, 228, 230, 232, 260
Wheatley, Margaret, 151
Whitehead, John, 377
Whole Foods, management practices of, 276, 279, 282, 285
Whyte, William, 136
Winblad, Ann, 183
Women: career development of, 134–135; as consumers of outside training, 136; entrepreneurship of, 139–140
Work-life balance, 220–221, 267
Workforce: aging, 110–112; changing demographics of, 266; diverse, 181–182; global economy and, 147
Workplace, changing nature of, 135, 138–140, 170
Wrigley, Philip, 235

X

Xerox: competitive failure of, 205, 206; competitive strategy of, 208, 210; formalized learning at, 211–212; Palo Alto Research Center, teamwork of, 317, 318

Y

Yield management, 165

This page constitutes a continuation of the copyright page.

Chapter Four copyright © 1998 by Doris Kearns Goodwin
Chapter Five copyright © 1996 by James M. Kouzes
Chapter Six copyright © 1997 by Herb Kelleher
Chapter Eight copyright © 1998 by Peter M. Senge
Chapter Nine copyright © 1998 by John P. Kotter
Chapter Ten copyright © 1997 by Gary Hamel and Jim Scholes
Chapter Eleven copyright © 1996 by Douglas K. Smith
Chapter Fourteen copyright © 1997 by Sally Helgesen
Chapter Fifteen copyright © 1997 by Esther Dyson
Chapter Sixteen copyright © 1997 by Margaret Wheatley
Chapter Seventeen copyright © 1997 by Kevin Kelly
Chapter Eighteen copyright © 1996 by Rosabeth Moss Kanter
Chapter Nineteen copyright © 1998 by Ann Winblad
Chapter Twenty copyright © 1998 by Kenichi Ohmae
Chapter Twenty-One copyright © 1998 by David A. Nadler and Mark Nadler
Chapter Twenty-Two copyright © 1997 by Franklin Covey Company
Chapter Twenty-Four copyright © 1996 by Jim Collins
Chapter Twenty-Five copyright © 1998 by Charlotte Beers
Chapter Twenty-Six copyright © 1997 by Noel Tichy
Chapter Twenty-Seven copyright © 1997 by Bob Nelson
Chapter Twenty-Eight copyright © 1998 by Jeffrey Pfeffer
Chapter Twenty-Nine copyright © 1998 by Linda A. Hill
Chapter Thirty copyright © 1997 by Leonard Berry
Chapter Thirty-One copyright © 1997 by Warren Bennis
Chapter Thirty-Two copyright © 1998 by Jon R. Katzenbach
Chapter Thirty-Three copyright © 1998 by J. Richard Hackman
Chapter Thirty-Five copyright © 1996 by John W. Gardner
Chapter Thirty-Six copyright © 1997 by Regina Herzlinger
Chapter Thirty-Seven copyright © 1998 by James E. Austin

The Drucker Foundation Future Series

Now Available in a Boxed Set!

All three hardcover volumes of the distinguished Drucker Foundation Future Series are available in an attractive gift set.

Boxed Set ISBN 0-7879-4696-6 $75.00

The Leader of the Future
New Visions, Strategies, and Practices for the Next Era
Frances Hesselbein, Marshall Goldsmith,
Richard Beckhard, Editors

In this *Business Week* best-seller, world-class contributors offer advice and insights about the future quality of our lives, our business, our organizations, our society—and the leadership required to move us into the exciting unknown. A selection of the Book-of-the-Month and Executive Program book clubs.

Hardcover ISBN 0-7879-0180-6 $25.00
Paperback ISBN 0-7879-0935-1 $16.50

The Organization of the Future
Frances Hesselbein, Marshall Goldsmith, Richard Beckhard, Editors

Best-selling authors, top-notch consultants, Fortune 500 CEOs, nonprofit leaders, and respected management scholars reveal strategies for confronting the challenges we face in building the organization of tomorrow. The authors underscore where, when, and how organizations and their leaders must evolve—not only to survive but also to prosper.

Hardcover ISBN 0-7879-0303-5 $25.00

The Community of the Future
Frances Hesselbein, Marshall Goldsmith, Richard Beckhard,
Richard F. Schubert, Editors

Managers and leaders from all sectors focus on the basis of our society itself—the community. They explore what our communities will look like tomorrow—how we will live, work, communicate, educate our children, and govern ourselves. This selection of the world's top thinkers shows us the challenges we face in building the communities of the future and what we need to do to meet them.

Hardcover ISBN 0-7879-1006-6 $25.00

FAX	CALL	MAIL	WEB
Toll Free	Toll Free	Jossey-Bass Publishers	Secure ordering at:
24 hours a day:	6am to 5pm	350 Sansome St.	www.josseybass.com
800-605-2665	PST:	San Francisco, CA	
	800-956-7739	94104	

Lessons in Leadership
Peter F. Drucker

Over the span of his sixty-year career, Peter F. Drucker has worked with many exemplary leaders in the nonprofit sector, government, and business. In the course of his work, he has observed these leaders closely and learned from them the attributes of effective leadership. In this video, Drucker presents inspirational portraits of five outstanding leaders, showing how each brought different strengths to the task, and shares the lessons we can learn from their approaches to leadership. Drucker's insights (plus the accompanying *Facilitator's Guide* and *Workbook*) will help participants identify which methods work best for them and how to recognize their own particular strengths in leadership.

1 20-minute video + 1 *Facilitator's Guide* + 1 *Workbook*
ISBN 0-7879-4497-1 $89.95

Excellence in Nonprofit Leadership
Peter F. Drucker, Max De Pree, Frances Hesselbein

This video package is a powerful three-in-one development program for building more effective nonprofit organizations and boards. *Excellence in Nonprofit Leadership* presents three modules that can be used independently or sequentially to help nonprofit boards and staff strengthen leadership throughout the organization. The video contains three twenty-minute programs: (I) *Lessons in Leadership* with Peter Drucker (as described above); (II) *Identifying the Needs of Followers*, with Max De Pree and Michele Hunt; and (III) *Leading Through Mission*, with Frances Hesselbein. The video comes with one *Facilitator's Guide*, which contains complete instructions for leading all three programs, and one free *Workbook*, which is designed to help participants deepen and enrich the learning experience.

1 60-minute video + 1 *Facilitator's Guide* + 1 *Workbook*
ISBN 0-7879-4496-3 $129.95

FAX
Toll Free
24 hours a day:
800-605-2665

CALL
Toll Free
6am to 5pm
PST:
800-956-7739

MAIL
Jossey-Bass Publishers
350 Sansome St.
San Francisco, CA
94104

WEB
Secure ordering at:
www.josseybass.com

The Drucker Foundation Self-Assessment Tool

Since its original publication in 1993, the best-selling *Drucker Foundation Self-Assessment Tool* has helped and inspired countless nonprofit boards, executives, and teams to rediscover the direction and potential of their organizations. This completely revised edition of the *Self-Assessment Tool* now offers even more powerful guidance to help organizations uncover the truth about their performance, focus their direction, and take control of their future.

The *Self-Assessment Tool* combines long-range planning and strategic marketing with a passion for dispersed leadership. It allows an organization to plan for results, to learn from its customers, and to release the energy of its people to further its mission. The *Process Guide* by Gary J. Stern provides step-by-step guidelines and self-assessment resources, while the *Participant Workbook* by Peter F. Drucker features thoughtful introductions and clear worksheets. Participants will not only gain new insights about their organization's potential, but also forge strategies for implementation and future success.

Multiple Uses for the *Self-Assessment Tool*

- *The leadership team*—the chairman of the board and the chief executive—can lead the organization in conducting a comprehensive self-assessment, refining mission, goals, and results, and developing a working plan of action.

- *Teams throughout the organization* can use the *Tool* to invigorate projects, tailoring the process to focus on specific areas as needed.

- *Governing boards* can use the *Tool* in orientation for new members, as means to deepen thinking during retreats, and to develop clarity on mission and goals.

- *Working groups from collaborating organizations* can use the *Tool* to define common purpose and to develop clear goals, programs, and plans.

Process Guide   Paperback ISBN 0-7879-4436-X $29.95
Participant Workbook   Paperback ISBN 0-7879-4437-8 $12.95

1+1 SAT Package = 1 *Process Guide* + 1 *Participant Workbook*
ISBN 0-7879-4730-X $34.50 **Save 20%!**

1+10 SAT Package = 1 *Process Guide* + 10 *Participant Workbooks*
ISBN 0-7879-4731-8 $89.95 **Save 40%!**

FAX	CALL	MAIL	WEB
Toll Free	Toll Free	Jossey-Bass Publishers	Secure ordering at:
24 hours a day:	6am to 5pm	350 Sansome St.	www.josseybass.com
800-605-2665	PST:	San Francisco, CA	
	800-956-7739	94104	

Leader to Leader

A *quarterly publication of the Drucker Foundation and Jossey-Bass Publishers*

Frances Hesselbein, Editor-in-Chief

Winner
1998 Maggie Award
1998 Apex Award

Leader to Leader is a unique management publication, a quarterly report on management, leadership, and strategy written by today's top leaders *themselves*. Four times a year, *Leader to Leader* keeps you ahead of the curve by bringing you the latest offerings from a peerless selection of world-class executives, best-selling management authors, leading consultants, and respected social thinkers, making *Leader to Leader* unlike any other magazine or professional publication today.

Leader to Leader is *not* written by journalists or business writers. Instead, it provides a forum for world-class leaders and thinkers to meet and share leading-edge insights *in their own words*—unfiltered, unbiased, unvarnished. You get direct access to innovative market strategies, management approaches, leadership models, and more directly from the people who are shaping and implementing them—people like Peter F. Drucker, Rosabeth Moss Kanter, Max De Pree, Charles Handy, Esther Dyson, Stephen Covey, Meg Wheatley, Peter Senge, and others. Think of it as a short, intensive seminar with today's top thinkers and doers.

"**Leader to Leader** is the ideal companion for the practicing manager. I find useful, hands-on material in every issue. I highly recommend it."
—John Alexander, president, Center for Creative Leadership

"I look forward to each issue of **Leader to Leader**. I find the articles challenging, provocative, and inspiring."
—Bob Goodwin, president and CEO, Points of Light Foundation

"**Leader to Leader** is a new and needed voice for both innovative and practical advice on how leaders make a difference. The articles are timely, interesting and helpful."
—Dave Ulrich, professor of business administration, University of Michigan School of Business

Subscriptions to **Leader to Leader** are $149.00.
501(c)(3) nonprofit organizations can subscribe for $99.00 (must supply tax-exempt ID number when subscribing).

Prices subject to change without notice.

FAX	CALL	MAIL	WEB
Toll Free	Toll Free	Jossey-Bass Publishers	Secure ordering, tables of
24 hours a day:	6am to 5pm	350 Sansome St.	contents, editors' notes,
800-605-2665	PST:	San Francisco, CA	sample articles at
	888-378-2537	94104	www.josseybass.com or
			www.leaderbooks.org